The Whig Party in Missouri

The Whig Party in Missouri

John Vollmer Mering

University of Missouri Studies Volume XLI
University of Missouri Press
Columbia • Missouri

To

CLARA VOLLMER MERING

and to the memory of

RAY DELAPLANE MERING

PREFACE

I AM deeply indebted to Professor Lewis E. Atherton for advice and encouragement in the preparation of this study. Dean James L. Bugg, Jr., read an earlier draft and made valuable suggestions for its improvement.

Librarians who have been especially helpful are: Miss Sarah Guitar, Mrs. Laura Crane, and Mr. Kenneth Holmes of the State Historical Society of Missouri; Mrs. Ann T. Rubey and Mr. Ambrose Easterly of the University of Missouri Library; Mrs. Ernest A. Stadler, Mrs. Benjamin D. Harris, Miss Dorothy A. Brockhoff, and Mrs. Lovelle Felt of the Missouri Historical Society; and Mr. Percy Powell of the Library of Congress. A grant from the Floyd Shoemaker Fund for Research in Missouri History and funds supplied by the University of Florida Graduate School helped finance research trips to St. Louis. My wife, Ellen Westfall Mering, aided me in numerous and important ways.

J.V.M.

Gainesville, Florida
May, 1966

CONTENTS

CHAPTER 1

TARDY WHIGGERY

MISSOURI's Whig party held its first state convention at Jefferson City in October, 1839. The candidates nominated for the 1840 elections formed Missouri's first Whig ticket, and the Whig State Central Committee appointed by the convention was Missouri's first continuing Whig administrative unit. This convention named delegates to the forthcoming Whig national convention, thereby forging the first formal link between Missourians and the national Whig party.[1] Thus, if organization and formal structure are requisite characteristics of political parties, there was no Missouri Whig party until 1839. Certainly that is the year the Whigs achieved an organization comparable to that of their Jacksonian counterparts.

Most political scientists, however, are at least as attentive to the symbolic factor of party label as they are to more corporeal anatomy in enucleating the concept of political party. After all, if Missourians who opposed the Jacksonian Democrats thought of themselves as Whigs and were so identified by their opponents, then there were Whigs in the state whether or not they had formally organized.[2] According to this criterion, the Whig party began in Missouri in 1838, one year before its first convention.

Prior to 1838, Missourians used the term *Whig* only fleetingly and irregularly in reference to the political structure of their own state. The St. Louis *Missouri Republican,* later the West's leading Whig newspaper, editorialized in favor of "Whig" organization in the fall of 1837, then ceased using the appellation altogether during the early months of 1838. As early as 1835, the *Missouri Intelligencer* of Columbia, near the center of the state, referred once to those Missourians who opposed Andrew Jackson's party as Whigs. This was an isolated instance, however, and the paper quickly reverted to the more familiar "Opposition" and "Clay Party."[3]

It is true that later recollections of the era abound with references to Whigs before 1835. For instance, Edward Dobyn, a St. Louisan active in the Democratic party, referred in his memoirs to the United States senatorial election of 1830 as a "Whig victory." Dobyn was writing in 1876, though, and his use of the term *Whig* is clearly an anachronism. The contemporary accounts of this election, which resulted in the elevation of Alexander H. Buckner to the Senate, uniformly characterized it as a victory of the "friends of the American System" over the "Jackson party."[4] Similarly, John F. Darby, prominent Whig and three times mayor of St. Louis, recalled in 1880 that a "large number of true and faithful Whigs" bade farewell to Daniel Webster after his visit to St. Louis in June, 1837. In 1837, however, Darby, as well as the other participants, shunned such nomenclature.[5]

Actually, it was six months after Webster's visit that the first group in the state with "Whig" in its title organized in St. Louis and appointed a St. Louis Whig Committee of Correspondence. Later still, in April, 1838, the *Missouri Republican* used the word *Whig* for the first time in reference to a specific state political contest. The paper had endorsed William H. Ashley as a candidate for Congress, but in discussing his candidacy it had at no time characterized him as a Whig. When Ashley died before the election, however, the editor, without commenting on his terminology, queried, "Who is to supply the place of General Ashley on the Whig ticket?"[6] Though Jacksonians continued to slander their opponents with the opprobrious Federalist label and Whigs frequently called themselves "the opposition," "Republicans," or "party of reform," from the spring of 1838 on, members of all parties increasingly spoke of the political division within Missouri as one between Whigs and Democrats.

Based on the criterion of party organization, then, 1839 marks the emergence of the Whig party in Missouri; if common usage of the term *Whig* denoted the existence of a party by that name, it appeared one year earlier. In either case, Whiggery arrived late in Missouri. In his standard work on the Whig party's origins, E. Malcolm Carroll reports instances of the use of the Whig label to designate a political organization opposed to the Jacksonian Democrats as early as 1832. Although the party did not hold its first national convention until 1839, Carroll clearly feels it was a going political organism by 1834.[7] More general works on American political history as well as most accounts of the Whig party in specific states have confirmed this chronology.

There is also wide agreement regarding the nature of the Whig genesis. That the national Whig party originated as a coalition of assorted political elements drawn together by their common antagonism to Andrew Jackson's Administration is one of the commonplaces of American political history, and contemporary analysts explained the Whig party in a similar manner. Indeed, in the first volume of the quasi-official *Whig Almanac*, editor Horace Greeley unabashedly listed five groups that combined to form the Whig party in the spring of 1834. Greeley climaxed his list with a reference to "Numbers . . . awakened from their apathy by . . . the imminent peril of our whole fabric of constitutional liberty," perhaps providing an example of Whig polemics rather than a historical datum. His other entries, however, describe the same elements that students of the Whig party from Greeley's day to our own have included as constituent members of the original Whig coalition. These were (1) champions of the American System who, under the National Republican label, had supported John Quincy Adams for the Presidency in 1828 and Henry Clay in 1832; (2) defenders of state rights who parted company with Andrew Jackson as a result of his response to South Carolina's Nullification Proclamation; (3) Democrats who opposed Jackson's policy toward the United States Bank, and (4) members of the Anti-Mason party.[8] In no single state were all of these components significantly present, but in states where the Whig party emerged earlier than in Missouri there was a fusion of two or more of them.

New York, Pennsylvania, and Massachusetts are examples of states where the Whig party resulted from efforts to merge the Anti-Masonic party with the National Republicans. Greater success attended the union in New York, where Masonry had declined enough to render futile a party dedicated to opposing it. The Anti-Masons of Pennsylvania were unwilling to abandon their name or organization in 1834, and the original appearance of the Whig party in that state represented little more than a change of name for the National Republicans. In Massachusetts also, the Anti-Masons rejected National Republican overtures to form a Whig party. Nevertheless, the National Republicans' purpose in donning the new mantle in both Pennsylvania and Massachusetts was to make themselves more appealing to the other anti-Jackson party, and it was hope for effective coalition that caused the birth of the Whig party in those states.[9]

Commingling of groups that hitherto had ardently opposed each other produced the Whig party in Virginia, North Carolina, and Mississippi. Representatives of Greeley's second category, champions of state rights who objected to Jackson's sponsorship of the Force Bill at the time of the nullification controversy, blended with National Republicans, whose bête noire was the removal of the federal deposits from the United States Bank. At first these forces found political intimacy distasteful, but their animosities toward the Jackson Administration quickly enabled them to overcome their fastidiousness.[10]

The pervading influence of Henry Clay in Kentucky politics cast the Whig nativity in that state in an exceptional mold. Clay first characterized his political allies as Whigs in a Senate speech in March, 1834; in July of that year a convention at Frankfort proclaimed the existence of Kentucky's Whig party. Under Clay's auspices, the National Republican party had developed sufficient strength in his own state to launch a potent Whig party merely by a change of name. Nevertheless, the new name apparently did make it easier for some former state-rights Democrats to join forces with Clay's supporters of longer standing.[11]

Across the river in Ohio, National Republicans coalesced chiefly with Democrats who were repelled by Jackson's financial and internal improvements policies, but these groups were also joined by Ohio's relatively weak Anti-Masonic party and even by a few disgruntled state-rights enthusiasts. Sensing the potential of the new party, John McLean's supporters for the Presidency began to weld these diverse elements into an effective Whig organization as early as 1833. Ironically, McLean's presidential prospects were concluded before the election of 1836, and another native son, William Henry Harrison, benefited from the well-formed party.[12]

The inception of the Whig party in all the states mentioned thus far occurred before 1836, the year of Martin Van Buren's election to the Presidency. Missouri, however, was not the only state without a Whig party during the campaign of 1836; Whiggery's arrival was late also in Tennessee, Illinois, and Georgia.

In Tennessee disaffected Democrats who supported Hugh Lawson White for the Presidency supplied the propelling force for the movement that eventually resulted in the Whig party. Though alienated from the Jackson-Van Buren wing of the Democratic party, these White adherents were slow to accept the label of a new party in whose councils Henry Clay was known to hold high place. Jackson's home state had nurtured few National Republicans, and this small band had little choice but to pool its votes and those of the White Democrats who became willing to answer to the name *Whig* only after the election.[13]

The White faction was also important to the anti-Van Buren coalition at Illinois. There, former National Republicans were more influential than in Tennessee, but despite their preference for William Henry Harrison, they found it prudent to treat gingerly the sensitivities of the numerous White Democrats in their midst. As a result, opponents of the Democratic party in Illinois frequently referred to themselves as White Democrats, and almost never as Whigs, until 1838.[14]

To some extent the White Democrat factor was operative in Missouri, where, as in Illinois, "White-Harrison" electors appeared on the ticket in 1836. But the situations in the two states were far from identical. In Illinois the presence of the hyphenated electors reflected an effort to compromise real rivalry within a political confluence, whereas in Missouri the "Harrison-White" designation is best explained as a device hopefully employed by a unified political group in an effort to woo additional voters to its standard. The increased percentage of the total Illinois vote garnered by the Harrison-White electors, compared with that won by Clay in 1832, further illustrates that effective coalition was in process in that state. A similar comparison for Missouri reveals only a negligible gain in the anti-Jackson vote for the later year.[15]

As instructive as Illinois' history in explaining the lateness of Missouri's Whig party is that of Georgia, where the Whig party appeared late in 1839 when a well-organized political party, the State-Rights party, cast its lot with the national Whig party. The similarities between Georgia and Missouri are found not in political ideology but rather in circumstances, for in neither state did the Whig party result from a coalition of two or more factions theretofore politically different. Consequently, the organizational pressures generated by efforts to unite divergent groups were missing in both states.[16]

The parallel between Missouri and Georgia can easily be overextended, however. In sharp contrast to the Georgia Whigs, all of those who cooperated in establishing Missouri's Whig party resembled the first group in Greeley's list, "National Republicans [who] had previously been known as supporters of Adams and Clay, and advocates of 'the American System.'" The National Republican label was never in common use in Missouri, but there were Adams men in 1828 who became Clay men in 1832, and these men consistently avowed their support of the American System. Other elements that contributed to the formation of the Whig party elsewhere either were not present in Missouri, or, if they were, they failed to unite with the Adams-Clay supporters in 1834 or later.

Although Missouri contained many seemingly zealous advocates of state rights, they did not become nullifiers, nor did they leave the Democratic party at the time of President Jackson's antinullification stand. In the early 1830's anti-Masonic sentiment was visible in the state, but this did not erupt into a political party as it did in some Eastern states. Some Jackson men opposed the financial policies of the Jackson Administration, but they did not "unite in condemning the high-handed conduct of the Executive" as Greeley's *Whig Almanac* indicated many nascent Whigs did. Instead, they continued to profess loyalty to Jackson and the Democratic party, even while differing on economic matters. It is true that Adams and Clay men often supported such candidates in elections, but members of both groups retained their respective identities, and no merger took place.[17]

A paradox, then, goes far to explain Missouri Whiggery's tardy appearance. The Whig party arrived late in Missouri because the group that finally did style itself *Whig* had a longer history than the party itself in states where it made its earliest appearances. To unite diverse political elements required a new party in which the various segments could assemble, but the nationalistic supporters of the American System in Missouri joined hands with no other opponents of Jacksonian Democracy.

The continuity of the Adams-Clay men of 1828 and later with those who adopted the Whig label in 1838 and organized a party in 1839 is exemplified by their attitudes toward these actions. The casual, indeed unannounced, change of the *Missouri Republican* from an Opposition to a Whig paper has already been noted. In its initial circulars the St. Louis Whig Committee of Correspondence did not call for the creation of Whigs. Rather, it assumed their existence and urged that they coordinate their activities. An examination of the personal correspondence of active members of the Adams-Clay group who later became Whig leaders reveals no feeling on the part of these men that a new party was being born. As in the newspapers, one notes a gradual shift to the term *Whig* to describe themselves and their political allies beginning in 1838, but the shift occurred without comment.

Nor did the Whigs of Missouri regard the convention of 1839 as heralding any new political alignments. Instead of the transformation of an old group or the creation of new platforms for candidates to run on, the purpose of this convention was simply to provide closer coordination for politicians who were accustomed to acting together in a less organized fashion. In the elections of 1838 the group suffered especially severe reverses, and, therefore, a new political approach seemed imperative. Rejecting the notion that their cause was basically unpopular and could never enjoy success, the leaders of the opposition to Jackson and Van Buren in Missouri sought to repair their losses through better organization. A Whig editor made clear the motivation behind the convention when he wrote: "There must be a better State,

County & Township organization, so as to enable the whole state to act with concert and energy, and have correct political information circulated among the people."[18] Clearly, the Jefferson City meeting was intended to rejuvenate an ancient political entity rather than to create a new one.

However, this conclusion does not mean that Whig beginnings in Missouri duplicated those in Georgia, where a well-organized political party changed its name, for formal organization was missing from the activities of Missouri's pre-Whig group. The Adams-Clay men of Missouri did possess one attribute of a political party, though, an attribute that a distinguished political scientist has labeled "in-group perspectives." Their "distinguishable set of perspectives, or ideology, with emotional overtones" did not in itself give them the characteristics of a political party, but certain common attitudes furnished Missouri's opposition with enough identity and cohesion to warrant beginning the study of Missouri's Whig party some years before there was a party by that name in the state.[19]

Chapter 2

ARMED NEUTRALITY

IN THE four-cornered presidential contest of 1824 Henry Clay won Missouri's three electoral votes by a comfortable majority. Of the approximately 3,400 votes cast, Clay received over 2,000, Andrew Jackson almost 1,100, and John Quincy Adams 218. There was no ticket of electors pledged to William H. Crawford.[1]

In the electoral college, none of these candidates received a majority, and the choice of a President from the leading three — Jackson, Adams, and Crawford — devolved upon the House of Representatives. To John Scott, who since territorial days had been Missouri's single representative, fell the task of casting the state's vote. John Quincy Adams was the beneficiary of his decision, a decision that hindsight would reveal was fraught with consequences for Missouri political history. Scott and Missouri's two senators, Thomas Hart Benton and David Barton, all supported Clay during the campaign, but only Barton concurred with Scott's preference for Adams over Jackson. According to Benton, the representative's vote defied the wishes of the people of Missouri, who, he asserted, clearly preferred Jackson. As Scott later pointed out, the General Assembly failed to provide instructions for the unique situation, and Benton's generalization about the meaning of the election returns depended upon interpretation of the overwhelming Clay vote. Still, it was Scott himself who told Adams shortly before the House ballot that his vote for the New Englander would be unpopular in Missouri. There was no question in Benton's mind that the action was a flagrant violation of the *demos krateo* principle, and he publicly and permanently severed political ties with the Representative.[2]

This division among Missouri's delegates to the national legislature quickly reflected itself in state political alignments. Rapidly, Benton assumed the dominant position in a pro-Jackson party that opposed "The Friends of the Administration," a faction consisting of the small number of original Adams men of 1824 and those Clay advocates who preferred Adams to Jackson when their favorite was no longer available. It was this group that, with negligible additions and losses, emerged as the Whig party in 1838 and 1839.

Only once following Scott's vote for Adams in 1825 did these pre-Whigs fail to act in concert. That was in 1826 when Edward Bates, later the sage of Missouri's Whig party, challenged Scott for the solitary congressional seat. Like Scott, Bates was Virginia-born. In 1814, when he was twenty-one years old, he migrated to Missouri Territory where his brother Frederick was governor; he himself achieved prominence at the convention that drafted the state's first constitution. Well-connected and brilliant besides, Bates already enjoyed an enviable legal reputation in the 1820's. Eventually his law and political careers culminated in the attorney general's post in the Cabinet of Abraham Lincoln. A member of that select band who voted for Adams in 1824, Bates had little cause for dissatisfaction with the incumbent's course, but he now seized the opportunity created by Scott's unpopularity to announce his candidacy. Declaring that "the expectation of finding any set of men . . . with whom one can agree in all things is idle and extravagant," Bates rejected the very notion of political combination and presented himself as a neutral in politics.[3]

Benton endorsed Bates for the office. Himself a candidate for re-election with only token opposition, he had no interest in fanning political flames in 1826. Further, the three-way division of the vote consequent upon the entry of a Jacksonian candidate would have increased the possibility of a Scott victory. As one Adams supporter wrote the President after Bates won the election, Benton might have even preferred Scott "had it not been for the attainment of his favorite object, to wit to sustain his repeated assertion that Mr. Scott's vote in your favor is reprobated by the people of Missouri." Benton's friends saw the election in a similar light. Complaining that the "majority" had no candidate, a pro-Benton paper concluded that the victory of one Adams man over another signified nothing of political sentiment in Missouri, "except on the single point of dissatisfaction with Mr. Scott." [4]

Never again did the Jackson party permit the Adams men the luxury of vying among themselves for the support of their opposition. In 1828 three Jacksonians indicated their willingness to represent Missouri Democracy in Congress. Bates also entered the contest, and again he concluded that neutrality was the most promising strategy. Informed of plans for a state Adams convention, he requested that the meeting not recognize his candidacy. "It is true it would amount to a committal of the bulk of the party," he confided to another Adams supporter, "but most of the party I shall get without a nomination, and from it I think there is some reason to fear an unfavorable reaction." This time Jacksonian leaders clearly recognized and labeled Bates as the Administration candidate.[5]

In the final analysis, the leaders of the Democratic party were able to use the Bates candidacy to good advantage. By stressing the danger from the common enemy, they convinced the contenders for place within their own ranks of the necessity for party discipline, and the three Democratic candidates for the congressional nomination submitted their claims to Benton for arbitration. He selected Spencer Pettis who, with a unified Jackson vote, retired Bates by the comfortable majority of 7,102 to 4,534.[6] A generation passed before anyone but an avowed admirer of Andrew Jackson held statewide elective office again.

With no more success than Bates, candidates for the state legislature also applied the neutrality policy. For example, Henry Clay's half brother, Nathaniel W. Watkins of Cape Girardeau, issued a circular refuting his opponent's claims that he was "brought out" by the Administration party in his race for the House of Representatives. Robert Wilson of Howard County made a similar statement in his local newspaper, but neither he nor Watkins was elected.[7] On the other hand, the results were no happier for Samuel Perry, candidate for lieutenant governor, who ran openly as an Adams man and received barely one third of the total vote.[8]

Of necessity those who hoped for Adams' re-election took a more open position in the presidential contest, since obviously they could not claim neutrality for Adams. Early in 1828 it appeared that the anti-Jackson group might organize a bona fide political party in the state. "The Friends of the Administration" held a convention in March and enthusiastically expressed their support of Adams, but the delegates did not succeed in furthering the Adams cause in Missouri. Most candidates for the state elections in August followed the neutralist pattern set by Bates and resisted identification with the Adams party. Following the August reversals the Adams leaders were pessimistic about the presidential election, and they put forth only a nominal effort. As one private correspondent noted to a relative in Kentucky, "Political matters are considerably at ease in this state, as the administration party have given up the ship."[9] Jackson's victory was indeed overwhelming; he received 8,372 votes, leaving only 3,407 for Adams; and he carried every county in the state.[10]

Typical of the anti-Jackson reaction to the election was the *Missouri Republican's* lament that the Battle of New Orleans had ever been fought, for the paper held the glory Jackson attained on that occasion responsible for his victory.[11] The elections clearly revealed the magic of the General's name in Missouri politics and demonstrated that his opponents were in a pitiful minority. Yet the Battle of New Orleans took place long before 1824, when Jackson ran a poor second in Missouri, and by itself it is an inadequate explanation for his high standing with the voters in 1828. More important in explaining the great swelling of Jackson's Missouri strength is the political deftness of those who proclaimed themselves his followers. Under Benton's leadership, they outgeneraled the Adams politicians on two observable fronts.

First, there was the matter of Scott's vote for Adams. Benton's denunciation of this action led directly to a sharper cleavage in Missouri politics, and it did so on terms decidedly advantageous to Benton's allies. More than he decried Scott's preference for Adams, Benton denounced his disregard of the obvious wishes of his constituents. From the beginning of this new division in politics, then, many Missourians equated preference for Adams over Jackson with rejection of democratic principles.[12]

Such an association in the public mind was indeed damaging. The historian Richard P. McCormick has recently emphasized that democracy did not "begin" in 1824 and that in very few states was the common man "apathetic or debarred" before that year. Missouri's situation fits McCormick's generalizations nicely. Universal white male suffrage dated from statehood; although participation in the presidential election of 1828 was markedly greater than in the preceding one, more people voted in the gubernatorial election of 1824 than in either presidential election.[13] Thus Benton did not originate what he called the *demos krateo* principle, though by capitalizing on Scott's violation of it, he undoubtedly augmented democratic fervor in Missouri. The point to be made here is that Scott's vote fastened an undemocratic image on the Friends of the Administration, an image hardly conducive to political success in a democracy.

If some of Adams' supporters were unenthusiastic about rule by the people, few were so unrealistic as to expect to win political power on a platform of avowed antidemocracy. Many therefore welcomed Bates's 1826 candidacy for Congress as a resolution of their dilemma, for it seemingly illustrated that it was possible to approve Adams and yet oppose the man who had aided in his undemocratic election. The voters agreed that Bates, "who gave only his own vote for Adams," was preferable to Scott, "who gave the vote of Missouri." But the antidemocratic taint clung to the supporters of Adams in Missouri. Once elected, even Bates could not convincingly combine satisfaction in the fact that Adams was President with dissatisfaction in the manner of his election.[14]

Crucial as Scott's vote was, it is a mistake to assume that Missouri politics in the 1820's turned exclusively on theories of democracy. Economic issues constituted the second front on which the Bentonians outmaneuvered their rivals.

Repeatedly, the Adams men named their belief in the American System as chief among their reasons for favoring Adams over Jackson. Their candidate, they pointed out at their meetings, was known to favor internal improvements by the federal government and a protective tariff, whereas Jackson was "mysteriously silent" on these subjects. As far as it went, this was sound political strategy. Focusing on economic matters drew attention away from the alleged political differences between parties, and most Missourians agreed that internal improvements were desirable and that tariff subsidy for Missouri's lead mines was a necessity.[15]

However, Missouri Jacksonians overcame whatever embarrassment they may have felt as a result of their leader's silence by supporting aspects of the American System that impinged on Missouri interests. Hence it was Benton, rather than Barton or Bates, who in 1828 most doggedly urged that Congress appropriate money to extend the Cumberland Road to Jefferson City. Reasoning that the high Tariff of Abominations would "give mortal offense to a large portion of the United States," Bates opposed the measure; but Benton overcame his misgivings and voted affirmatively, since the bill did at least provide protection for Missouri's lead.[16] Consequently, Benton canceled benefits the Adams party might have derived from its tariff and internal improvement views. However, a different economic matter, the question of public lands, was of even greater interest to Missourians.

Well before the 1824 election, Benton made himself the champion of cheap land when he introduced his Graduation-Donation bill, providing for lower land prices and, in some cases, actual donations to bona fide settlers. Realizing that these proposals enjoyed nearly universal approbation in Missouri, John Scott urged that the Adams Administration publicly favor a similar plan. For this advice Scott received a stinging response from Henry Clay, who characterized the suggestion as treasonable. Clay did more than rebuke Scott; he in effect abandoned Missouri to the Jacksonians. Others besides Scott had impressed upon him that he who would carry Missouri must espouse a generous land system. This necessity Clay acknowledged to Adams, but the Kentuckian thought that the "madness for the public lands" existed only in Missouri and that her three electoral votes hardly merited a change in policy. Before Scott gave his vote to Adams, he attempted to extract assurances from the New Englander that Clay would receive a Cabinet appointment, perhaps in hopes that Missouri's favorite would make the new administration more palatable to his constituents. If Clay's presence in the Cabinet ever had any such influence, it ceased to do so after his views on the public lands became known. Henceforth, Clay's coattails were of little more benefit to Missouri politicians than were those of John Quincy Adams.[17]

The course of David Barton, Benton's Senate colleague, intensified the difficulties the Adams men encountered because of Adams' and Clay's opposition to downward graduation of land prices. While the party in Missouri maintained a discreet silence on the subject, Barton took the lead in

Washington in opposing Benton's proposals, and in a roll-call vote in 1828, he was the only Southern or Western senator to vote against the measure. Missourians saw confirmed their suspicions that Adams men opposed not only political democracy but economic democracy in the form of cheap land as well.[18]

These developments resulted more from political infelicity than from the sacrifice of expediency to principle. For a state party to find the policies of its national leaders embarrassing is not unusual in American politics, but in contrast to Benton's course on the tariff and internal improvements, Missouri's anti-Jacksonians found no antidote for the unpopular land policy. Yet it is doubtful that many in the state affiliated with Adams because of his views on public lands. With the exception of Barton, they consistently ignored the subject, and even Barton alleged that he feared speculation more than erosion of land values.[19] The apparent opposition of Missouri's minority party to graduation-donation was more a result than a cause of the state's political alignment during the 1820's. But it was a costly result, nonetheless.

In large measure, then, conditions peculiar to Missouri explain the unusually weak position of Adams' supporters there, but this should not obscure the determining effect of national party alignments on Missouri's political profile.[20] The minority's effort to create the impression that presidential preferences were irrelevant to state elections was a political stratagem rather than a description of reality. Aware of the gains that would accrue to them through opposite course, the Jacksonians made neutrality impossible.

The Jacksonian strategy in 1828 led to an active campaign; the Adams methods dictated organizational quiescence. Since Benton's party emerged with a vigorous organization and campaign experience, it was in a position to consolidate its strong position. By the same token, the Adams party was handicapped in its future efforts to control the state. It is incorrect, however, to conclude that the Adams men of Missouri abjured party activity because of apathy, lack of ability, or reasoned arguments about the propriety of campaigning. Rather, neutrality was a tactic consciously adopted by men who hoped to win elections. Over the long pull it was probably a miscalculation, since it left the party organizationally retarded, but for the year 1828 the supposition of Adams' friends that their best hope for victory lay in efforts to conceal their identity appears well founded.[21]

While election results in 1828 indicated that the followers of Jackson formed an enormous majority in Missouri, the plethora of would-be Jackson candidates for Congress in that election portended future difficulties of a similar nature for the Democrats. Not surprisingly, a majority so great attracted many ambitious men, among whom there were many disagreements. The Democratic division furnished the pre-Whig minority with another tactic besides neutrality. Except in rare individual cases there were no mergers of disaffected Jacksonians and the Adams or, as it was commonly called after Adams' defeat, the Opposition party. With increasing frequency, however, the Opposition did offer its support to the highest Jacksonian bidder.

Chapter 3

MEASURES, NOT MEN

IN 1828 Missouri's Jacksonian legislature proposed constitutional amendments requiring popular election of circuit court judges and changing the terms of those officers from life tenure to four years. Under constitutional procedure the 1830 session of the legislature had to accept or reject these proposals, and through a skillful combination of neutrality and support of quasi Jacksonians, the Opposition brought about their rejection.[1] The anti-Jacksonians were seemingly unanimous in their desire to preserve the judicial *status quo*, an understandable conservatism in view of the scanty gains their own party could expect from any extensions of direct democracy. By themselves they could not hope to defeat the amendments, but not all Jackson candidates for the legislature concurred with the pro-Jackson press in supporting their passage.

Thus, the leading anti-Jackson newspaper, the *Missouri Republican,* endorsed William Carr Lane and Francis Nash, men who professed devotion to General Jackson but also indicated opposition to the amendments. Within the Opposition itself neutrality was the watchword. The candidate for representative from St. Louis County confessed his 1828 vote for Adams, but he denied having any real opinions about the Jackson Administration. Opposition to the amendments, he asserted, was his entire platform. According to William Jewell of Boone County, the very concept of party was a distraction in politics, and he protested all such unnecessary causes of "public disturbance." [2]

The antiamendment forces scored substantial victories in

St. Louis, and returns from the rest of the state foretold the doom of the amendments. Exulting, the *Missouri Republican* announced a rout of "the Jackson troops." Yet, as the editor of a Jackson paper retorted, a comfortable majority of the members of the new legislature were committed to the support of the Jackson Administration, their views on amendments notwithstanding.[3]

The first actual test of these rival analyses came not on the amendments but in the election of a United States senator. Noting that Jacksonians were ascendant in the General Assembly, Thomas Hart Benton expected the election of a colleague more congenial to himself than the pro-Adams, pro-American-System David Barton, whose seat was at stake. Benton's announced choice was Governor John Miller. However, in the final balloting Miller placed second, and Barton did not figure at all. The position went instead to another Jacksonian, Alexander Buckner of Cape Girardeau.[4]

The explanation for this unexpected result was soon forthcoming. Seeing the impossibility of electing Barton or any other of their own number, the members of the anti-Jackson party "acted as prudent men . . . should act; they have chosen the best man in the opposing ranks." The "best man in the opposing ranks" combined in his political philosophy an admiration of Andrew Jackson with avowed support of the essential components of the American System, a protective tariff and internal improvements by the federal government.[5] One week later the House of Representatives rejected the controversial amendments by a majority of one vote, and the almost exact correlation between the votes for Buckner and against the amendments showed there was a dissident faction within the Jackson-Benton party which when combined with the Opposition formed a slight majority.[6]

These groups did not merge into a new political party. Indeed, Buckner characterized as "base" suggestions that the method of his election implied an affinity for Henry Clay.

The events of 1830 did suggest that the Opposition might reap greater rewards through support of "counterfeit Jacksonians" than through an easily exposed attitude of neutrality or an open stand as the anti-Jackson party, but the anti-Jacksonians were not yet ready to abandon their own nominations.[7]

Because of a special ruling by Missouri's legislature, the congressional election that would normally have taken place in 1830 did not occur until 1831, thus inaugurating a five-year period when Missouri elected her congressman in odd years, in different elections from those for state offices. Months before the 1831 election, Spencer Pettis, the choice of Thomas Hart Benton in 1828 and victor over Edward Bates, announced he was a candidate for re-election.[8] Three other politicians also aspired to shoulder the Jacksonian standard, and the Democrats again were aware of the inconveniences that could accompany the overwhelming majority they enjoyed in Missouri. Although the Clay party, as the opposition to Jackson was increasingly characterized, had made no nomination as late as June, Democratic leaders felt this signified "more of evil to our party than good." "The whole force of the opposition," worried Lieutenant Governor Daniel Dunklin, "can be brought to any point and on very short notice, such is their discipline, while ours at this time, is too much disjointed to be very efficient."[9]

Dunklin was correct that members of the Opposition were capable of unified action; they delayed in making a public nomination only because the candidate of their choice was unwilling to run. From all parts of the state, Abiel Leonard, a graduate of Dartmouth who left New Hampshire for central Missouri in 1820, received letters encouraging him to campaign for the office. The state's leading lawyer outside of St. Louis, Leonard inspired a loyal following of admirers who for forty years persistently besought him to be their candidate for high office. Just as persistently, Leonard declined to canvass, but his reluctance in no way damaged his influence among his partisans. Within Whig councils his power was exceeded by none and rivalled only by such men as Edward Bates. Leonard's correspondents emphasized that they realized their party was in a minority, but they thought the Jacksonian divisions made victory possible. Bates himself joined in the urgings and pointed out to Leonard that his prospects were brighter than his own because "You have not been scorched in the furnace of party strife." [10]

National as well as local Democratic schisms were expected to assist Leonard's candidacy. In Washington relations between Vice President John C. Calhoun and the President were noticeably strained, and members of the Clay party in Missouri predicted a rearrangement of parties beneficial to themselves. "All the friends of Calhoun," said Bates, "are in their hearts — some will be in their mouths openly against Jackson." However, the intended nominee agreed with another adviser that "this Jackson fanaticism still prevails over sound principle," and he refused to file for the office. [11]

Leaders of the Opposition in St. Louis felt that the scramble of competing aspirants within the Democratic party created an occasion too auspicious to ignore. Styling themselves "Friends of the American System," they held a meeting and nominated ex-Senator David Barton for the congressional seat. Their political associates in other parts of the state acquiesced in this move, and the Clay party entered the contest united. [12]

Just as they had done after Bates announced that he was a candidate for Congress in 1828, leaders of the Benton wing of the Democratic party used the threat of a common enemy to establish control over recalcitrant Jacksonians. All of the Democratic contenders but Pettis withdrew, and he defeated Barton by an even more decisive majority than he had won over Bates two years earlier. [13]

Some members of the Opposition attributed the enormity of their loss to an incident that occurred only a few days before the election. In St. Louis Thomas Biddle, brother of Nicholas Biddle and a director of the St. Louis branch of the United States Bank, flogged Pettis with a cowhide in retaliation for what he considered attacks on his character. This event, Clay leaders reasoned, solidified an unenthusiastic Democratic party behind Pettis, and many who might have stayed away from the polls went to avenge their martyred candidate.[14]

Perhaps Leonard would have made a better showing than Barton, who more than any other Missourian was known as an opponent of Benton's land proposals. Certainly, Barton could not have seriously entertained hopes of support outside his own party, and all recognized that such support was a prerequisite for success in a two-sided contest.

However, a more satisfactory explanation of the election than either Barton's personal standing or Biddle's indecorous behavior was the unity the Jackson majority achieved after an Opposition candidate entered the field. The course of events during the Adams Administration had created an invincible Democratic majority in Missouri, and by 1830 it was an understood fact of politics that if the Jacksonians were united they won elections. Bates's nomination in 1828 and Barton's in 1831 had been the very catalysts that had brought about this dreaded unity.

Another election was not far in the future, for soon after Pettis' victory he and Biddle fought a duel that was fatal to both.[15] Missouri's only congressional seat was again vacant, but this time the Opposition made no nomination. Instead, the Adams-Clay men returned to the policy so successfully pursued within the legislature at the time of Alexander Buckner's election to the Senate. Having twice learned that taking an open stand served only to unify the overwhelming majority they struggled against, members of the pre-Whig group began a regular practice of supporting the least offensive Jacksonian candidate.

Pursuing this course did not reduce the Opposition to choosing among ambitious Jacksonians on the basis of personality; for, as the election of Buckner illustrated, genuine differences of principle prevailed within the majority party. Allegiance or nonallegiance to Andrew Jackson determined political affiliations in Missouri, but the minority who opposed Jackson shared other common ground as well, which furnished them both greater unity than the more developed Jacksonian organization was able to command and a definite basis for selection of Jacksonians with whom to cooperate. From the time the Adams men met in the winter of 1828, they consistently coupled endorsement of the American System to their demurrers in regard to Jackson's qualifications for office. Before he won the Presidency, Jackson did not make known his stand on this nationalistic program, but anything short of enthusiasm was sufficient to convince the Missouri pre-Whigs that Adams, who openly espoused internal improvements by the federal government and the protective tariff, would be a safer man to have at the country's helm.[16]

In 1828 when men said they favored the American System, they meant they were for internal improvements and a protective tariff. By 1831 there was still doubt as to where Jackson stood on the tariff, but his Maysville Road Veto of 1830 seemed to confirm the prediction that a Jackson Administration boded ill for internal improvements. However, the question lent itself to sophistry in Missouri, for Jackson's veto of this bill providing federal funds for construction of a road in Kentucky was worded in such a way that a politician could still favor improvements "of a truly national character" without openly differing with the President. Missourians' chief concerns were the improvement of the Missouri and Mississippi rivers for navigation and the westward expansion of the

Cumberland Road. By placing these in the "truly national" category, Missouri Jacksonians successfully straddled the internal improvements issue.[17]

To the American System's provisions for tariff and internal improvements a third ingredient had been added since Jackson's inauguration, the United States Bank. In his messages to Congress of 1829 and 1830 Jackson questioned the constitutionality of the institution, but it was Missouri's Senator Benton who, in a speech delivered to the Senate in February, 1831, opened the battle to prevent renewal of the bank's charter. The bank issue thus forced its way into Missouri politics, and the middle ground was impossible to locate. Jacksonians had hitherto refused to tolerate ambiguity on the matter of presidential preference; now neither party would permit a man's views on rechartering to remain unknown.[18]

Assimilating approval of the bank to the rest of the American System was not difficult for the members of the Opposition. In their minds proposed destruction of the bank offered a leading example of the Jackson Administration's revolutionary unwillingness to utilize the resources of the national government for promotion of the nation's development and prosperity. Democrats, however, found their problems of disunity compounded by the new issue, and the nebulous division within their party became distinct when some Jackson followers refused to concur with the antibank policy.

Cooperation with these dissenters from the Benton doctrine instead of action as a party that made its own nominations occurred to some leaders of the Clay group before Barton's disastrous defeat. "Bucknerize" was already part of the Opposition vocabulary, and Bates suggested that if no "true man of our own side" would enter the contest, the process might be applied to Pettis through supporting John Thornton, one of Pettis' rivals for the Democratic nomination. Thornton refused to state publicly his views on the United States Bank, and Bates either knew or surmised that this meant disagree-

ment with Benton and Pettis. Noting in May that "the virulence of party strife had caused our most qualified men to
retire from the controversy," the *Missouri Republican* also
suggested the possibility of supporting the most amenable
Jacksonian.[19]

In the first congressional election of 1831 the temptation
presented by the divided Jackson party ultimately out-
weighed such considerations, but Barton's defeat pushed
them forward in the plans of the Opposition for the second
election. Anti-Jackson newspapers publicly proclaimed that
their party would have no candidate, being careful, however,
to assert that this did not signify an acceptance of Jacksonism
by any members of the minority party. Eschewing every
branch of the Jackson party, the *Republican* ejaculated, "For
the good of the country, we hope they will break each other's
necks politically as soon as possible."[20]

Later, the same paper summarized the position and philosophy of Missouri's Opposition when it editorialized:

> We have said before that our party is a minority, and the
> question now presents itself whether we can support our prin-
> ciples by giving our votes to any one of the numerous candi-
> dates now presented by our opponents. Our State is deeply
> interested in the continuance of the tariff policy — the system
> of internal improvements — and the re-chartering of the United
> States Bank. These are measures to which our present adminis-
> tration are [*sic*] unequivocally hostile, although a great portion
> of its friends give to them a cordial support. In our own State
> the dominant party is divided upon these measures. . . . We
> must select, in exercising our elective franchise, from among
> our opponents, the man whose principles accord the nearest
> with our own and whose personal character will attach some-
> thing like respectability to the office he holds. This is all we
> can effect now; we must look forward to other and better
> times.[21]

Jackson men, then, were not joining the Opposition party,
and certainly Clay, or Opposition, members were not endors-

ing the Jackson Administration. Rather, the anti-Jackson men had decided that they could best serve the cause of the American System by acting as a pressure group instead of as a political party. The policy was suitable for the pre-Whigs. Although antipathy to Andrew Jackson was their identifying characteristic, they also were unanimous in their approval of the American System's principles. Having no unanimity other than its professed devotion to a political leader, the Jacksonian majority contained many who, as did Alexander Buckner, gave to the American System a "cordial support," thus furnishing the Opposition with opportunities to support its principles, if not its men.[22]

CHAPTER 4

PRESSURE GROUP

POLITICAL scientists conventionally distinguish between political parties and political pressure groups. A party, by definition, seeks to supply the officials of government, and in a democracy this necessarily means nominating and campaigning for the election of candidates. A pressure group, on the other hand, does not aspire to fill offices from its own ranks but rather endeavors to influence government policy by voting for candidates, regardless of party, who champion certain interests and principles.[1] From David Barton's defeat in the first congressional election of 1831 until the Whig convention of 1839, Missouri's anti-Jacksonians resembled a pressure group more than a political party. In other words, they seldom entered candidates of their own in political contests but supported Jacksonian Democrats who were friendly to the Bank of the United States.

Availability of an especially palatable pro-bank Jacksonian expedited execution of the new strategy. Of the fur-trade magnate and director of the St. Louis branch of the United States Bank, William H. Ashley, members of the Clay group could truly feel that "politically we agree or nearly so except as to the Presidency." When he announced his candidacy for the congressional seat vacated by Pettis' death, Ashley eloquently endorsed the Bank of the United States, proclaiming that "its advantages reach every citizen in the community, however obscure his condition or limited his means."[2] Refusing to abide by the results of a Democratic nominating convention, Ashley narrowly defeated Robert Wells, the regular nominee. At once the Opposition rejoiced that, though this was not a victory for their party, it did show the power the Clay group could wield when it properly directed its efforts. And if not a victory for party, it was a victory for principle, because "though a friend of Jackson he [Ashley] was a greater friend of the American System." [3]

This election inaugurated an era of cooperation between pro-American-System Jacksonians and Missouri's pre-Whigs. Ashley was the perennial favorite of the combination, and it succeeded in re-electing him to Congress in 1832 and again in 1835. With the same support he ran for governor in 1836, but he lost that election. When Ashley was busy elsewhere, the Opposition and pro-bank Jacksonians turned to Dr. John Bull of Howard County, who had served as a Jackson elector both in 1824 and 1828. This remarkable Virginian concurrently practiced medicine, politics, and the Methodist ministry. He almost won the governorship in 1832 when he was only twenty-nine years old, and in 1833 he won the special election called to fill the additional congressional seat Missouri gained as a result of the 1830 census. [4]

So successful was the pressure-group policy that in 1835 members of the Clay group were confronted with a problem more familiar to the majority party. James H. Birch, scion of a prominent Virginia family, must have cut a commanding figure, his over-six-foot frame invariably clad in a swallow-tail coat with brass buttons; but he had another distinguishing characteristic besides his appearance. This politically ambitious newspaper editor from Howard County held the most inconsistent record in Missouri politics. When he sought to share Opposition endorsement with Ashley in the first election in which Missourians elected two representatives simultaneously, the Clay group refused. Many disliked and distrusted the erratic candidate, but chiefly they feared his dubious political reputation would detract from Ashley's powerful candidacy. [5] However, in the next election, when Ashley was running for governor and Bull had retired from politics,

Birch and Samuel Owens, another professed Jacksonian, both received affirmative nods from the Opposition in their campaigns for Congress. By then the more regular Jacksonians had found means of combatting the American System combination, and, lacking the stature of Ashley and Bull, the two were severely beaten.[6]

The support Ashley, Bull, and Alexander Buckner gave to the national bank in Congress demonstrated that the Clay men had not misplaced their confidence. In an effort to determine whether introduction of a bill for rechartering would be premature in 1832, the Clay forces tested congressional sentiment, and Buckner was among those consulted who agreed to support such a measure. Ashley joined Buckner in voting affirmatively when the bill was presented, leaving only Benton of Missouri's three national representatives to be counted among the nays. Although not yet a member of Congress at the time of the contest for rechartering, Bull was able to affirm his loyalty to the bank in 1833 by voting for resolutions condemning Jackson's removal of the government deposits.[7]

It was not only in state-wide elections that the pre-Whigs applied pressure-group tactics during the 1830's. Although in certain localities where they enjoyed unusual strength Clay men did run for General Assembly seats, they relied to a great extent upon persons who pledged allegiance to Andrew Jackson for achievement of their two major legislative aims: blocking the renewed efforts to weaken the independence of the judiciary and prevention of the establishment of a state bank. Thus, a Columbian described a situation that was not unique when he wrote of election results in his county, "The whole number elected are anti-amendment-anti-state bank & for a National bank. Yet [they] are called Jackson men." In spite of Jacksonian majorities in both legislative houses, the Democratic governor found the success of his programs uncertain. Even in St. Louis, where the influence of the Opposition reached its apogee, there were occasions when the Clay party found it convenient to support congenial Jacksonians. Gloomily commenting on the victory of Opposition-supported Elliot Lee over Hugh O'Neil for state representative in 1836, the *Missouri Argus* could find consolation only in the observation that it required a Jackson man to defeat a Jackson man.[8]

Supporting nonconformist Democrats brought less success to Missouri's Opposition in its attempt to dominate the state legislature than in its quest for control of the state's representation in Washington, as the complete failure to "Bucknerize" another senatorial election indicates. However, passage of the constitutional amendments pertaining to the judiciary was delayed until 1835, and they finally emerged in a somewhat modified form.[9] The General Assembly did create a state bank in 1837, but the charter reflected pre-Whig influence. Furthermore, since their distaste for such an institution stemmed largely from fears that its existence would prove a burden to those in Congress who still struggled to keep the Bank of the United States alive, Clay men had less reason to oppose a state bank after the expiration of the national bank's charter in 1836.[10]

Because political parties in Missouri were homologous to presidential parties, application of pressure-group tactics to presidential elections would have meant loss of identity for the pre-Whig group, and this did not occur. Jacksonian triumphs in the national elections of 1832 and 1836 demonstrated vividly the Opposition's need for cooperation with part of the majority party if it would entertain any hopes of success.

Early in 1831 "Friends of the American System and Henry Clay" held a meeting in St. Charles, but the state-wide organization they advocated never formed. Missouri was unrepresented at the National Republican convention at Baltimore that nominated Henry Clay and John Sergeant, and only at the eleventh hour did a Clay electoral ticket enter the field. In the spring of 1831 the *Missouri Republican* noted that many Democrats were "standing aghast or falling into our ranks," but as the contest approached it became increasingly clear that this was more hope than fact; and the Clay campaign was carried on, when at all, with an air of futility. Jackson, of course, carried the state overwhelmingly, receiving 8,904 votes to 4,760 for Clay.[11]

Admirers of the Kentuckian could reflect sadly on his changed fortunes in Missouri. In 1824 he carried the state by a comfortable majority; now he received scarcely one third of the vote cast. Perhaps greater exertion by the Clay party would have produced a less doleful result, but campaigning could not alone have diverted Missouri from its Jacksonian course. Indeed, the man who had done more than any other to make Missouri a Jacksonian stronghold felt impelled to apologize for the majority of 4,000. "We could have given you double the number," wrote Thomas Hart Benton to Vice President-elect Martin Van Buren, "but there was no question of the result, and the vote was a thin one." [12]

The candidacy of Tennessee's Hugh Lawson White for the Presidency appeared to furnish an ideal opportunity for collaboration with disaffected Democrats in 1836, for White insisted he was a Jacksonian who had differed with Jackson only on his choice of Martin Van Buren for the succession.[13] However, the Clay men of Missouri preferred William Henry Harrison, who more completely identified with the national Whig party. Eventually, the Opposition leaders forgave White his Jackson taint sufficiently to condone a scheme whereby a common set of electors served for both Harrison and White, the votes, in the event of victory, to go to the man the voters indicated by write-ins they preferred.[14]

Henry Clay had advised his Missouri followers that he considered it expedient to countenance White's pretensions, for it required two candidates to "represent the feelings and interests of each of the two great divisions of the party."[15] Considerations of the wisdom of this policy on a national scale aside, it was clearly unrealistic to expect favorable results from its application within Missouri. "Two great divisions" did not exist within the Opposition party there; the problem was to appeal to Jacksonians who were unenthusiastic about Van Buren. With the candidacies of White and Harrison so intimately linked through the same electoral ticket, voting for the former too nearly resembled identification with the anti-Jackson party, and Van Buren's carrying the state by a ratio almost equal to Jackson's in 1832 indicates that few voters were willing to take the step. The contrast between the state and presidential elections of the 1830's demonstrated convincingly that, though some Democrats were unwilling to follow Benton's lead in economic matters, these dissidents and the anti-Jackson minority had not united in a "new party."[16]

Benton contended that such a union had taken place, and his biographer agrees with him. Following Ashley's election to Congress in 1831 the Senator warned a political confrere:

> Do not deceive yourself about the new party; do not think it is to vanish soon, it is of long preparation, deep & extensive roots, & will be permanent. . . . The B. U. S. [Bank of the United States] is the turning point. That *political engine* of the old federal monarchical party, will draw the line between parties. . . . Every Jackson-bank man in this quarter belongs to the New Party. Nearly the whole of the old Adams & Clay party belong to it.[17]

Benton's frustration is understandable, for he was chiefly responsible for the fact that identification with the party of Andrew Jackson was a *sine qua non* for election. Now, as one of the fruits of his labors, he saw politicians clinging to the label that he had made so valuable and, at the same time, rejecting his leadership. However, his remarks are better regarded as an accusation than as an analysis; had the new party been a reality, Missouri would have led instead of trailed the nation in witnessing the creation of a Whig party. If an actual merger between the "Adams & Clay party" and the "Jackson-bank men" had taken place, both groups would have contributed candidates to the party's tickets. However, during the entire period of cooperative effort, a candidate for lieutenant governor in 1836 was the only authentic Clay man to receive joint endorsement in a state-wide election.[18]

That there was no permanent coalition of the Clay group and contumacious Jacksonians is also apparent from the fact that the friends of Henry Clay never ceased to regard them-selves as members of a separate political organization, pos-sessing its own identity. In endorsing Jacksonians, Opposition newspapers consistently stressed that these were not their own candidates but that they were choosing the best avail-able men in a *different* party. Even more revealing is that a small number of Clay men never fully accepted the collabora-tion policy and that in the gubernatorial elections of 1832 and 1836, as well as in the congressional election of 1833, there were efforts to launch genuine anti-Jackson candida-cies. Indeed, George C. Sibley of St. Charles, who opposed John Bull for Congress in 1833, seemed to echo Democratic leaders when he complained that Bull's coupling of enthusi-asm for the national bank with professed devotion to Andrew Jackson was a devious attempt to serve two masters.[19]

Unlike the divisions within the Democratic party, these were differences over strategy only and not over principles. The rest of the Opposition always sympathized with the de-sires of some of their political brethren for political purity and disparaged their campaigns, not on the grounds that they constituted infidelity to party, but because they showed a naïve blindness to the unfortunate political reality that Clay men could not win elections in Missouri.[20]

This reasoning was implicit also in a central Missourian's letter vetoing plans for an Opposition state convention. John

Wilson and his correspondent, the aforementioned Sibley, shared a common political label and a devotion to American System principles, but their similarities did not embrace political methodology. Sibley, the deeply religious founder of Lindenwood College, abhorred anything short of complete candor in his politics. Wilson, who in 1848 was the first Missouri Whig to sense the winning qualities of Zachary Taylor as a presidential nominee, was not perturbed by the use of practical expedients to achieve his political aims; in fact, he was impatient with those who failed to see the need for them. Asserting that he himself looked forward to nothing with so much enthusiasm as the day when the anti-Jackson party could compete on equal terms, Wilson on this occasion reminded Sibley of practical political considerations:

> I have seen a request signed by several highly respectable gentlemen of your county calling a meeting of those of your citizens who are opposed to the reelection of Gen'l Jackson . . . and I see the design is to get up a convention etc at Columbia. . . . I now wish to inform you before the meeting what is the opinion pretty generally up here among *our* friends — So far as I am informed it is that it is perfectly hopeless to attempt an opposition ticket. . . . One thing has been whispered to us here, if that it should prove true *we* might change our opinions as to the propriety of an opposition ticket in this state. It has been said here that Gen'l Ashley intended *soon* to make a full renunciation of Jacksonianism in public print. . . . Now if Ashley should . . . make a full and decided renunciation — then it is my own opinion [that there is] *some* prospect (tho I should not be sanguine then) of our success. . . .[21]

The debate over the wisdom of pressure-group tactics was not between city and country either, for the *Missouri Republican* soon joined in advising against a convention. Since Ashley's impending disavowal of Jackson proved mere rumor, none took place.[22]

Internal divisions did not plague the minority Opposition.

Although the Jacksonians possessed more of the attributes usually associated with a political party, their devices for party discipline were not as effective as the natural control that common interest furnished to the smaller Opposition. Prevention of the proposed convention and the minute vote polled by Clay candidates who did not withdraw show that the minority party retained its discipline as well as its identity during this period when it gave a surface impression of being too disorganized to participate in politics.[23]

From the Jacksonian side also there is evidence that the Democrats who were willing to cooperate with the Clay party did not join them. Possibly Ashley was in the process of doing so when death intervened in 1838, but in the last election in which he ran for office a Democratic editor frantically pointed out that Ashley's claims to Jacksonism were false. John Bull permanently retired from politics in 1836, never having retracted his allegiance to Old Hickory. Alexander Buckner died of cholera in 1833 in a similarly unconfessed state.[24]

Eventually all leaders of the Benton wing of the Democratic party repudiated Ashley, Buckner, and Bull; but some were quite slow in doing so. Lieutenant Governor Daniel Dunklin's reply to Governor John Miller's urgings that he publicly refute allegations that he had supported Ashley for Congress in 1831 must have been less than satisfying: "It is litterally [sic] true that I did not support Gen. Ashley, not even with my vote. This is truth. But the *whole* truth is this, had I not been prevented by high water from reaching an electoral precinct in time, I should have *voted* for Ashley." [25] Perhaps the chief reason for the delay in clarifying the division within the Democratic party was that not all of Benton's followers agreed with their leader that the national bank was the pivotal political issue. Certainly the Clay group did. But, as Dunklin wrote to Senator Alexander Buckner, "I was in favor of General Ashley's election although I knew he differed from me upon this question [banking] and so long as this may be the only political question in which we differ, I shall continue the same relationship to him." Dunklin, correctly, did not sense any great difference between himself and either Ashley or Buckner on internal improvements. Further important areas of agreement, Dunklin felt, were their acceptance of Van Buren as Jackson's heir apparent and their condemnation of Calhoun and the doctrine of nullification.[26]

Jackson's controversy with Calhoun raised hopes of some members of Missouri's Opposition prior to the presidential election of 1832 that a rearrangement of parties would occur that would alienate enough Jackson followers to destroy the overpowering majority enjoyed by the Jackson party; but, unlike states farther south, nothing of the sort transpired in Missouri. Instead, virtually all Missourians joined in denouncing Calhoun and nullification. State rights advocates in the Democratic party, not carrying their doctrines as far as Calhoun did, felt perfectly secure under Andrew Jackson. Indeed, for a brief period after the President requested Congress to pass the Force Bill in 1833, it appeared that some individuals in Missouri's Opposition might become Jackson converts, so agreeable did they find his strong stand against Calhoun.[27]

Contrary to Henry Clay's suggestion, then, it was not feasible to use Hugh Lawson White's candidacy to appease state rights devotees or nullifiers, because there were none in the state. Rather, the White movement in Missouri appears to have been a futile device whereby the Birch brothers, James H. and Weston F. of central Missouri, attempted to appeal to the Gargantuan prejudice in favor of Jackson and at the same time be acceptable to the Clay minority. The Birches later joined the Whig party, and thus it is arguable that the White movement approximated what occurred in other states: a union of disaffected Jacksonians with the supporters of Henry Clay, resulting in the birth of the Whig party. Before taking such a conclusion too seriously, however, it is well to note certain unique features about White's support in Missouri.

A study of the Birch brothers' political careers during the 1830's is immensely confusing, partly because there were two of them, but more so because their paths are checkered with unsuccessful attempts to gain the support of all Missouri political factions. In 1831 Weston was rejected by the Opposition as a candidate for the state legislature on an anti-Benton ticket that never materialized, only months after his pretensions to be the congressional candidate of the same party had been ridiculed. The next year he opposed Benjamin Reeves, one of the few anti-Jackson men who ran for office during the pressure-group period in the contest for General Assembly representative from Howard County.[28] In 1833 James, claiming to be a Jacksonian, announced his candidacy for Congress but was scorned by the Democrats. He then made an appeal to the Opposition, but, concluding that "the reform of a rake is ever problematical," that party ignored him and threw its support to John Bull instead. The 1835 congressional contest again saw his rejection by both sides, and finally in 1836, running as a "White" candidate, he received Opposition endorsement.[29]

Whether one agrees with an admirer of James's rival newspaper editor that these brothers were guilty of political amorality or looks upon them as truly independent men in politics, it is obviously not certain whether they were new additions to the pre-Whig ranks, or if they had previously been members. In either case the disparity in the returns of 1836 between the White-Harrison vote, as well as James's own vote in the congressional race, and that received by Ashley in his attempt to become governor indicates that the Birch-

White following added little to the strength of any coalition in which it may have participated.[30]

By withdrawing from electoral contests and concentrating its strength on Jacksonians who were sympathetic to its economic views, Missouri's Opposition enjoyed more than occasional triumphs for American System principles between 1830 and 1836; but, failing to make any permanent alliances, it did not succeed in altering the imbalance between political parties. Missouri's meaningful political conflict was within the Democratic party. When the Adams-Clay party pitted itself against this massive force, as it did in presidential contests, the outcome was never in doubt.[31] As experience elucidated this situation, the minority, not surprisingly and not unwisely, increasingly took advantage of the breaches within the opponents' camp.

It is unfair to criticize those who employed pressure-group tactics as opportunists, as men who eyed only the main chance. Certainly, if sacrificing principle for political preferment is what constitutes opportunism, the charge cannot be levied against the pre-Whigs, for their entire course consisted of placing American System principles ahead of office seeking. For them the opportunistic move would have been to profess loyalty to Andrew Jackson, but assuming poses of neutrality was as far as they would go in that direction.

Even to characterize bank-Jacksonians as opportunists is to concede that it was Thomas Hart Benton's prerogative to draw the lines of political battle in Missouri. Benton himself voted contrary to the wishes of the Jackson Administration on tariff and internal improvement bills when it suited his political convenience to do so; and, after David Barton left the Senate, no Missourian again tried to build a political career on opposition to Benton's land proposals.[32] "Counterfeit Jacksonians" were indeed bank-Jacksonians. There is nothing logical about singling out the bank issue as a test of party loyalty, except that it alone lent itself satisfactorily to Benton's purpose of conserving his leadership of Missouri's strong Democratic party.[33]

Perhaps the real opportunist in Missouri politics during this period was a nonresident of the state, Andrew Jackson. His name engendered the support of more than two thirds of Missouri's voters; his principles only an undependable majority; and he took no steps to cull his followers.

CHAPTER 5

FULL-FLEDGED WHIGGERY

PRESSURE-GROUP tactics, so rewarding during the first half of the 1830's, failed Missouri's anti-Jackson party in the 1836 elections. After all, the policy's efficacy required convincing some Democratic voters that the candidates supported by the pre-Whigs were sound Democrats who merely interpreted Jacksonism in a different light than Thomas Hart Benton did. Benton and his followers early saw that their task was, through persuasion and party discipline, to create the impression that this was not possible; and by 1836 they had at least temporarily succeeded. James H. Birch and Samuel Owens, the allegedly Democratic candidates supported by the pre-Whigs for Congress, failed to attract any Democratic support and, polling only the normal Opposition vote, suffered severe defeat. Unable to convince enough Democrats that he remained one of them, even the redoubtable William H. Ashley lost his race for the governorship, although he did fare better than the congressional candidates. Ashley's death in 1838 and the consequent loss of the most attractive amenable Jacksonian marked the final transition of the Opposition to open Whiggery.

It has already been shown that the appearance of the Whig party in Missouri did not signify the coalescence of politically opposed or even politically differentiated groups. From 1828, those who were variously known as Adams men, Clay men, the Opposition, or anti-Jacksonians consistently acted together, with only mild internal dissensions over political methods. Whiggery's advent resulted when this group embraced a label already common in other parts of the nation, an action coincident with efforts to achieve a stronger organization. Thus, the Whig party in Missouri conceived itself; from its first appearance it had unity and a tradition of concerted effort and needed only the adornments of tangible structure and party nominations to qualify as a full-fledged political party.

The continuity between the Opposition and the Whig party lends coherence to the narrative, but at the same time it obscures the motivation behind the change from pressure-group tactics to open political warfare. Since the party was not new, its spokesmen saw no reason to explain its existence. Because there was no confusion over who wore the Whig label, editors could and did simply begin to use it without explanation. While Missouri's Whig leaders frequently discussed what they hoped to gain through party organization, one looks in vain for an exhortation to Missouri's Opposition to call itself Whig, let alone for a reflection on the merits or demerits of the new designation. Typical was the *Missouri Republican's* plea in September, 1837, for a state convention, which the editor unexpectedly characterized as a potential gathering of Whigs.[1] Reaction to this and other pronouncements in favor of Whig organization showed that Missourians of all political creeds knew intuitively who the Whigs in the state were.

Although the Whigs themselves did not make clear their purpose in emerging as a distinct political party, a number of reasons for their doing so in 1838 and 1839 may be adduced. There is no evidence that the Whigs of Missouri adopted their new course at the behest of politicians in other states to identify more openly with the national party, but, of course, Missourians were aware of and influenced by national political trends. Within most states the Whig party was well organized before 1836, but in the presidential election that year these state parties only loosely affiliated with each other. The party held no national convention, nor did it agree on a presidential nominee. Following the failure of the Harrison-White combination to prevent Martin Van Buren's election, however, Whigs began efforts to concentrate their national strength. In 1837 Whig members of Congress recommended that the party hold a national convention in June, 1838, and selection of Missouri delegates was the chief task the *Republican* assigned to the state convention it urged Missouri Whigs to hold.[2]

Within Missouri itself paradoxical stimuli existed for the anti-Benton group's coming forth as a recognizable Whig party. On the one hand, the defeats of the bank-Jacksonians it supported in 1836 showed the Opposition that such a strategy was no longer dependable. As 1838 approached, it became apparent that Democratic party discipline was again certain to prevail, thus preventing the divisions within that party that were necessary to give the friends of the American System a decisive voice in elections. The General Assembly's creation of the Bank of Missouri in 1837 allayed much discontent that rose from Jacksonian financial principles within the Democratic ranks, but even more important was the fact that the legislature elected in 1838 would have to consider whether Thomas Hart Benton should be returned to the United States Senate. There were visible efforts within the Democratic party to prevent the re-election of Benton in 1844; but, while some members may have been reluctant, the party agreed in making his return to Washington its cause in 1838. Unity in support of Benton ruled out schisms over financial doctrine, for the hypocrisy in working for both the re-election of "Old Bullion" and a national bank would have been too patent, even for Missouri politicians.[3]

The popular Ashley seemed to offer the Whigs their only hope; and from January, 1838, when he announced his candidacy for Congress, until his death in March, the word *Whig* utterly disappeared from the Missouri lexicon. No other strong independent was available to replace him, and the

Democratic unity confronted the Whigs with the alternatives of abandoning all political designs or of taking an open stand and making their own nominations. There are no indications that they ever considered the former course.

However, pessimism alone did not dictate the new policy. As the memory of the defeats in 1836 receded, there was a rising optimism within the Opposition, especially in St. Louis where devotees of the American System enjoyed a local majority. As one city member of the Opposition wrote to a more timid collaborator in the country, "It is manifest that Van Buren is not near so strong as Jackson was, that the Pressure of the times and the hard money humbug have changed the views of many." [4]

The reference to the panic of 1837 lacked validity, for Missouri was largely spared the effects of that financial disaster until after 1840. [5] In the final analysis, the belief that Democratic preponderance in the state rested on association in the popular mind of Andrew Jackson with the Democracy also proved faulty, but surely it was as reasonable for the Whigs of the 1830's as it is for historians of our own day to suspect that a good part of the Democratic party's success depended on the personality of the old hero.

Granting the presence of a modicum of optimism, it is understandable that members of a politically conscious group would desire to operate their own party. Although cooperation with bank-Jacksonians had given the pre-Whigs the pleasure of seeing men sympathetic to their views achieve office, they themselves had been denied such opportunities. Even those who shunned the risks and expenses of political campaigns, a type well represented in the Whig leadership, could find no party councils to dominate without an organization of their own.

At a meeting on November 24, 1837, St. Louis Whigs endorsed resolutions favoring a state convention for the purposes of selecting delegates to a national convention and nominating candidates for Congress. By appointing the Whig Committee of Correspondence to promote interaction with political friends throughout the state, this meeting created the first perceptible Whig instrumentality in the state. In December "The Whig Young Men of St. Louis" organized and urged that young Whigs throughout the state take similar action.[6]

This enthusiasm for organization did not extend to central Missouri, and Whigs of that region forestalled its accomplishment in 1838. On his own initiative, John Wilson of Howard County announced that he was a candidate for Congress, thereby forcing convention advocates to abandon their plans or risk the appearance of division within the party. Personal ambition and fear that a convention would be St. Louis-dominated may have been factors in Wilson's action, but a Democratic newspaper struck closer to the core of the matter. The *Jeffersonian Republican* accurately explained that those in the "old Federal party" who opposed a convention did so neither because of honest rivalry within their party nor because of serious philosophical consideration on the subject of republican nominating procedures, but rather because they "saw it *was arousing the old Democrats in every county in the state.*" Not having known the successes that the St. Louis Whigs had experienced, the country branch of the party remembered better the dire results of a unified Democracy.[7]

Reaction in St. Louis to Wilson's announcement showed that, just as in the pressure-group years, the Whigs were divided only over procedure. The *Missouri Republican* at first objected to Wilson's candidacy because of the effect on convention plans, but it carefully averred the highest respect for him and the certainty that his motives were not "improper." Soon the paper admitted that a convention that did not embrace the entire state would have no value, and it coupled Ashley's name to Wilson's on an unlabeled congressional ticket, both halves of which it supported ardently. The St.

Louis Whig Committee of Correspondence also agreed to forego a convention, although in doing so it urged that Whigs in each county formally organize themselves, for that alone would "greatly assist in revolutionizing the state."[8]

The convention crisis abated only to be followed quickly by another. Ashley's unexpected death in March left the Whigs with only one candidate for Congress, and a replacement was not forthcoming. Despite their enthusiasm for open Whiggery, St. Louis Whigs as well as others were unwilling to heed the admonition of their Committee of Correspondence that "the present [is] an emergency in which no man has a right to deny his services to his country." Recognized leaders of the party, such as Edward Bates and Henry S. Geyer of St. Louis and Nathaniel W. Watkins of Cape Girardeau, all refused to undertake the arduous campaign.

This situation was not untypical in Missouri Whig annals. Many of the party's leaders were, as these three lawyers, sufficiently wealthy that the pecuniary emoluments of elective office did not tempt them. On the other hand, their modes of living were expensive and their acquisitive instincts fully developed. Satisfaction of these personal interests demanded attention to their often extensive investments. Edward Bates, for instance, was not poor by ordinary measurements. Yet, to please his refined tastes and to provide for his twelve children in accordance with his high standards, he complained to a friend that "it took all the money that lawyer Bates could make to support farmer Bates." Needless to say, such commitments left little time for political campaigning.[9]

Finally, Beverly Allen, another prominent St. Louis lawyer, consented to undertake the candidacy. Reputed to have "none of the gifts of oratory," a graduate of the College of New Jersey at Princeton, and one-time law partner of John Scott, Allen was zealously devoted to his profession and only a dilettante in politics. This campaign was his sole political venture; in the future he, too, would find the sacrifices of bearing the minority standard more onerous than he could endure.[10]

Greatly relieved to have replaced the late Ashley at last, the *Missouri Republican* endorsed Allen without qualification. This endorsement marked the beginning of the paper's permanent identification with the Whig party, for, unlike Ashley, Allen could not plausibly claim membership in any Jacksonian genus. In other parts of the state Wilson and Allen traveled without benefit of party label; in St. Louis, however, they were known as "The Whig Reform and Internal Improvements Ticket." [11]

Despite the emphasis on internal improvements implied by the St. Louis label, different financial policies constituted the graphic issue between the followers and opponents of Benton in 1838, as in earlier years. When the Independent Treasury bill first occupied the attention of Congress in 1837, Missouri Whigs approved of a strategy set forth by some of their national leaders "to permit the quacks to exhaust their store of nostrums," which, while it might result in temporary disaster, would be the quickest method of awakening the country to the need for a national banking institution. However, the appearance in Virginia and in her neighboring states of "Conservatives," who opposed creation of *any* federal depository for government funds, unexpectedly enabled the Whigs to table the measure in the House of Representatives and raised hopes of Whig-Conservative control of the next Congress.[12]

Certainly, neither Missouri party could be charged with evading financial issues in the campaign of 1838. With no reluctance, Allen and Wilson opposed the Independent Treasury bill and, since there were no Conservatives to conciliate in Missouri, advocated restoration of a national bank as well. The Democratic candidates took the opposite stand with equal frankness. In the contests for seats in the General Assembly the issue was the same, only there it was phrased in terms of the election of a United States senator.[13]

Throughout the campaign Whig attitudes ranged from un-
bounded optimism in St. Louis to severe circumspection in
Howard County, where the party did not even muster a slate
for the legislative and county offices. Allen buoyantly declared, "I really believe my vote throughout the state will
be larger than our lamented friend Ashley would have attained." To James S. Rollins, a young Whig of Boone County
just entering the political arena so unpropitious for members
of his party, a St. Louis editor wrote, "Courage, Sir, Courage! We are gaining upon the enemy, and if our friends do
their duty Benton will be left alone. There is a change operating throughout the state, which . . . will do the business
for him." [14]

More nearly correct, however, was the forecast of one of
the Democratic congressional nominees, Albert G. Harrison,
a lawyer from Fulton in Callaway County. Unlike most Whig
leaders, Harrison "was well read in his profession, but em-
barked too early in political life to distinguish himself as a
lawyer." The Democrat confidently predicted that the "feds"
would suffer the "severest drubbing" they had yet received
in Missouri, not because of the reticence of mid-state Whiggery, but rather because "they have foolishly taken an open
position, which will rouse up the democracy to bring out their
entire strength. This they cannot stand." Harrison's party defeated the Whigs as decisively as they had earlier beaten
Opposition candidates who were unable to draw Democratic
support. The Whigs did not receive their "severest drubbing," but they surpassed by only 1 per cent their usual 40
per cent of the total vote cast. [15]

Benton's re-election to the Senate soon reflected the similarity of the result in the struggle for control of the state legislature. When the members balloted in November the famous
incumbent received 75 votes, his Whig opponent, 48. [16] That
opponent was Abiel Leonard, the Howard County lawyer who
refused to shoulder his party's colors in the doubtful con-

gressional race of 1831. Still disdainful of political risk, Leonard resented his party's subjecting him to this certain defeat; for it required no oracle to foretell Benton's victory. Nevertheless, the unsolicited support he received from all but one Whig member of the General Assembly, who "when drunk he is a *loco foco* & when sober a whig," attests to the party leadership that Leonard's admiring biographer attributes to him.[17]

This senatorial election signified more than either Whig deference to Abiel Leonard or continued Democratic hegemony. It was the first united effort by the Opposition to contest a Senate seat since the combination with dissident Democrats in 1830 that resulted in the election of Alexander Buckner, who was, after all, a Democrat. Seeing no similar opportunities, anti-Jacksonians had been content to scatter their votes as complimentary gestures to various individuals, and in 1836 they had acceded to making Lewis F. Linn's election unanimous.[18] Despite its futility, then, Leonard's candidacy is an important milestone in Missouri Whig chronology.

The Whig members of the legislature logically followed their support of Leonard with an equally unanimous recommendation that the party hold a state convention in 1839. Missouri's political minority, which had possessed unity since 1828 and had sponsored its own candidates in 1838, prepared to organize formally; and thus acquire the one characteristic of a plenary political party it yet lacked.[19]

This time Whigs from all parts of the state concurred that conspicuous Whiggery would benefit the cause. Even Abiel Leonard, still cautious about permitting himself to be brought forward as a candidate, took the lead in organizing central Missouri county conventions to select delegates for the state gathering. New Whig newspapers appeared, optimistic that if the Whig party became "united and persevering . . . even Missouri may yet witness a release from an influence under which she groans."[20] In October the delegates met and created a full-scale Whig organization for Missouri. Besides appointing a state central committee and a committee of correspondence, they nominated candidates for governor, lieutenant governor, congressmen, and presidential electors. All of the members of this first complete Whig ticket in Missouri stood firmly on a platform of opposition to hard money policies and condemnation of the Independent Treasury.[21]

The Whigs expected too much from organization, largely because they erred in interpreting their past reversals in terms of its absence. "Union of the Whigs for the sake of the Union" was a euphonious slogan, but union was the one advantage the Whigs and their antecedents already possessed.[22] When a Whig newspaper declared "Without organization the Whig party are as a militia contending against a regular deciplined [sic] party," it decried a shortage of coals at Newcastle.[23] Only John B. Clark, who accepted the Whig nomination for governor, seemed to remember in 1839 the chronic disinclination of Whigs to run for office and the more than occasional triumphs Democratic disunity had provided for Whig principles:

> They [the Democrats] have many aspirants, and therefore have to apply the screws, we have but few, for it is rather a hazardous undertaking with us at best and but few are willing to try it and none anxious. All that is necessary for us is to name the man and all will at once agree to run him.[24]

The elections of 1840, even after the injection of William Henry Harrison and the accompanying din of hard cider and log cabins into the campaign, were to disappoint Whigs who hoped for great changes as a result of organization; but those who earlier had advocated passively awaiting shifts in the political complexion of the state had not been vindicated either. Since the Whig position in Missouri was consistently a minority one whether the party had organization or lacked it, whether it boldly attacked or avoided giving offense, it appears that either the Whigs themselves or their doctrines must have been basically unpalatable to Missourians. The next chapter describes the men who associated themselves with this minority and suggests reasons why they remained in a minority.

Chapter 6

WHIG CHARACTERISTICS

In his presidential address before the Mississippi Valley Historical Association in 1934, Professor Jonas Viles explained that Missouri's Whig party contained strikingly divergent interest groups. According to Viles, only the willingness of the "rural slaveholding wing" to profess unfelt enthusiasm for tariff measures and internal improvements made political cooperation between that faction and the St. Louis "business classes" possible.[1]

This interpretation microcosmically applied to Missouri the then widely held view that the national Whig party was an opportunistic combination of Northern businessmen, who favored an active role for the federal government, and Southern planters, who recoiled from programs that threatened the position of the state governments. U. B. Phillips and Arthur C. Cole are the two historians commonly credited with the development of this thesis, and in their respective studies of Southern Whiggery both concluded that upper-class solidarity was the cement in this otherwise unnatural alliance. Anti-Jackson expediency, as opposed to either economic interest or conviction, accounted for the advocacy of nationalistic programs by the actually dedicated state-righters of the South.[2] If one accepts this view of the national party, there is indeed an appealing logic in the presence of both Northern and Southern elements in border Missouri.

However, in 1954 Charles G. Sellers, Jr., convincingly challenged the Cole-Phillips thesis and in effect questioned the validity of distinguishing between Northern and Southern brands of Whig philosophy. Pointing out that "the size and importance of the urban middle class in the old South has yet to be fully appreciated," Sellers denied that Whigs in that section espoused a protective tariff or a national bank merely to placate Northern allies. Instead, the Southern as well as the Northern branch of the party had a predominantly business orientation, and the platforms in both sections were reflections of business interests. Although he granted a modicum of state rights influence in the Whig organizations of the deep South, Sellers asserted that in the border slave states "Whiggery was simply National Republicanism continued under a new name."[3]

Certainly the Whig party in Missouri did present a consistently united front as the bulwark of nationalistic principles. Debate over federal versus state power sometimes erupted within the Democratic party, but not within the Whig camp. The form that Whig nationalism assumed indicates that the party sought to further commercial and industrial expansion. Although the willingness of even hard-shell Benton Democrats to tolerate improvements of "a truly national character" at federal expense and to support tariff protection for Missouri products such as hemp and lead blurred these two issues, the fact remains that it was the Whigs who unreservedly favored both. In the fields of banking and finance, the Whigs articulately expressed their fears of the hard-money, anticentral-bank policies of the dominant wing of the Democratic party; and they plainly insisted that Whig financial programs were desirable because they promoted commerce. While they recognized that Missouri Whig pronunciamentos uniformly rang with these endorsements of Henry Clay's American System, Phillips, Cole, and Viles considered these professions out of harmony with the true sentiments of the party's dominant wing.[4]

Sellers' revision extended only to the economic interests of the Southern Whig party. That its members were propertied men who rallied to Whiggery "as a bulwark against mobocracy" he accepted without question, thereby, as one writer has pointed out, retaining as much of the Phillips-Cole thesis as he rejected.[5] Recent studies of candidates and officeholders in Alabama and New York have revealed no significant social and economic differences between Whigs and Democrats in those states, and other investigations have supported the conclusion that both parties were oriented around a middle-class norm.[6]

For Missouri, however, both segments of Sellers' interpretation serve rather adequately. A survey of persons active in politics during the Whig period hardly indicates a struggle between an aristocracy and a proletariat; indeed, the mere size of the Whig minority challenges such an assertion. It does appear, though, that the Whig party represented more wealth and contained a higher proportion of professional and educated men than did the Democratic party. Furthermore, Missouri's Whig party seems to have been primarily a business party with nothing forced, conciliatory, nor hypocritical in its nationalistic expressions.

These generalizations rest in part on a comparison of census data pertaining to members of the two parties. Both parties held state conventions in 1848 for which the newspapers conveniently published complete lists of delegates. Names of delegates at the Whig convention of 1839 and at the Adams or "pre-Whig" convention of 1828 were also available. No complete list of delegates to the Democratic convention of 1839 was published, but it was possible to determine who the delegates from most of the counties were. One newspaper classified all members of the 1850 state House of Representatives according to party, and the two-way division between Whig Abiel Leonard and Democrat Thomas Hart Benton in the senatorial election of 1838 made it possible to include the representatives of that year as well.[7] Those from ten representative counties were checked against the manuscript Census of 1850,[8] which revealed three facts about each individual located: his occupation, the value of his real estate holdings, and the number of slaves he owned.[9] The various categories furnished 77 Democrats and 79 Whigs from the ten counties, of whom 63 and 66, respectively, were located in the census.

Farmers predominated among the samples for both parties, though to a greater extent among the Democrats. Forty-two, or exactly two thirds, of the members of that party told the census-taker they were farmers, while thirty-two, or just under half, of the Whigs classified themselves in that manner. Two Whigs, however, were "tobacconists," which evidently meant large-scale growers of tobacco, for both valued their real estate holdings at high figures and, by Missouri standards, owned large numbers of slaves.[10] Nine of the Democrats and eighteen of the Whigs were lawyers. Also represented in the Whig sample were six merchants, a grocer, an editor, two clerks, three physicians, and a Disciples of Christ minister; the Democrats shared the company of five physicians, two land agents, two editors, a merchant, a tanner, and a wagonmaker.

Besides the sample used in connection with the census, occupations of St. Louisans were available from *Green's St. Louis Directory*.[11] To the various gatherings from which the sample derived, Saint Louis Whigs sent sixteen lawyers, five merchants, a superintendent of Indian Affairs, a county surveyor, a "trader," and a man who listed his occupation as "investments." The Democratic representatives included nine lawyers, a physician, a lumber merchant, an assignee in bankruptcy, and a farmer. While it would be an overstatement to say that persons engaged in semimenial occupations were prominent in the Democratic party, the appearance of two St. Louis tavernkeepers and two carpenters at the 1839 Democratic convention plus the already noted tanner and wagonmaker among the rural Democrats lends some basis to the speculation that such persons more frequently found their interests identified with the Democratic party. Members of comparable occupational groups were completely absent from the Whig samples.[12]

Turning to real estate valuations, one finds considerably more wealth of this nature concentrated among the Whigs. Of the thirty-two Whigs who classified themselves as farmers, all but nine claimed ownership of real estate worth more than $5,000. Of the forty-two Democratic farmers, only twelve owned more than that amount. One Whig farmer owned $10,000 worth of real estate; two others surpassed the $20,000 mark. Two Democrats claimed $40,000 and $60,000; but the Whig tobacconists had the highest valuations with $65,000 each.

Equally significant is a comparison of real estate owned by nonfarming members of the two parties. Two Whig lawyers boasted $50,000 worth of investments in real estate, one $40,000 and the other $25,000. Eight other Whig attorneys claimed over $10,000, as did two Whig merchants and the minister. None of the nonfarmers in the Democratic sample surpassed $5,000. Granting full allowance for the possible vagaries of this portion of the census that might result from modesty, boastfulness, or miscalculation, it seems evident that there was not only more wealth among Missouri Whigs than Democrats, but also a higher percentage of men who speculated in land or at least invested in real estate for purposes other than farming it themselves.

A comparison of the slaveholdings of the two groups supports this conclusion. Only twenty-six Whigs were slaveholders; thirty-one Democrats were. Such disparity does not reflect the residence of a disproportionate number of Democrats in large slaveholding counties, for from the three counties in the sample with the largest slave populations, Boone, Howard, and Callaway, there were twenty-six Democrats and twenty-four Whigs. Twenty-one of the Democrats from those counties held slaves, while only thirteen of the Whigs did.

The largest slave holding in the entire sample was fifty-eight, belonging to one of the Whig tobacconists. A Democratic farmer owned forty-four Negroes. The other Whig tobacconist, a Whig lawyer, and two Whig farmers owned between twenty and thirty slaves, while five Democratic farmers fitted into this category. The remainder of the slaveholders of both parties owned an average of eight slaves each, and among these smaller investors the evidence of a greater concentration on agriculture among the Democrats persists. Only six nonfarmers of that party held slaves; thirteen Whig nonfarmers did. Whigs who owned slaves were apparently likely either to use them as house servants or to regard them as incidental investment; slaveholding among Democrats was more often directly related to their predominantly agricultural interests.

The preceding sample dealt with the middle level of Whig and Democratic decision makers, though, of course, a few very prominent men in each party were incidentally included. A comparison of the leadership of the opposing parties further supports the thesis that the Whig party controlled more wealth and contained more men whose primary economic interests lay in fields other than agriculture than did the Democratic party. A list of fifty Democrats was compiled, including all candidates for offices elected by the entire state, all candidates for Congress, and a few others of obvious prominence. All Whig candidates for major offices were included in the list for that party; but since the Whigs frequently did not enter candidates and never had two contenders as the Democrats sometimes did, construction of the two samples on an exactly parallel basis would have resulted in too few Whigs. Therefore, the Whig sample consists largely of those who the available manuscript collections indicate shared in making the party's decisions. The Whig list thus derived contains sixty-six names.

Those who resided in the ten representative counties used in connection with the manuscript Census of 1850 were checked in that source, but the comparison of the two groups is based mainly on information from biographical reports on the individuals.[13] While these did not yield data on property holdings, they did uniformly furnish data about both occupation and education. Lawyers predominated among the leaders of both parties, though to a lesser extent within the Democratic organization. There were twenty-five Democratic attorneys, four doctors, twelve farmers, four businessmen,[14] one editor, and four for whom no occupation was ascertained. Forty-four of the Whigs were lawyers, and six were editors, four of whom were also qualified to practice before the Missouri bar. There were three Whig farmers, nine businessmen,[15] and one physician; and the artist George Caleb Bingham was a prominent Whig. Not surprisingly, then, both parties conformed to the traditional American political pattern of lawyer domination. However, while it is quite possible that most lawyers, just as most Missourians, supported the Democrats, within the Whig party men of that profession were more frequently given the reins of control. The purely agricultural interests in the Democratic party yielded dominance to lawyers at this higher level, but they reserved more of the prominent places for themselves than the Whig farmers did within their party.

Twelve Democrats and sixteen Whigs in the leadership sample were located in the portion of the census checked, and the tendency toward greater wealth among the Whigs remained true at this level. Seven of the Democrats claimed over $5,000 in real estate investments, compared to fourteen, or all but two, of the Whigs. Only two Democrats surpassed $20,000, and both of these were farmers owning a large number of slaves. Thirteen of the Whigs were above the $20,000 mark, and only one of these was a farmer. One was a physician, and the rest were lawyers or merchants, substantiating the earlier conclusion that the large landholders in the Whig party were likely to be wealthy investors rather than actual farmers.

The largest slaveholders located in the census were the two Democratic farmers who owned more than $20,000 worth of real estate, one possessing sixty-nine Negroes and the other forty-four. Four Democratic lawyers and one smaller farmer owned less than ten slaves. Ten of the Whigs were slaveowners. The wealthy Whig farmer owned twenty-four, two lawyers owned over twenty; and a merchant owned seventeen. The other six, five lawyers and a merchant, owned fewer than ten. Again, a smaller proportion of Whigs were slaveholders, and those that owned Negroes were less often farmers.

The educational attainments of the leadership of the two parties provide striking contrast. Almost all of the biographical sketches either specifically mentioned their subjects' college attendance or noted the lack of such training. For fourteen of the fifty Democrats college experience was definitely indicated; for twenty-nine, the biographers made it clear that there was none, and seven of the sketches did not mention education. Forty of the sixty-six Whigs definitely attended college; only twenty definitely did not; and in six cases the matter was left in doubt.

The well-known colleges Princeton and Yale each claimed two of the Democrats. Three Whigs were alumni of the former; two graduated from Yale; and one held a degree from Dartmouth. Harvard seems to have been unrepresented in Missouri politics. The outstanding difference that emerges from a comparison of the institutions attended by the college men of the two parties is that eighteen Whigs attended Transylvania College in Lexington, Kentucky, either as undergraduates or as law students, while only two Democrats had been students there.[16]

More important than the possibility that this aristocratic institution of the Blue Grass region may have been a Whig indoctrination center is the far greater proportion of college people in the Whig leadership. That the era was one when such opportunities accrued to the few is apparent from the statistic that in 1829 the number of students in all American colleges was 3,400, and this out of a population of thirteen million.[17] Here is a strong indication that the Whig party was not only wealthier and more business and professionally inclined than the Democratic party, but also that the Whigs attracted more men with whom privilege and position were matters of long standing rather than attributes newly acquired on the frontier.

Another approach frequently employed in studies of state politics, besides consideration of characteristics of politically active individuals, is analysis of county election returns. Examining those for Missouri, one can note that only 29 of the 108 counties that existed during the period 1836–1852 ever yielded Whig majorities in a presidential election. Only three of these — Boone, Marion, and Montgomery — were consistently faithful to the Whig cause during all five of the elections involved, but seventeen others might properly be regarded as Whig counties. The remaining ten more commonly returned Democratic than Whig majorities.[18]

Two common characteristics of the Whig counties are immediately apparent. Most, as the map on page 264 illustrates, touched either the Missouri or the Mississippi River, and almost all could be classified as "old" counties in that they were established before 1830. Since water transportation and, to a lesser extent, long-established settlement are factors that might be expected to contribute to the growth of commercial interests, the formula "river plus age equals Whiggery" seems to have merit. However, a cursory glance at the map reveals that as many river counties were Democratic as were not. Furthermore, some of the oldest consistently gave over-whelming support to Democratic tickets. Cole, Franklin, and Gasconade counties on the Missouri River were all in exist-ence by 1820; yet, in none of these was a two-party system a reality. In the seven other Democratic counties founded by 1820, the normal Whig vote was over 40 per cent of the total, but the Democratic party regularly maintained its ascendancy. Thirty-two of Missouri's counties could trace their origins to 1830 or earlier. Of these sixteen displayed Whig tendencies, and sixteen were Democratic.[19] Therefore, while it is reasonable to conclude that Whig counties tended to be long established and located on rivers, it would not be accurate to say that either old or river counties were espe-cially likely to be Whig.

It has been suggested that Whiggery in Missouri thrived in the counties with the largest populations.[20] Twenty coun-ties in the state had a population larger than 10,000 in 1850, and eleven leaned in a Whiggish direction, which is certainly a higher proportion than chance alone explains. Further-more, only three of the other eight bona fide Whig counties would appear in the lower half of a table of counties arranged according to population, although three others ranked below fortieth.[21] Granting, nevertheless, that the Democrats enjoyed a near monopoly in Missouri's sparsely settled county units, the fact remains that the majority party also exercised its share of influence in the more populous ones, and a further identifying feature of Whig counties is necessary.

One correlation sometimes put forth is that between slav-ery and Whiggery.[22] All but five of the sixteen Missouri coun-ties whose Negro population in 1850 was over 20 per cent of the whole were Whig, but the Whig vote exceeded 40 per cent in all of them. None of the twelve counties with less than 1 per cent Negro population was Whig, and in only three of them was the minority party strong enough to constitute any challenge to the Democrats. Closer examination, however, indicates that it is wise to proceed cautiously in interpreting these statistics. If slavery explains Whiggery, why did the party receive support from Washington, Grundy, Clark, and Audrain counties, which in percentage of Negro population ranked thirty-third, sixty-fifth, forty-second, and twenty-ninth, respectively? [23] Why were the Whigs shunned by many counties with a higher ratio of Negroes to whites? And why was not doubtful Howard, whose 35.29 per cent Negro population outranked all others, the banner Whig county instead of Boone with its seventh-ranking 24.56 per cent?

Certainly, the survey of individuals in Missouri politics indicated that slaveowners tended to identify with the Democratic party, a possibility not ruled out by even the largest Missouri Whig majorities, which in only one county exceeded three-fifths of a county's total vote. Perhaps the best evidence that slavery and the interests its presence generated do not explain a Missouri county's Whiggery comes from those who have found a close relationship between slavery and Whig strength in states farther south. Arthur C. Cole, the most noted exponent of the slavery-Whig interpretation, found a "decided coincidence between the Whig strongholds and the regions where the slave population was in a majority or nearly so." More recent scholars who have shared an area of agreement with Cole have been even more specific that Whiggery prevailed in counties with nearly 50 per cent Negro population. Counties where the ratio between races was two whites to one black tended to be doubtful; where the ratio was three to one the counties tended to be pronouncedly Democratic.[24] Thus, if a "Little Dixie" political psychology was operative in Missouri, the state's slaveholding counties should have been staunchly Democratic; for the population of all but three was over 70 per cent white. Only Howard with its two-to-one racial distribution and its vigorous two-party system was playing its assigned role.

An index that relates more closely to a county's political complexion than slavery, geographic location, age, or population is the average size of farms. Although farmers appear to have exercised more influence in the Democratic organization, even a party that consistently occupied the minority position the Whigs did in pre-Civil War Missouri was necessarily dependent for the major portion of its voting strength on persons engaged in agriculture. The 1850 census indicates that, excluding St. Louis County, there was a ratio of one farm to every 1.85 white males over twenty years of age. Making additional allowance for persons who worked on, but did not own land, it is clear that Missouri was an overwhelmingly agricultural state.[25]

The average Missouri farm of 1850 contained 52 acres of improved land. In only two of the nineteen counties that were normally Whig was the average farm acreage below this mark. In four it was over 80, in nine over 70, in two over 60, and in two between 52 and 60. There were 81 normally Democratic counties treated in the 1850 census, and the farms in only nineteen of these surpassed the state average.[26] Howard's and Pettis' mean sizes of 100 and 98 acres were the largest. The figures for three other Democratic counties were over 80; one was 78; and two others were between 52 and 60. Quite obviously, then, large per capita size of farms did not ensure Whig victories any more than did large population or large percentage of Negroes. However, taking a normal Whig vote of 40 per cent or more as the mark of a viable two-party system, it is true that in all the counties where farms averaged over 52 acres both parties were vital organisms. In the sixty-four counties below the state average the Whigs polled respectable votes in only eight, including the two they actually carried. Among Missouri's twenty-nine counties with average farms smaller than 40 acres only St. Louis' next-door neighbor Jefferson County regularly returned a Whig vote in excess of 40 per cent.

Of course, if slavery was the controlling influence in the average size of a county's farm units, the above analysis would be little more than confirmation of the association between Whiggery and the presence of large numbers of Negroes. Howard's high average holding of 100 acres and the fact that all but one of the counties with over 20 per cent Negro population were above the state mean attest that slavery was one factor in larger per capita landholdings. However, something besides slavery is needed to explain the difference between Boone's mean of 74 acres and Chariton's of 53, since the counties' percentages of Negroes were 24.56 and 24.34, respectively. The Whig counties of Clark and Audrain showed average farm sizes of 71 and 78 acres, while Negroes comprised only 9.30 and 13.06 per cent of their populations. Dodge County, which almost evenly divided its small vote between the two parties, had a Negro population of less than 1 per cent and an average farm size of 84 acres. Whiggish Grundy boasted an average farm of 61 acres and less than 5 per cent Negro population. Almost one quarter of the inhabitants of Democratic Mississippi County were Negroes, but its average landholding was 54 acres. Consistently Whig Monroe's Negro population was less than 20 per cent, but farms there averaged 80 acres.

The study of county statistics shows, for one thing, how predominantly Democratic Missouri was. While there were counties in which the Whig vote was 10 per cent or less,[27] it was only in Boone County after 1840 that Democrats failed to receive at least 40 per cent of the total. In areas where the per capita wealth was above the average, Whig victories did not necessarily occur, but the party at least became visible.

A full explanation of Whiggery's failure to achieve majority status in some of the counties where it became established and its success in others must rest with detailed county studies. However, a glance at some of the unique features of neighboring Howard and Boone counties does suggest the type of local conditions that influenced county politics. Howard's Democratic tendencies in the face of so many Whig characteristics possibly related to the already noted cautiousness of her Whig leaders. Unwilling to exert themselves in doubtful contests, the Howard Countians roused the ire of Whigs in other parts of the state who warned, perhaps correctly, that such a passive policy would result in nothing but doubtful contests.[28]

Boone County's preponderant Whiggery may have stemmed from its high proportion of residents originally from the strongly Whig county of Madison in Kentucky. "It seems strange," wrote Boone's chronicler, "that so many people could have left one county without in a great measure depopulating it." Local Whigs were instrumental in securing the location of the state university at the county seat, which, judging from the number who were willing to contribute money in its behalf, must have been popular with Boone Countians. In any event, the legislature passed the University Bill in 1839, and in 1840 Boone planted itself even more firmly in the Whig column.[29]

Regardless of the local conditions that tempered the precise political result in a county, it is not surprising that the index that corresponded the most closely to wealth should prove the most reliable weathervane of Whiggery. Leaders of both parties were relatively well-to-do, but those in the Whig group were more so. At the middle level of decision making the gap between average Whig and Democratic wealth was greater, and the county analysis merely lends credibility to the assumption that there was a financial distance between the rank-and-file voters of the two parties as well. The Whigs were the party of business as well as the party of wealth; and although all of Missouri except St. Louis remained agricultural, such a party would create less distrust among more prosperous farmers than among self-sufficient ones. The formers' operations more nearly resembled those of business, and they were more likely to have other interests besides their agricultural ones. Furthermore, diversified purchasing power, along with dense population and river location, contributed to the development of stronger commercial and professional classes.

Members of these groups set the course of Missouri's Whig party. There was no "growing divergence of interests" between the business elements of St. Louis and a "rural slaveholding wing" of the party.[30] Democrats did at times face a dilemma of that sort, but common interest continued during the 1840's to furnish the Whigs the unity it provided them during the 1830's. As long as financial issues were paramount, Missouri Whigs held together firmly. When the focus shifted to slavery, the party began to sunder; but the rupture occurred both within St. Louis and within rural Missouri.

Besides the dubious validity of crediting Missouri's twenty individuals who owned over fifty slaves — or even her 365 who possessed over twenty — with such great political influence, Whig leaders in rural Missouri were not typically of that class. Abiel Leonard, for instance, did not nominally endorse American System principles as a concession to the St. Louis wing of his party. Leonard, the Whig nominee for senator in 1838 and perennially in demand by his party as a candidate for office, was a Howard County lawyer whose chief activity seems to have been speculation in land. In 1850 he owned nine slaves and real estate that he valued at $50,000. Leonard's dislike of democracy is said to have been "equal to that of Chancellor Kent."[31] Perhaps it was, but not because of the possible consequences for plantation agriculture. If Leonard feared democracy, he did so because he feared business and investment opportunities would suffer at its hands.

James S. Rollins, Whig candidate for governor in 1848, was a Boone County lawyer and landowner. An agnostic who at death's door affiliated with the Presbyterian Church, he shared Leonard's enthusiasm for land speculation and later added profitable railroad promotion to his financial ventures. Rollins, descendant of the fashionable Rodes family of Madison County, Kentucky, and husband of well-to-do Mary Hickman of Franklin, Missouri, owned twenty slaves in 1850. In 1858 he estimated his wealth at $100,000. Besides his slaves and the land that he actually farmed in Boone County, this evaluation included 4,000 acres on the North Missouri Railroad near Centralia, land situated at the crossing of the North Missouri and Hannibal and St. Joseph railroads in Macon County, and two hundred mules that he expected to sell to the government at $175 apiece. His actions hardly governed by his slavery interest, this member of Indiana University's first graduating class spoke for himself as well as for Missouri when he said, "So far as the mere slave interest of the state may be compared to her other great interests, it sinks into utter insignificance." [32]

Rollins' fellow Boone Countian Eli Bass is an example of a man whose wealth was more strictly agricultural. Owner of forty-four slaves and "living in princely style at his elegant country residence," this Baptist from Tennessee inherited a large fortune, but he confined his investments chiefly to farming on a grand scale. He consistently supported the Democratic party. [33]

George R. Smith, the Whig founder of Sedalia in Pettis County, was a native of Kentucky who forsook the Baptist faith of his ancestors for the Christian denomination. His salient pursuits were a continuing quest for patronage and an unparalleled zeal in the promotion of railroads. When in 1854 he wrote, "We want the best men, and it matters not whether they are Whigs or Democrats, just so they are right on this subject," the subject did not pertain to the eight slaves he owned. Rather, Smith spoke of his overriding political passion, legislative aid to railroads. [34]

William B. Napton, a Democrat of Saline County, correctly sensed the relationship between slavery and the political philosophy of these and other leading Whigs. In 1857, after the Whig party had all but disappeared from the scene, he warned against the moderate slavery policy advocated by many ex-Whigs, including Leonard, Rollins, and Smith. To those who protested that these men could surely be trusted for they were slaveholders themselves, Napton's answer was that they differed greatly from "those of us whose entire property consists of large bodies of land and considerable numbers of slaves."[35]

Missouri Whiggery's business orientation undoubtedly goes far to explain its poor reception in an overwhelmingly agricultural state. Yet, examples of probusiness elements did exist within the Democratic party, and if there had been a union between these disaffected Jacksonians and the Whigs, Missouri politics would have had a stronger two-party flavor. Temporary, sporadic alliances were the rule instead, and the Whigs remained a decided and also distinct minority.

One obstacle in the way of union between Whigs and Democrats who held similar views on financial policy was Whig snobbery. Indeed, the aristocratic aura that clung to the Missouri Whigs may have harmed the party's fortunes quite as seriously as its economic program. Certainly, contemporary Democrats delighted in painting the Whigs as reactionary aristocrats resisting the march of democracy, but circumspection in accepting the adversary's estimate is well advised, of course.[36] Excessive caution should not obscure, however, the greater wealth of the Whig party and the more impressive educational attainments of its leadership. Besides, Whig word and deed, as well as Democratic propaganda, can be cited in support of the aristocratic description.

Such characterizations of their victorious opponents as "the despotism not of a single tyrant, but of a thousand" are not unnatural for members of any minority, but in the hands of opposing politicians they could be made to sound like outright repudiation of democratic principles.[37] When the Democratic party divided over currency and banking in 1844, the Whigs naturally preferred the branch whose views most nearly accorded with their own. Endorsing the "independents," one Whig paper editorialized:

> It is most true, that it is a nauseous pill to every Whig, and to none more bitter than ourselves, to vote for such men as even the independent candidates; but believing that the medicine, under existing circumstances, is necessary, and may be beneficial to the public health, we will apply our thumb and finger to the nasal organ and gulp them down.[38]

Condescensions of this nature were hardly conducive to permanent collaboration.

The year 1840 is commonly characterized as marking the Whigs' final reconciliation to the inevitability of mass participation in government and their reluctantly setting out to convince "the people" that they liked them.[39] In Missouri, where the normal Whig vote increased only from 35 to 40 per cent of the total, their success was limited. In Eastern states, where by virtue of dilutions from the ranks of Anti-Masons and disenchanted Jacksonians the Whig leadership included some new elements, the convincing presentation of a new public image was an easier matter. Since the composition of the party had actually changed somewhat, the switch to log-cabin tactics had a logical as well as an opportunistic basis.[40] Missouri Whigs did not respond happily to the Eastern idea of supplanting Henry Clay with William Henry Harrison, and their final acceptance of hard-cider and log-cabin campaign methods came late and artificially.

As Pennsylvanians were developing their pseudo-frontier policy, Missouri's leading Whig newspaper discovered that Harrison was not really such an unsuitable candidate, because, after all, he did have considerable "capacity of intellect." When St. Louis Whigs finally organized a Tippecanoe Club, it was at first an exclusive affair; and only belatedly did they realize that the purpose of such an organization was not to strengthen their own solidarity, but rather to entice new people into the Whig ranks. When in May Missouri Whigs held their first log-cabin raising, the site selected was "the beautiful square in front of Mrs. Ashley's mansion," and many Whigs attended wearing kid gloves.[41]

All this is not to imply that Missourians renounced Whiggery because its aristocratic tendencies especially offended their frontier natures. Missouri Whigs were simply not convincing in their professions of devotion to the common man; it is doubtful that Americans anywhere have ever responded favorably to politicians whom they regarded as snobs.

CHAPTER 7

URBAN WHIGGERY

THE special case of the Whig party in St. Louis warrants one further interruption in the chronological narrative of Missouri Whiggery. This is not to say that St. Louis Whigs constituted a breed apart, for indeed a theme of the preceding chapter is that there was no marked divergence, either of interest or of type, between St. Louis and rural Whigs. Whigs of the latter category seldom engaged in exclusively agricultural pursuits. Rather, their occupations and investments tended toward the most "urban" sectors of their communities' economies, and frequently their interests transcended their own localities. In the 1850's, after slavery issues replaced economic ones at the forefront of political concern, there was conflict within Missouri's Whig party. That is the subject matter of the latter part of this study. Here it is sufficient to stress that the clash occurred within St. Louis Whiggery and within rural Whiggery, but not between the two.

Because urban and rural Whigs had overlapping interests, it does not follow that St. Louis Whigs were without special problems. After all, they were residents of a city whose population was 16,469 in 1840 and 77,860 in 1850. In the latter year St. Louis County contained slightly less than one sixth of the state's population and was three times as large as the second ranking county.[1] The Whigs were strong in this urban constituency, but Democratic strength was also considerable, and two-party politics flourished in St. Louis as in few other Missouri places. Every April the parties contended for control of St. Louis. This chapter focuses on these annual elections.

St. Louisans voted for a bewildering variety of public officials during the period of the Whig party's existence. A
charter amendment in 1839 established a bicameral city council, consisting of the Board of Delegates elected annually and
the Board of Aldermen elected biennially. There were six
wards in the city, and each had two representatives in both
of these houses. The mayor's term was for one year. Elaborate
as this machinery was, the powers of the city government
were subject to the pleasures of the state legislature. To bor-
row money, levy new taxes, establish licensing requirements,
or amend its charter, St. Louis had to seek the permission of
the General Assembly, grantor of its corporate charter.[2]

Logically, one might expect to find a continuing debate in
St. Louis city politics over what to request from the legislature. Such was seldom the case, however. St. Louis delega-
tions to Jefferson City, often composed of members of both
parties, tended to vote solidly on St. Louis matters; and the
Democratic legislature regularly respected the wishes of the
St. Louis delegation in regard to city business, whether that
delegation was predominantly Whig or Democratic. On one
occasion, when a group of St. Louis Democrats directly approached the rural Democratic leadership in the General Assembly, a Democratic representative from St. Louis promptly
consulted the Whig mayor to find out if he and the council
held the same views.[3]

Thus, despite the two-party character of St. Louis politics,
campaign issues were few and often trivial. The *Missouri Republican* candidly acknowledged that a major Whig interest
in the city elections was the opportunity they afforded for
"sustaining here that complete and paramount organization"
so useful in the important state contests.[4] St. Louis campaigns
provide classic examples of personalities overshadowing issues. Whigs were justly aggrieved when the Democratic organ, the *Argus*, branded self-made John F. Darby a "notorious
speculator." In a different mayoralty contest the *Republican*

piously objected that the Democratic candidate was "only a politician." Another year the same paper called for a Whig majority on the city council because the character of the Democrats was such that if they won, "money cannot be borrowed on the faith of the city on fair terms."[5] Unproved charges and countercharges of corruption were yearly editorial themes. Yet, disturbing accusations of defalcations disappeared from the press following elections, leaving the historian wondering whether the recriminations were so unfounded that their perpetrators were happy to let them vanish, or if the accused benefited more by the postelection silence.[6]

Although issues of substance were scarce in Missouri's urban politics, the two parties did present contrasting images. Here, as elsewhere, the Whigs found themselves saddled with a reputation for undemocratic principles. Among the provisions of the original St. Louis charter passed by the legislature in 1822 were a taxpaying qualification for voters in city elections and a minimal real estate qualification for office holding. In his study of American suffrage, Chilton Williamson points out that similar provisions in city charters were not unusual in this period, even in states like Missouri where state-wide suffrage restrictions never existed.[7] Probably no one was prevented from seeking office by the provision, and since the charter was vague about what kind of tax was obligatory for voters, payments no larger than a dog tax sometimes sufficed, depending however on the inclination of the election official.

This vagueness led to misunderstanding but not to any agitation for repeal of the restrictive clauses. In 1840, however, Democrats began to make political capital by emphasizing that the restrictions were undemocratic and by asserting that Whigs were responsible for them. Whigs had controlled the St. Louis representation to the legislature in recent years, yet never once had they introduced charter amendments providing for universal suffrage, reasoned the *Missouri Argus*. Vainly the Whigs retorted that Democrats had never suggested repeal in any campaign and that there had been some Democratic legislators from St. Louis who had been equally indifferent to the notorious clauses. Nevertheless, the Whigs were on the defensive. Ineptly, they permitted their defense of their legislative record as guardian of St. Louis' interests to include approval of the charter as it was. Seeming to flaunt an aversion to unrestricted voting, a Whig newspaper editorialized: "Demagogues may prate as much as they please about the provisions depriving men of the right to vote who have not paid a city tax. . . . We never hear these complaints when the assessor and collector are going around." [8]

The Whigs belatedly tried to revise their stand by advocating a 37-cent poll tax as sufficient to establish eligibility, but not until 1841 did they emulate the Democrats in calling for the end of all property and tax qualifications for voting and office holding. The requirements were soon abolished, and under Whig auspices at that. Still, because the Whig response was not automatically in favor of this extension of democracy, charges that the party lacked sympathy with workingmen carried more weight. [9]

Only in St. Louis were laborers a potent political force. Before Whigs realized this important fact, their ineptness cast them in a light more repellent to labor than realities merited. When workingmen advocated legislation to establish a ten-hour day in 1840, Whigs quickly voiced opposition, contending that such a law destroyed freedom. The Workingmen's Association endorsed candidates sympathetic to the ten-hour principle in the August state elections of 1840; and all of these, mostly Democrats, ran ahead of the other candidates on the same ticket. Once labor's strength was thus apparent, St. Louis Whigs quickly dropped their opposition to the ten-hour day. In the following legislative session, every Whig

from St. Louis save one voted for a law making it manda-
tory.[10] Just as they had done in regard to the suffrage restrictions, the Whigs had first taken an unpopular stand on a
matter about which they did not feel strongly. Though they
willingly reversed themselves as soon as they saw the disfavor of their position, the antilabor stigma clung. By
contrast, the Democratic press expressed its approval of a
ten-hour-day law immediately after the Workingmen's Association raised the issue.[11]

Whig aversions to democratic suffrage and labor are easily
exaggerated, but the third element in the composite Whig
image was more real. That element was nativism. So preva-
lent were antiforeign sentiments within St. Louis Whiggery
that some years the native branch of the party completely
controlled the local campaign, and refused to cooperate with
Whigs who would not openly subscribe to the nativistic platform that called for long United States residence as a prerequisite for voting eligibility.

The eminently practical editor of the *Missouri Republican*,
A. B. Chambers, furnished the leadership for a segment of the
party that contended that nativism could only harm St. Louis
Whiggery, an analysis that proved correct. In the first place,
the issue divided the Whigs. St. Louis nativism was the source
of the only consequential split within Missouri Whiggery before the 1850's, and it naturally weakened the normally unified party. Many Whigs, either from considerations of expediency or from conviction, simply would not act with their
erstwhile political associates under a Native American banner. Secondly, nativist proclivities repelled more supporters
than they attracted from outside of the ranks of regular Whiggery. There is virtually no evidence of customary Democrats
aiding either the Whigs or Native Americans when antiforeign principles were publicized. On the other hand, the claim
of the *Republican* that nativism automatically drove away
the foreign-born appears incontrovertible. The nativist re-

sponse to this argument was that almost no foreigners voted the Whig ticket anyway. Perhaps few did, but the distinction between cause and result is blurred. The nativistic aspect of the Whig image in effect prevented the party from participating in the city's growth, to which the foreign-born contributed disproportionately.[12]

A compact survey of St. Louis city elections between 1836 and 1854 demonstrates the generally declining fortunes of the Whig party and also indicates the strong connection between nativism and that decline. The year 1838 has been established as marking the birth of the Whig party in Missouri. St. Louis elected a Whig mayor in 1838, and her mayors had come from the precursors of the Whig party since 1829. By the slightest stretching of the evidence, one could even argue that pre-Whig tenure in the St. Louis mayoralty extended all the way back to the origins of the office. St. Louis' first mayor, William Carr Lane, served continuously from 1823 until 1829. A supporter of Clay in 1824, Lane preferred Jackson to Adams in 1828, but this affinity was short-lived. He was one of the few Missourians who later deserted Jackson in favor of the Adams-Clay persuasion. By 1830 his conversion was accomplished, and in 1838 he once again became St. Louis' mayor, this time as the first bona fide Whig to fill the office.[13]

The three mayors who served between Lane's two incumbencies all later acted with the Whig party. Until 1839 the balance between the two parties in the city council was often precarious, and in 1838 St. Louis' council majority was Democratic, while her mayor was Whig. However, Whig organization brought dividends within St. Louis, resulting in Whig hegemony in the city government from 1839 until 1842,[14] the first year the Native American party entered a separate ticket. In 1840 the Native American Association had openly supported the Whig candidates, but the *Republican* had just as openly deplored the alliance, reasoning that association of

nativism and Whiggery in the popular mind could only drive
all foreigners permanently into the ranks of the Democracy.[15]

Resentful of the *Republican's* "domination" nativistic
Whigs encouraged the formation of an "American" ticket for
the 1842 elections, headed by a Whig of good standing, Joseph Charless, Jr. Charless' father had founded Missouri's
first newspaper, the *Missouri Gazette*, which later spawned
the *Republican*.[16] So split was the party that Whig efforts to
organize were "all in vain," and 1842 witnessed the anomaly
of the *Republican's* supporting the Democratic candidate for
mayor. Theorizing that "the success of the Whig party would
be more jeopardized by the election of a Native American
candidate than by the temporary ascendancy of locofocoism,"
the newspaper discouraged "real" Whigs from voting even
for Wilson Primm, a lawyer who at the eleventh hour independently announced his candidacy and appealed for support from Whigs who rejected nativism. Although the *Republican* heartily endorsed Primm's qualifications, it felt he
had no chance and that his candidacy might serve to furnish
Charless with a decisive plurality.[17]

The Americans, as nativists in politics referred to themselves, protested that the *Republican's* attitude was an attempt to dictate to the rest of the party. After all, Charless
had merely added distrust of foreigners to his Whiggery. He
was, claimed the American newspaper, a Whig candidate
nominated through the Native American Association. On
what grounds, asked the *American Bulletin*, did *Republican*
editor Chambers feel that he was certified to pass on Whig
nominations?[18]

Had it been possible, Chambers very likely would have
dictated to the St. Louis Whigs in order to swerve them from
what he considered a senseless course. Before the election,
however, the dissenters were unwilling to submit to coer-
cion, and instead, Chambers had to rely on maneuver. By
ensuring Democratic victory he inflicted on the Native Ameri-

can party a serious wound. Although the *American Bulletin* continued to avow its distrust of the Whig party under *Republican* tutelage, almost immediately after seeing their city turned over to the opposite party, errant Whigs began to return to the fold. Before the state and county elections in August the Native American party considered disbanding. It did not do so, but it entered candidates for only a few minor county offices and gave its endorsement to Whig candidates for the General Assembly. Dedicated Americans denied that they were a branch of the Whigs, but the group increasingly reverted to the status of a private organization rather than a political party. Soon after the August elections the *American Bulletin* ceased publication. Its editor, Vespasian Ellis, embraced Tylerism and began a new paper dedicated to the interests of that movement.[19]

Nevertheless, nativistic sentiments persisted. A Whig party reappeared in the city elections of 1843, but it was not the invincible organization of 1839 to 1841. John Wimer, the Democratic "Workingmen's candidate" defeated the well-known Whig John F. Darby, who had earlier served two terms in the office. Darby was among those Whigs who had shunned any connection with the Native American Association. Democrats, however, found it good campaign tactics to suggest that, since so many of his supporters were members, some of the taint must have rubbed off on the candidate himself.[20]

Not until 1844 did the Whigs regain control of the city government. A united party, drawn together to a great extent by its enthusiasm over the presidential nomination of Henry Clay, succeeded in electing a mayor and a majority of the other city officers. A year later, however, resurgent nativism once more offered its own slate of candidates, headed by Peter G. Camden, a dry-goods merchant and St. Louis business agent for the wealthy widow of William H. Ashley. This time Whigs who opposed nativism effected an arrangement with the Democratic leadership whereby the Democrats made no nomination for mayor and the Whigs abstained from the contests for city councilmen. The strategy worked for the Whigs, who saw Bernard Pratte elected for his second term, but the Native American candidates won every other office in the city.[21]

Unable to repeat this cooperation with the Democrats in 1846, the Whigs abandoned the field again. Contending against a Democratic party divided on state issues, the nativists were victorious. This was the only time the Native Americans controlled both the mayor's office and the council, although the later Know-Nothing party scored a similar success in 1855. Democrats regrouped their forces in 1847 and regularly defeated competing Whigs and Americans for the next three years.[22]

Finally, in 1850 a compound of Whig unity and Democratic disunity brought the former party back into power. Thomas Hart Benton's re-election to the Senate was at stake, and throughout the state the Democratic party was fiercely divided into Benton and anti-Benton factions. Benton himself insisted on "applying the test of Benton or no Benton in all elections, city and county, State and Federal, Congress, and all."[23] The chance for plurality victories offered by the Democratic rupture was a powerful incentive for the Whigs to put their own house in order.

Another contribution to Whig reunification came from the *Missouri Republican.* Without actually espousing nativism, the editors softened their stand against it. The change may have resulted from a practical desire for compromise, but it also seems to have been related to the increased prevalence of a free-thinking, agnostic element among the foreign-born of St. Louis. Vocally leading this group was Henry Boernstein, a German intellectual who arrived in Missouri in the mid-forties after having been on the fringe of revolutionary movements in his native land. He established a German-language newspaper that attacked slavery, the Jesuits, tax exemptions for churches, and Sunday closing laws for liquor-dispensing establishments. To the *Republican* editors these views were not only nefarious but "foreign" as well. Expressing satisfaction over the Whig victory of 1851, the newspaper harangued its readers: "It is a rebuke . . . to those who would rear the hydra-headed factions of Socialism, Red Republicanism, Communism, Revolutionism, and infidelity in our midst. We glory in it as a signal rebuke to those who would burn churches or sack convents to carry out their revolutionary purpose."[24] Only Americans whose nativism rested on a virulent anti-Catholicism could fail to find comfort from such editorials.

Further evidence of a *rapprochement* between the two Whig branches is furnished by the history of the man who was the party's successful candidate each year from 1850 to 1853. Luther Martin Kennett, a wealthy manufacturer, had run for alderman on the Native American ticket in 1845 and 1846.[25] Now that he was again under the Whig label, the *Republican* saw no reason to question his past.

The Whig restoration always rested on divisions among the Democrats, and it promptly terminated when Democrats overcame their internal differences for the election of 1854. By the following year the Know-Nothing party was born. Whiggery's split reasserted itself, and the nativistic party won a plurality victory in the three-way election.[26] There was never another Whig ticket in a St. Louis election. In 1856 those Whigs who, like the *Republican* editors, could not abide the Know-Nothing party associated themselves with one of the Democratic branches.[27]

A nativistic component was unique to St. Louis Whiggery. Only in the city did Whigs have to overcome the strife that nativism inflamed among themselves and the unfavorable image it engendered among other parts of the electorate. Other Missouri Whigs bore the burden of appearing snobbish and unsympathetic to the aspirations of the common man and, as already suggested, the St. Louis party was afflicted with a similar reputation. The preceding chapter presents evidence that Missouri's Whig party, while not an aristocracy, was in fact more affluent than its Democratic rival. A comparison of occupations of city Whigs and Democrats supports a similar conclusion.

St. Louis political parties customarily appointed Vigilance Committees at each election. Officially, their purpose was to observe the polls and to prevent fraud by the other side, but it is likely that they also were a means whereby leaders recognized the party faithful. In any event, the St. Louis newspapers sometimes published lists of the members of these committees, thus providing a basis for comparing the status of rank-and-file party members.

For the year 1848 committee memberships of both parties in the First, Third, and Fourth wards appeared in the local press.[28] The *St. Louis Directory* for 1848 furnished information on the occupations of most of the individuals, data that admittedly require interpretation. This particular directory often indicated occupations only by a firm's initials, for example, B&H. At least one of the initials invariably corresponded to that of the individual in question, leading to the assumption that he was a partner, rather than an employee, in some independent enterprise. However, the lack of an index of business establishments makes it impossible to determine the nature or the size of the business.[29] Still, if the somewhat nebulous category of "businessmen" can be tolerated, some clear occupational differences between the Whig and Democratic samples emerge.

The lists contained the names of 96 Whigs and 146 Democrats, and the directory listed occupations for 79 and 105 of these, respectively. Among the Whigs there were nine attorneys as opposed to only two Democrats from that profession. Whig businessmen on the vigilance committees numbered forty-four, while Democrats in that broad classification to-talled twenty-five. Druggists and merchants were counted with the businessmen; tailors were not. There were four Democratic tailors as opposed to one Whig from that trade.

Tavernkeepers and brewers certainly were businessmen, but they were not included in the above computation be-cause they so unanimously chose one party. There were twen-ty-one individuals connected in some way with the liquor in-dustry, every one of whom appeared on the Democratic list. Aside from the already remarked sympathy of the *Republi-can* for Sunday closing laws, this writer is unaware of de-bates over liquor issues in St. Louis politics. Students of nativism have commented on a connection between that movement and temperance societies. Perhaps the tavern-keepers of St. Louis were simply reacting to the Whigs' repu-tation for nativistic inclinations.[30]

The other outstanding difference between the two samples is the far greater incidence among the Democrats of laboring, blue-collar occupations. No Whigs were identified simply as "laborers"; ten Democrats were. Occupations such as car-penter, brickmason, plasterer, and caulker accounted for only eleven Whigs, but for thirty-four Democrats. On the other hand, eight Whigs were clerks, bookkeepers, or collectors; only three Democrats were clerks, and they all worked for the United States Post Office. The Democratic committees included the only watchmen and sextons.[31]

Among the candidates for the city council also, Whigs generally engaged in occupations of higher status. In addi-tion to four attorneys, the Whig candidates of 1848 followed such diverse occupations as physician (2), mill owner (2), foundry owner, businessman (5), and Unitarian pastor. One attorney sought office on the Democratic ticket, as did an architect, a physician, and three partners in business firms. They ran in company with two grocers, a livery stable pro-prietor, one tailor, a gunsmith, a wheelwright, and two plasterers. There were no candidates from the Democratically inclined liquor interest nor any from the ranks of unskilled labor.

Whig candidates for mayor further demonstrated the party's business and social ascendancy over the Democrats. Unsuccessful candidates included Pierre Chouteau, scion of one of the city's founding French families and known as "the prince of the fur traders," and James H. Lucas, head of the wealthiest family in St. Louis. In 1851 the real estate within the city limits owned by these two men was assessed at $290,000 and $452,000, respectively.[32] Closely associated with these two socially and in business was Bernard Pratte, a descendant of a leading Ste. Genevieve family. Pratte was mayor for two terms during the 1840's. Though not connected with old Missouri families, Luther Martin Kennett was definitely a product of a privileged background. Educated at private schools, he came to St. Louis permanently only in 1842. He was then thirty-five years old, and after several years of leisure in Europe he was ready to turn his attention to business investments, at which he was spectacularly successful.[33]

John F. Darby's origins were less exalted, but on his arrival in St. Louis in 1827 he was a well-connected young man. He had studied law under John J. Crittenden of Kentucky and bore letters of introduction to Hamilton Rowan Gamble and Henry S. Geyer, leaders of the St. Louis bar. Darby, incidentally, was the only practicing lawyer who was a Whig candidate for mayor, though leading St. Louis lawyers, including Edward Bates as well as Geyer and Gamble, were all Whigs.[34]

Quite different from these Whigs was John Wimer, the Democrat who was elected mayor in 1843. A very large man, Wimer was a blacksmith when not engaged in politics and, according to one St. Louis historian, was the prototype of the political boss, ruling the First Ward from his blacksmith shop.[35] More nearly resembling the Whig mayor candidates, though certainly not a wealthy man, was John M. Krum, who was mayor in 1848. He came to St. Louis in 1840 from Alton, Illinois, where he had been mayor at the age of twenty-seven. A lawyer and later judge of the St. Louis circuit court, Krum was assessed for only $50 worth of city real estate the year of his election. Before his death in 1885, John How, elected in 1853, became known for his philanthropy to Washington University. His great success in mining ventures came after the Whig period, however.[36]

There is no intent here to suggest that sharp class conflict was characteristic of St. Louis politics during the decade before the Civil War. Certainly, both How and Krum would properly be found on the side of the exploiting class in a Marxian struggle, and there were members of St. Louis' elite group in the Democratic party. Fully as "aristocratic" as the Whig leaders was Bryan Mullanphy, Democratic mayor in 1847. This bachelor inherited a large fortune from his father, an astute merchant who was one of the first non-French settlers in St. Louis. As had Lucas, Mullanphy studied in France and did not return to St. Louis until his father's death left him in control of an estate valued at five million dollars. The elder Mullanphy acted with the pre-Whig Adams party before his death, but Bryan chose different political allies.[37] Another Democrat of large wealth and high social standing was Lewis Vital Bogy, who, like Bernard Pratte, was a descendant of one of the leading French families of Ste. Genevieve, and like so many well-to-do Whigs, a graduate of Transylvania College in Kentucky. Successful in the practice of law, Bogy's St. Louis real estate was assessed for $191,000 in 1851. Benton's chief lieutenant in St. Louis, Frank P. Blair, Jr., would also qualify for upper-class standing. One of the few graduates of Princeton College in Missouri politics, he was connected with the famous newspaper family and was independently wealthy.[38]

The membership of the parties in St. Louis, then, would tend to support the apparently controversial generalization that "unless fine criteria are used, . . . both parties can be said to have recruited their leaders from *the same social and economic strata.*" [39] However, these memberships will also support the conclusion of the preceding chapter, namely, that in Missouri a comparatively upper-class Whig leadership was not as successful as a somewhat less affluent Democratic leadership in winning the sympathies of the humbler members of the electorate.

An aristocratic image was harmful to the Whigs in St. Louis as it was elsewhere, but the Whigs' reputation as a party of business was not so damaging in St. Louis. Rather, in the state's metropolis a reputation for agrarianism embarrassed the Democrats. In his study celebrating the importance of Western cities, Richard C. Wade alleges that Thomas Hart Benton's power rested on an urban base.[40] Initially it may have done so, but Benton's advocacy of hard money in the 1830's and 1840's had a rural appeal. St. Louis Democrats were apt to apologize for Benton's policies and even to oppose them.

Benton's position in Missouri was a state rather than a city issue, however, and therefore it belongs in the context of the state study. The next chapter resumes the chronological narrative of the Whig party in Missouri.

CHAPTER 8

TRADITIONAL WHIGGERY

ONE of the more notable recent revisions of American political history avers that 1840, rather than 1828, properly marks the advent of truly mass participation in American presidential politics. In support of this thesis, Richard P. McCormick has marshalled statistics demonstrating that the later contest between William Henry Harrison and Martin Van Buren drew to the polls a significantly greater proportion of the eligible voters than the earlier election when Andrew Jackson was the central figure. McCormick also shows that until 1840 there was consistently more interest in state than in national elections.[1]

In some respects, Missouri furnishes a textbook illustration of these findings. Almost three times as many people expressed their presidential preferences in 1840 as did in 1836, and the vote in 1840 was fully four times as large as that in 1832. There was more to the increase than just population growth, impressive as that was during the decade; for fully three fourths of the qualified males visited the polls in 1840, breaking the 1828 record, when slightly over half of the eligible voters participated. Moreover, nearly as many voted in the 1840 national election as did in the earlier state election. In 1836, by way of contrast, the number of votes cast in the two elections was 27,000 and 18,000, respectively; whereas the comparable totals for 1840 were 49,000 and 53,000. Undoubtedly, as McCormick suggests, much of the heightened interest in national politics was due to the presence at last of two organized and active national parties in the state.[2]

Yet, the rest of the Missouri story does not conform to McCormick's schema. Going beyond mere documentation of the electorate's expansion, McCormick considers it especially significant that when the "flood of democracy" occurred, it "engulfed the Jacksonians." The Harrison-Tyler campaign is, of course, famous as the Whigs' "great commotion," and a major purpose of McCormick's article is to show that the Whigs lured ordinary Americans to the polls more effectively than had the earlier Jacksonians. In Missouri, however, the Democratic party retained the offices, the electoral vote, and almost as large a percentage of the popular vote as it had become accustomed to expect during the previous decade.[3] Part of the explanation for this divergence from the national pattern lay in the failure of the Missouri Whigs to capture the enthusiasm that pervaded so much of their party in 1840.

Three related reasons contributed to this lack of zeal. Not least among them was the aristocratic nature of Missouri's Whig party, described in an earlier chapter. Distaste for Jacksonian campaign methods permeated the Whig leadership, and to few Missouri Whigs did rowdy campaign tactics come naturally. Secondly, the record of overwhelming Democratic victories naturally generated a pessimism, well-founded, but contributing nevertheless to the prophecy's self-fulfillment. As important as pessimism and campaign queasiness, however, was the disappointment felt by Missouri Whigs that Henry Clay, the leading champion of active governmental programs to foster commerce, was not the party's presidential nominee.

Following instructions from the state convention, the small Missouri delegation to the first Whig national convention was among those that remained unanimously loyal to Henry Clay throughout the balloting. When Missouri Whigs did dutifully chorus their endorsements of William Henry Harrison after the nomination, they did so "with a feeling of regret that forbids concealment," and privately they complained to each other, "Have not the Whigs done a poor business at their Harrisburg convention?"[4]

True, as the canvass progressed, the party's enthusiasm for Harrison became more convincing. Whig activity contributed to the wresting of centrally located Cooper, Lafayette, Ralls, and Saline counties from the Democrats; but these gains were offset by Democratic successes in newly settled areas. "Like the cat in the well that gained two feet through the day but fell back three at night," philosophized a Fayette editor, "every change which has been effected in older sections of the State has, perhaps, been more than counterbalanced by immigrants, chiefly from Tennessee, who brought the seed of political error along with them." Tennessee's political tendencies were more pronouncedly Democratic than those of either Virginia or Kentucky, and the editor may have been partially correct in attributing the election results in the recently organized counties to the political traditions the settlers brought with them. However, Cooper, Lafayette, Ralls, and Saline counties had voted Democratic before 1840, despite a preponderance of residents with Kentucky and Virginia antecedents. The analysis in the preceding chapters suggests that meager per-capita wealth and the absence of strong commercial interests in the newly established counties were at least equally important as ancestry in determining their preference for Democracy.[5]

More to the point here is the quiescence of Whigs in sections of the state where their party had a chance. What effects campaigns have on election results is always open to question, but certainly the Eastern strategists who were instrumental in Harrison's nomination viewed the candidacy as a principal ingredient in a campaign designed to identify the Whig party with popular aspirations. At least a few Missouri Whigs saw their party's needs in a similar light. "I do believe," wrote one, "that the people are seeking light & if they were once convinced that the Whigs are contending for &

not against Democracy they would do right." The instruments at hand for dispelling these misapprehensions, if such they were, were log cabins and hard cider; but Missouri Whigs were chary in their use.[6]

As already observed, the log cabin symbol was slow to make its appearance in Missouri politics. During the campaign there were only two authentic log cabin rallies of any size in the state, both of which were in counties where the Whigs already enjoyed majorities. St. Louis was the scene of the exquisite gathering on the lawn of Mrs. Ashley's mansion referred to in an earlier chapter, and it did not prevent a slight decline in the Whigs' share of that county's vote. In Boone County, however, the Whigs improved their already favorable position.[7]

The Boone County celebration, held at the small river town of Rocheport, was the one occasion when Missouri Whigs clearly reflected the boisterous Tippecanoe spirit. Offering a number of out-of-state speakers, though none of national prominence, the meeting lasted three days and attracted thousands, who encamped in tents and covered wagons. According to the report of a Jefferson City Democrat, the members of the St. Louis delegation "made quite a display of their deficient cerebrums in our town — both during their trip up and down the river, carrying with them emblems of ridicule of the present administration, singing songs and creating riots equal to any set of intoxicated boys within my knowledge."[8]

Such indecorous passion for the Whig cause, always rare in Missouri, was nowhere visible between the state defeats in August and the presidential election in November, and even before the state election the Whigs were beset by familiar difficulties. The convention of 1839, with its buoyant optimism and pledges of sacrificial devotion to the cause of Whiggery, seemed ludicrous by the spring of 1840. Of the four nominees selected at that gathering, only the candidate for governor, John B. Clark, remained active in the canvass. Joseph Bogy, member of one of the old French families in Ste. Genevieve and candidate for lieutenant governor, let it be known in March that because of business and family considerations he would continue in the race only on the condition that he would not be expected to campaign. Not surprisingly, the Whig Central Committee acquiesced in this demand, for the two supposed congressional aspirants had both withdrawn in February, and replacements were not forthcoming. Thornton Grimsley stated that his St. Louis business, supplying the Army with the military, or dragoon, saddles he had invented, required his full attention. Woodson J. Moss, a Clay County physician, asked to be excused on grounds of ill health.[9]

Solicitations to James S. Rollins, Edward Bates, Henry S. Geyer, and Beverly Allen to fill the vacancies all proved futile. Finally in June the ever conscientious George C. Sibley of St. Charles and E. M. Samuel, a prosperous Clay County merchant who later moved to St. Louis and established the Commercial Bank, agreed to run. Optimistic as these men were about the prospects of "the cause of truth, justice, & the Constitution," they knew that their necessarily brief visit to the "rabid loco foco counties" of the still undistricted state would be insufficient to change the character of Missouri's congressional representation.[10]

Even Clark's gubernatorial nomination probably resulted from the unwillingness of the real leaders of the party to undertake the canvass. This man was one of the first to break Whig ranks when slavery issues began to split the party in 1850, and he afterwards was a moving force in the ultra-Southern wing of the Democratic party. His stature in 1839 and 1840, however, was by no means equal to that of some of the St. Louis leaders. All seems to have gone placidly at the convention, and there is no evidence of a city-country rivalry. If a central Missouri nominee was the desideratum, though, Clark's more widely known fellow Howard Countian, Abiel Leonard, would have met that condition. A Democratic member of Congress furnished the following estimate of Clark's prestige: "The *Fed* nominations are but poor affairs — John B. Clark for gov. . . . what a commentary on all the talents [of the Whig] party in Missouri — it will be but sport to beat such a team." [11] The slur on Clark's abilities may have been partisan, but the prophecy of his defeat proved correct.

Missouri's Whig campaign of 1840 differed from that in other states in another respect besides the reluctance of its candidates. At their national convention the Whigs did not draft a platform, and in most states the party imitated this noncommittal example by concentrating on hard cider, corruption, and executive usurpation. Platitudes were not unknown to Missouri Whigs, but neither was frank discussion of issues. Toward the tariff the Whigs' attitude did remain obscure, their sole pronouncement on this subject being that they considered the matter settled by the compromise tariff of 1833. A case could be made that the party was evasive in its positions on public land and internal improvements, for it proposed nothing specific in regard to these issues. However, statements favoring "any" land policy conducive to actual settlement and advocacy of liberal federal expenditure "for objects of a strictly national character" are more accurately construed as illustrations of the essential agreement between the two Missouri parties on these matters.[12]

No such bipartisan approach to financial problems existed, and the Whigs contributed fully to that issue's lucidity. At last complying with the wishes of President Van Buren, a Democratic Congress passed the Independent Treasury Act in 1840. The Whig party in Missouri denounced this "experiment," but it also opposed a continuation of depositing federal funds in selected state banks, the policy inaugurated under Andrew Jackson. Rather, Whig spokesmen boldly advocated re-establishment of a national bank.

Confident that the ruinous character of the Independent Treasury would soon lead to its abolition, Whigs predicted, "This scheme abandoned, the State deposite [sic] system exploded, we must necessarily recur to the re-establishment of a National bank." [13] His alleged residence in a log cabin was not the only charm assigned to Harrison. To Missouri Whigs, his willingness to countenance a "properly restricted" national bank, as opposed to Van Buren's obdurate negativism on the subject, was a prime reason for favoring the hero of Tippecanoe, and it was Clay's more open association with the bank cause that endeared him so warmly to Missourians of his party. Deploring Democratic opposition to national banking, one Whig declaimed: "We ask whether the reflecting citizens of this giant young State, with her resources undeveloped and all her interests paralized [sic] by the failure of all the 'experiments' of the past few years, are ready thus to TIE THEIR HANDS." [14] The appeal to the "reflecting citizens" and the frank espousal of an economic program set Missouri Whigs apart from their party in the nation at large. As previously stated, the results of the election did also. The Van Buren electors carried the state by 8,000 votes, and Whig candidates in the state elections were defeated by a slightly larger margin.

Still, Harrison did win the Presidency, "demonstrating to the skeptical," said the *Missouri Whig's* editor, "that the American people are capable of self-government." Whether the journalist was conscious of his implication that Missourians were not so qualified is unknown, but his statement testified to one of the continuing difficulties of Missouri's Whig party. In a year when most Whigs strove to convince the average American of their confidence in his abilities, the Missouri party remained aloof — and out of power. [15]

Repeated failures in their own state merely whetted the appetites of Missouri Whigs for patronage favors, once a Whig President was in a position to grant them. Seemingly affluent and well-established men were interested in patronage. Among Missouri Whigs who sought federal employment in 1840 were Samuel B. Churchill, a St. Louis editor and newly elected member of the legislature; George C. Sibley, founder of Lindenwood College at St. Charles; George Mc-Gunnegle, a successful St. Louis merchant; and two physicians, Hardage Lane of St. Louis and Woodson J. Moss of Liberty. Not infrequently there were references in patronage letters to the "degrading," "mortifying" aspects of office seeking. Nevertheless, requests for recommendations poured in to party leaders such as John Darby, who as mayor of St. Louis was the only Missouri Whig holding important elective office, and John O'Fallon, an aide to General Harrison during the War of 1812 and probably closer personally to the President-elect than any other Missourian. Either because they realized their influence was limited or, possibly, because they simply did not care to devote large amounts of time to party matters, the response of these men to their supplicants was indifferent at best. For example, O'Fallon, president of the St. Louis branch of the Bank of the United States during its existence, complained both when asked to campaign for Harrison and when asked to make recommendations to him that their relationship "begins to occasion me much annoyance." In the end, O'Fallon made exactly three recommendations to his old chief.[16]

Nor did O'Fallon and Darby, or even more established party leaders such as Edward Bates and Abiel Leonard, seek appointments for themselves. Their private affairs superseded interest in run-of-the-mill appointments, and Missouri Whiggery's known preference for Henry Clay over Harrison did not enhance their claims for high office. In short, though many sought federal employment, no one stepped forward with a design to use patronage as a builder of Whig strength in Missouri.

National leaders also failed to furnish direction or strategy. Indeed, one of the striking features of Missouri Whig history is the sparsity of communication between famous Whigs in Washington and leaders of the Missouri party. Letters from such men as Henry Clay, Daniel Webster, and Thurlow Weed are rarities among the papers of Missourians; and only infrequently does one come upon a letter from Missouri to one of them. When he does, it is apt to resemble two that Daniel Webster received shortly after Harrison's election. Both writers, though locally active in Whig politics, were unknown to Webster either personally or by reputation; and, in fact, they wrote more as private citizens than as fellow politicians.[17]

Lacking leadership from either state or national figures, Missouri's patronage situation drifted aimlessly throughout Harrison's brief Administration. When the new President's death only a month after taking office relieved O'Fallon of his bothersome influence, Missourians turned increasingly to James H. Birch of Fayette to represent their patronage claims.

This chameleonlike politician, once scorned by both parties, came to Missouri Whiggery almost unaccompanied through the door opened by the presidential candidacy of Hugh Lawson White in 1836. In 1840 he served energetically on the State Central Committee, and following the election he promptly departed for Washington to seek employment. Dismissed by O'Fallon as deserving but hardly competent to fill a position "of the grade to which he aspires," Birch was recognized even before Harrison's death as having considerable influence over Missouri patronage. He quickly paid homage to the new chief magistrate, John Tyler, and Missourians thereafter made Birch the chief recipient of their supplications. Before the Howard Countian had an opportunity to test his persuasiveness, however, Tyler vetoed the first United States Bank bill passed by the newly elected Congress. At once the Whig party in Missouri denounced this "traitorous course" and effectually alienated itself from the President.[18]

Few Whigs from Birch's state continued their interest in appointments from the Tyler Administration. After all, they had publicly proclaimed their devotion to the national bank principle during a campaign when members of their party elsewhere were expediently reserved on that issue, and even before the first bank bill passed Congress, Missouri Whigs reacted irately to Tyler's insistence on provisions permitting a state to exclude a branch from its borders. With the actual veto, then, it is no wonder that the Whig party in Missouri should be among the first to discover that the "President-by-accident" had "suffered himself to be elected under false and delusive expectations." Not only were Missouri Whigs prompt in their denunciation of Tyler; they were almost unanimous.[19]

Hunger for patronage motivated the few who did not break with the Virginia President. In the forefront of this small group was Birch himself, who, notwithstanding his spirited defense of a national banking institution during the campaign of 1840, now asserted that it was but natural for him to be a "Tyler Whig" in view of "my uniform opposition to any bank similarly constituted." Birch did not become Commissioner General of the Land Office as he hoped, but his flexibility was rewarded by a much sought-after appointment, registrar of the newly opened land office at Plattsburg.[20]

Even more arrantly opportunistic was George R. Smith, a recent immigrant from Kentucky who later gained fame as a promoter of railroad interests. Smith sought the receivership of the land office at Springfield, an appointment he eventually received, in no small measure due to the exertions of Birch. Before he would recommend Smith, Birch required

assurance of his fidelity to Tyler and "old school republicanism." The fact that Smith received the appointment, coupled
with his extensive correspondence with Tyler Democrats
about strategy to nominate their favorite in 1844, indicates
that he complied. That Smith's professed enthusiasm for the
controversial President was merely for the sake of employ-
ability, however, is shown both by his sudden re-entry into
the Whig party in 1844 and the remarks of a Kentucky relative.

> I am glad to hear that Tylerism has made no progress with
> you, although the Captain has thought proper to give you an
> appointment. It might be well enough, however, for you to
> be somewhat prudent in your expressions of disgust toward
> him before those who would report the facts to your injury.
> The Captain's time is short, but you had as well hold on to the
> end of his term, if you can.[21]

Unlike Smith, Birch was at least consistent in his incon-
sistency, and from a tactical point of view he might be regarded as an unusually constructive Whig politician. Missouri
Whigs chronically awaited a realignment of parties; Birch
alone had a record of actually trying to create one. His support of Hugh Lawson White for President in 1836 could be
construed as such an effort, albeit an unsuccessful one. When
charged with treachery by Whigs during the Tyler era, Birch
declared his attackers ignored "all I *have* done & am *yet* doing (in my own way) to bring about a change of things in
Missouri." To Abiel Leonard, who "at least used to have some
sagacity in political affairs," he wrote:

> It [a union of Tylerites and Whigs] will utterly defeat & over-
> throw Benton — and that object accomplished, the liberal, en-
> lightened & honorable men throughout the state can write
> their policy & their names where they long since would have
> done, but for the rashness & blunders of their associates who
> assumed the lead as to the Presidency. . . . I cannot for-
> bear remarking that, had anything like the same fair and tol-

erant spirit been manifested toward Tyler by the Whigs of
Missouri, as was in Massachusetts, Mr. Benton had already
been as powerless here as he is there.[22]

Actually, it is doubtful whether Birch's plan would have
significantly altered the political situation, for Tyler failed to
command the support of any substantial faction of the Democratic party either. Besides Birch and Smith, the only two
important Missouri Tylerites were two St. Louisans, Silas
Reed and Vespasian Ellis. Reed, owner of one of the early
steamship companies, was apparently drawn to Tyler through
personal friendship and was not politically active before or
after the Tyler Administration. Ellis was associated neither
with Whiggery nor Democracy, the Native American Association of St. Louis having been his sole political haven prior
to Tylerism. The letters of these Tylerites reveal that, in contrast to the Whigs during Harrison's short regime, the supporters of the new President consciously designed to build
their party through executive appointments, but the raw ma-
terials were not available in Missouri. Already enjoying enormous majorities, Democrats were not tempted by the offers
of the shadowy Tyler figures. To the Whigs, victory that did
not lead to the establishment of a national bank was no victory
at all.[23]

Never happy with the Harrison-Tyler expedient of 1840,
the editor of the leading Whig newspaper seemed almost relieved when it became evident that the scheme had boom-
eranged and he could properly call for a renewed surge of
activity in behalf of Henry Clay, the dependable champion
of sensible fiscal policy. Even John Wilson, usually so impatient with Whigs who eschewed glamour for tradition when
their principles were at stake, now turned to Clay as the most
likely to succeed in the enactment of Whig measures.[24]

Missouri delegates to the Baltimore convention in 1844,
which nominated Henry Clay for President, returned home

happier than those who had attended the 1839 gathering at Harrisburg, Pennsylvania. George C. Sibley, recipient of an allocution from Wilson in 1833 on the wisdom of supporting amenable Jacksonians rather than Whigs, was chairman of the Missouri delegation; and he felt the actions of the national meeting vindicated his long crusade for unsullied Whiggery. Having "regretted the necessity" of running Harrison in 1840, Sibley was confident the Baltimore ticket would win, both in Missouri and in the nation. Furthermore, he found the nomination of Theodore Freylinghuysen for Vice-President as pleasing as Clay's for the Presidency. In addition to the former's indisputable Whiggery, to Sibley's mind his devoutly religious nature augured well for the party's future course.[25]

Clay inspired a more vigorous campaign than Harrison had in the famously energetic contest four years earlier. There were spirited Whig rallies at Boonville and St. Louis, both described as larger than the one at Rocheport in 1840; and Democrats had to be alert to prevent the Clay party from using state-owned artillery pieces to enliven its boisterous meetings.[26]

Augmenting the spontaneous response to Clay's candidacy was thirty-three-year-old Charles Daniel Drake, who essayed the role of campaign director. Drake, whose only official title in 1844 was Corresponding Secretary of the St. Louis Clay Club, is most famous as the leader of Missouri's Radical Republicans during and after the Civil War. Also, he served briefly in 1850 as Treasurer of the Board of Foreign Missions of the Presbyterian Church, an office he resigned when it belied his understanding "that it was in no sense inferior or subordinate to any of the other offices of the Board."[27] In 1844 Drake goaded Missouri Whigs to greater efforts, and he presumptuously sought assistance from Whigs outside the state in a plan to saturate Missouri with Whig literature. Very early in the campaign he wrote to Hamilton Fish, a leading

Whig congressman from New York, "In the course of two months I shall have the names of 1200 to 1500 active Whigs in every section of our State. Should I send those names to Washington City, will the Whig members of Congress do anything toward supplying them with Whig documents? If so, how far will they be willing to work for Missouri?" Fish's reply gave evidence once again of the essential indifference of Eastern Whigs to the plight of their party in the small and distant state. Naturally, any Whig triumph in Missouri would be hailed "as an unexpected ray of light in a hitherto benighted region," but the press of affairs was clearly too great for Whig members of Congress to commit themselves to aiding the cause there.[28]

More successful in exhorting Missourians, Drake even prodded the usually lethargic Howard Countians to unwonted zeal. The year 1844 was the only time this second most populous county in the state returned a Whig majority in a presidential election. In January Drake berated Abiel Leonard for Howard County's procrastination in forming a Clay Club; by fall Leonard was orating at campaign festivals throughout central Missouri. It was significant even that there were fall rallies. In 1840 the Whig campaign ended after the state defeats in August, but for Clay, Missouri Whigs worked to the end.[29]

Not many Missourians were converted by the enthusiasm; Clay received almost exactly the same proportion of the total vote that Harrison had in 1840. However, Whigs themselves, who were never very successful in convincing others anyway, certainly found canvassing for Clay a more congenial activity than shouting "Tippecanoe and Tyler Too!" The Boonville members of the party enjoyed the campaign so thoroughly that they decided to climax it with a "Clay Ball" after the election, even though there was no victory to celebrate.[30]

The controversy over the annexation of Texas portended momentous changes in the politics of Missouri as in the nation, but the Whigs of the state gave the matter little notice during the presidential campaign of 1844. Endorsements of Benton's stand against immediate annexation did not signify, as some anti-Benton Democrats charged, an alliance between the Senator and the minority party. On election day when Benton appeared at the polls in St. Louis to cast his ballot, a Whig challenged his right to do so on the puerile grounds that the Senator spent too little time in the state to qualify as a legal resident. Eventually, Missouri was to witness an astonishing rapport between Old Bullion and *some* Whigs, but clearly that development was still in the future in 1844.[31]

In fact, the Whigs during the early 1840's cooperated closely with the anti-Benton faction of the Democratic party in state elections. After 1840 the minority party did not enter congressional candidates again until 1848, and in 1844 it did not participate in the gubernatorial contest. Instead, Whig support went to the branch of the Democratic party that opposed Benton's financial policies. The following chapter deals with the reasons for and the results of this reversion to the pressure-group tactics of the 1830's.

CHAPTER 9

PASSIVE RESISTANCE

MISSOURI's minority party regularly waged campaigns in behalf of the National Republican and, later, the Whig presidential nominees. However, a synopsis of its actions in state elections shows an almost cyclical oscillation between two courses: the one, making its own nominations, the other, supporting Democrats whose financial views accorded most nearly with American System principles.

The congressional candidacies of Edward Bates and David Barton in 1828 and 1831 served only to unify the Jacksonian party, and both Adams contenders consequently suffered overwhelming defeat. Following these reversals, the predecessors of the Whigs ceased to enter candidates of their own. Instead, they gave their support to bank-Jacksonians, a type best exemplified by William H. Ashley. Until 1836 that policy was relatively successful, but by then the Benton followers had established the principle that dissent from Benton doctrine equalled disloyalty to the Democratic party. As a result, the renegade Jacksonians received scarcely more than the normal anti-Jackson vote.

Faced with Democratic unity, the opposition transformed itself into the Whig party. In 1838 and 1840 Whigs entered candidates from their own ranks in congressional and gubernatorial races, but defeats ensued both years. More than a few Whigs looked wistfully toward former days when they had at least been able to choose the lesser of Democratic evils.

In the fall of 1841, the *New Era*, a St. Louis Whig newspaper, advised party members to refrain from nominating candidates for the 1842 congressional elections. The elections of 1838 and 1840 had demonstrated to the editor that an open Whig position unified the Democratic party under Bentonian hegemony, leaving the Whigs not only defeated but governed by the most undesirable Democrats as well. The *Missouri Republican*, constant prodder of lethargic Whigs and leader of the organization movement in 1839, at once rejected this suggestion.

Whereas the editor of the *New Era* recalled the successful election to Congress of the satisfactory Democrats Ashley and John Bull in the early thirties, A. B. Chambers of the *Republican* remembered that in 1836 the Democrats had achieved unity even in the face of Whig quiescence. Chambers, a Pennsylvanian who practiced law as well as journalism, was not of the same mold as the pious George C. Sibley, who rebelled against anything less than open Whiggery, chiefly on grounds of moral and intellectual honesty. Eminently practical, Chambers found support of bank-Jacksonians entirely palatable as long as the method worked. Sensing its failure in 1836, however, he became a champion of Whig organization. For one thing, he argued, Whig defeats were but unpleasant milestones on the road to Whig victory, and only by keeping its name constantly before the voters could the party ever hope to dominate Missouri. Of equal importance to Chambers was the effect of organization on Missouri Whiggery's voice in councils of the national party. How could Whigs, he asked, who did not participate in the party wars expect to exert influence over the selection of presidential nominees or to receive attractive patronage favors? [1]

In 1838 and 1839 the disagreement over the wisdom of organization was largely between the Whigs of St. Louis and those of central Missouri. No geographical division existed in 1841, however, and the *New Era* found its proposal condemned by the *Columbia Patriot* as well as by the *Republican*. The editor of the Boone County newspaper was William F. Switzler, a native of Switzerland now twenty-two years old, who later edited the widely known *Missouri Statesman*. The Whigs of Boone County, declared Switzler, were "for war, 'war without truce, and war without quarter.'" On the other hand, the *Boon's Lick Times*, Howard County's Whig paper, concurred fully with the *New Era*. Noting that there were at least thirty Democrats with congressional ambitions, the *Times* surmised:

> So long as a Whig Convention or Whig organization is probable, loyalty to the party and devotion to the convention will be the rallying cry of our opponents. But once satisfy these aspirants that Whig organization and Whig opposition is abandoned, and that our thirty thousand votes will be thrown as a reward to decency and moderation in the canvass, and rebuke of ultraism, and our word for it, the key to all their bugles will be so modulated as to suit the occasion.[2]

Chambers' and Switzler's enthusiasm for organization did not prevail over the reasoning of the *New Era* and the *Times*, and by February the latter was able to report that "the propriety of our suggestion is generally acquiesced in." Even the *Republican* now agreed that it would not be profitable for the Whig party to seek to do more than win what seats it could in the legislature. "The Whigs with us, are used up," confided one Democrat to another, noting the new mood of the minority party.[3]

The former advocates of continued activity never explained their shift, and their failure to do so is understandable. When the *New Era* boldly declared that disharmony within the Democratic party would probably result from the absence of a common enemy, it alerted Democratic leaders. "I send you the *New Era* in which you will observe under the editorial head of the calculations made by the Whig party of running democrats in this state for Congress," warned a correspondent of the Lieutenant Governor's. "Divide and conquer will be their watchword."[4] Having ample advance warning, Democrats were in a position to take steps to quash plans of any members of their party who might look upon Whig support with a covetous eye. Wiser was the approach of the *Patriot* and the *Republican,* who, once reconciled to the absence of Whig nominees, said as little as possible about it. There was only one Democratic ticket in 1842, and early exposure of Whig strategy alone did not prevent a division of the Democratic party. Certainly, though, the statements of the *Boon's Lick Times* and the *New Era* contributed to their opponents' harmony.

Hopes for a Democratic rupture were not without foundation during the winter of 1841–1842. The legislature's creation of the Bank of Missouri in 1837 greatly mollified the discontent of Democrats who rejected extreme hard-money doctrines, but the conservative policies pursued by that institution, coupled with renewed efforts by the followers of Thomas Hart Benton to implement the Senator's views, revived the old controversies. In keeping with Benton's hard-money principles, Thomas Reynolds, the Democratic governor elected in 1840, urged the General Assembly to pass legislation restricting the circulation of "foreign" small bank notes within Missouri. That currency derived from banks located in nearby states not subject to the same conservative restrictions as the Bank of Missouri, whose charter forbade issuance of notes under ten dollars. To supply smaller denominations and also to augment larger ones, a number of corporations actually chartered as insurance companies were, in effect, engaging in banking. By receiving on deposit notes of banks in other states — which often as not had suspended specie payment — and then by lending these notes, such corporations made a handsome profit. Moreover, they circulated a type of currency that was anathema to Benton and his followers.[5]

Hard-money members of the legislature sponsored measures to curb these quasi-legal operations before 1840, and at least one Whig thought even then that the issue would fatally divide the Democratic party. In 1838 a bill was introduced, providing that any person who passed or received a bank note smaller than twenty dollars (other than one issued by the Bank of Missouri) should be liable for the amount of the note and that any agent, dealer, or broker who violated this act should be subject to a fine of $10,000 in addition to being disqualified from holding office in the state. Samuel Knox, a St. Louis merchant, commented:

> From the papers I perceive that the Loco Foco members of the Legislature are determined to make themselves look as rediculous [sic] as possible to the world. It seems that they have put on and are resolved to wear the collar made by their infamous, empty headed leader, T. H. Benton. How a reasonable man can, for a moment think of passing a bill like the one entitled "A Bill to regulate the Currency" I am unable to conceive. It is generally hoped, as far as I know, by the business men of our city that this Bill of abomination will pass and become a law. I think it would make a fine funeral dirge (if adopted to music) to be sung at the burial of Loco Focoism in this state. I think it might be well, for a party so *notorious* to begin soon to look for music for this occasion; for if we may judge from appearances, its obsequies cannot be far distant.[6]

Apparently, the Whig members of the legislature either did not agree with Knox that enactment of the bill would sound the death knell of their opposition or else thought its passage too high a price to pay even for Democracy's funeral; for in combination with dissident Democrats they defeated the measure. Then, as the campaign of 1840 gained momentum, attention shifted to the Independent Treasury, and the "foreign currency" question subsided until after the election.[7]

By the end of 1841 the matter was again paramount among political issues. The Governor's pronouncement in favor of restrictive legislation, added to similarly forthright declarations by Benton and by the Democratic state committee, promised extreme discomfort for anyone in the Democratic party who disagreed. A bill similar to that introduced in 1838 was brought forward in 1841, narrowly passed the House of Representatives, and was defeated in the Senate by one vote. The overwhelming Democratic majorities in both houses could, of course, have passed the measure if the party had been united in its favor; yet the Whigs, together with those Democrats who opposed it, formed a bloc barely strong enough to forestall the legislation. Small wonder that some Whigs saw the seeds of a situation similar to that which had existed from 1831 to 1836 when a coalition of bank Democrats and anti-Jacksonians had almost equally divided political sway with the Benton wing of the Democracy.[8]

Whigs who hoped their own passivity would stimulate Democratic cleavage could see faint signs early in 1842 of another majority party fissure besides the one that resulted directly from the currency issue. Closely related to that controversy was resentment toward the "Central Clique," a group of Democratic politicians residing in central Missouri who specialized in hard money, Benton worship, and monopoly of the important offices for their section of the state. So potent had the Clique's influence become that in 1840 the Democratic candidates for governor, lieutenant governor, and the two congressional seats were all residents of the central part of the state. Naturally, Democrats from other areas chafed under the direction of such a discriminatory oligarchy; and though the protests in 1842 were minuscule compared to those of a year later, disgruntled rumblings were audible. For example, the *Ozark Eagle*, a Democratic paper published at Springfield in southwest Missouri, commented little on the actual currency question. Rather, it denounced the Central Clique and Benton's acceptance of its domination.[9]

Well founded as the expectations of Democratic discord were, they were not fulfilled. Two factors intervened, both of which reinforced the Whigs' decision not to make congressional nominations while at the same time helping to conserve Democratic unity.

The first of these was a rare phenomenon in Missouri Whig history, disunity within the minority party itself. Only in St. Louis did this occur, but it was of a far more serious nature than the usual Whig differences over political methodology. The defection of a considerable body of St. Louis Whigs to the Native American Association and the resultant Democratic victory in the city elections of April 1, 1842, was discussed in the chapter on St. Louis Whiggery. The connection here is that nativists kept the St. Louis Whigs in such turmoil throughout the spring of 1842 that they were unable to give the rest of the state the leadership and cajolery in behalf of organization that they traditionally supplied. Thus, one important force that might have disturbed the Whig decision not to run congressional candidates was eliminated. At the same time the Democrats of St. Louis smothered personal ambition and discord in order to be in a unified position to take advantage of the unexpected opportunities at hand.

The other factor besides disunity in St. Louis which reinforced the Whig decision to pursue a passive policy in the congressional elections resulted from Missouri's increased congressional representation as a result of the 1840 census. There was no question that the state would be entitled to more than the two congressmen it had heretofore sent to Washington; but until Congress passed the necessary legislation to implement the census findings, no one could be certain of the exact number or of whether the change would take effect before the August election. The uncertainty virtually suspended Democratic congressional plans throughout the spring of 1842. Not knowing whether he would have to struggle for one of two or for one of seven places on the ticket, it was impossible for a congressional aspirant to plan his strategy; and all adopted a wait-and-see attitude.[10]

The Democratic state convention met as scheduled early in June. By that time the United States House of Representatives had passed an apportionment bill providing for seven

Missouri congressmen, but it appeared likely that the Senate would reduce the number fo five. Undismayed by the nebulous situation, the Democrats adroitly used it to restore party harmony. Seven candidates were nominated. Each drew a number, and it was agreed that the two nominees who held Numbers Six and Seven would withdraw should the state be entitled to only five representatives. With so many vacancies on the ticket, it was possible to satisfy all factions of the party. The Central Clique reserved three places for itself; two were allotted to outright foes of the currency regulation bills; and there was even a spot for the editor of the aforementioned anti-Central Clique *Ozark Eagle*, John P. Campbell.[11]

The designs of the *New Era* and *Boon's Lick Times* to sunder the Democrats through nonresistance were foiled. The latter paper found some comfort in the nominations of Judge James B. Bowlin of St. Louis, "a very good man, tolerably well educated," and James M. Hughes, a Liberty merchant, "possessed of good common sense," but these consolations were far removed from the competing Democratic tickets the editor had hoped to see in the field. The nearest approach to opposition encountered by the regular Democrats came from John P. Campbell, Number Six among the nominees. Under the apportionment bill finally passed after the convention, Missouri was entitled to only five representatives, but Campbell refused to abide by the rules of the convention and did not withdraw. Denounced by Democrats of all varieties for this breach of political decency, he received barely one fourth as many votes as the legitimate nominees.[12]

Simultaneously with enactment of the apportionment bill, Congress also passed a law requiring each legislature to divide its state into single-member congressional districts. Had Missouri complied with this direction, Whigs might yet have seen a divided Democratic party; or, perhaps, they might have been motivated to enter candidates themselves. Politicians of the majority party, however, saw no reason to undo the sutures so deftly sewn at their convention. Whigs demanded that the Governor either call a special session of the General Assembly to district the state or postpone the election until the legislature had complied with the congressional act in regular session. When it became evident that no action would be taken, the Whig press had to content itself with denunciation of the election as "illegal and nullifying." Whigs were urged not to mark congressional ballots at all, and apparently they followed these instructions, for the total congressional vote was slightly under that received by the Democratic candidates alone two years earlier. Bowlin and Hughes, the two candidates most approved by the Whigs, received 1,000 and 2,000 more votes than the other candidates, perhaps indicating that a few Whigs did attempt to demonstrate the potential fruits of Whig favor.[13]

Clearly the Whigs had right on their side in this controversy, and the Democratic rulers of Missouri committed an act of nullification when they ignored the directive of the Whig-controlled Congress. However, before praising the Whigs for abstaining from an illegal election, it is well to remember that their choice of nonparticipation was taken months before the districting issue existed. No Whig nominees withdrew in the face of the Democratic outrage; no plans for a Whig nominating convention were canceled. Rather, the expedient ground already occupied by the minority party metamorphosed into the high ground of principle.

Might triumphed in this case. Congress passed from Whig to Democratic hands as a result of the 1842 elections; and, though the districting legislation was not repealed, the Missouri Democrats took their seats and kept them for the full term. Amply supplied by the indignant George C. Sibley with evidence of the outrageous fraudulence of the "pretenders'" claims, Whigs in Congress periodically challenged their right to remain. But Democrats were not of a mind to reduce their majority, and the Whig efforts were of no avail.[14]

CHAPTER 10

DEMOCRATS DIVIDED

SUCCESSFUL as their coup had been, and despite their endeavors to share the victory with all branches of their party, Democratic managers had not heard the last of the districting controversy. Although the Central Clique had countenanced distribution of places on the 1842 congressional ticket among all sections of the state and all factions of the party, some Democrats feared that this generosity would prevail only when circumstances dictated its absolute necessity.

John P. Campbell's persistent candidacy in 1842 furnished an early example of Democratic dissatisfaction with the 1842 convention compromise. Confronted with the fact that his political preferment not only depended on the whims of Democrats from another area but was further subject to the vagaries of chance, Campbell was a districting enthusiast. In a separate electoral unit he, or at least someone from his section of the state, could be assured of an opportunity to go to Congress.[1] Undoubtedly, the difference between Democrats in southwest Missouri and Democrats from the central part of the state was accentuated by the former's confidence that they could be even more victorious in a districted election, while central Missourians feared that no matter how artfully the legislature gerrymandered the state, they would find themselves in a district where Whigs were capable of offering effective opposition.

When it became clear that the Central Clique did not favor compliance with the Districting Act even for the forthcoming 1844 election, many joined Campbell in rebellion. Benton's endorsement of the antidistricting position made the contest more obviously one between Benton and anti-Benton Democrats. A proposal to nominate candidates by districts and to elect by general ticket would have coupled local autonomy with maximum security to all Democratic congressional nominees, but the suggestion came too late. Politicians who opposed Benton and the Central Clique knew that districting was a potent issue among Whigs and independent voters. Since it appeared unlikely that the two wings of the Democratic party would be united at the next election, they refused to exchange it for a halfway measure.[2]

Even had the districting compromise proved acceptable, Democratic dissension would have continued, for other matters also cleft the majority party. Chief among these was the currency issue that had aroused such high Whig hopes for a Democratic split in 1842. The wound remaining from this battle reopened soon after the new legislature convened and turned to the regular election of a president and board of directors for the Bank of Missouri. Once again, the Whigs had evidence of the potentialities of cooperation with "Soft" Democrats, as those who rejected the hard-money position of the Benton-Central Clique wing of the party were frequently characterized. Together, the Whigs and the Softs defeated the "Hard" candidate for the presidency and elected instead Ferdinand Kennett of St. Louis, brother of Luther Martin Kennett, a Whig mayor of St. Louis during the 1850's. The brothers cooperated in numerous business ventures, but they remained in opposing political parties. On financial issues they shared a wide area of agreement, however. Ferdinand had already been a director of the Bank of Missouri for two years, and he had a consistent record of advocating liberal, or soft, note issue policies for that institution.[3]

Following Kennett's election a newspaper war broke out between the *Jefferson Inquirer* of Jefferson City and the *Missouri Reporter* of St. Louis. Declaring that "you have commenced the war and we shall defend to the last ditch," the *Inquirer* inaugurated a series of relentless harangues in behalf of hard money and against the "St. Louis masters," to be answered by the *Reporter's* equally vehement condemnations of the Central Clique. Other Democratic presses rapidly aligned with one side or the other, while the Whigs stood by, rubbing their hands over the fratricidal strife in the enemy's camp. There were no calls for Whig organization between the elections of 1842 and 1844.[4]

If any doubt remained that Thomas Hart Benton was the central figure in the intraparty feud, Shadrick Penn, editor of the *Missouri Reporter*, eliminated it in the fall of 1843. Penn, a Kentuckian who removed to St. Louis only in 1841, is credited by a historian of that city with the first editorial in the nation to urge the claims of Andrew Jackson for the Presidency. The two men had a great deal more in common in 1819 when Penn endorsed the General than they did in 1843, for, just as Jackson did in Tennessee, Penn took a strong stand in Kentucky against the relief party, assailing stay laws with great vigor.[5] Now, with Jackson elevated to the role of hard money's patron saint, Penn assumed the editorial leadership of Missouri's paper currency forces. In a series of letters publicly addressed to Benton through his paper, he accused the Senator of a multitude of sins ranging from party dictatorship to sycophantic submission to "centralism." The legislature elected in 1844 would decide whether Benton should return to the Senate, and long before Penn's attack the editor of a hard-money paper had written, "Another object of the coalition [Softs and Whigs] is the overthrow of our distinguished Senator Thos. H. Benton. They dare not say so openly, but they war upon him in disguise." Shadrick Penn stripped what was left of the disguise, and from the time of his "Benton Letters," it was clear that Old Bullion would have to fight to keep his seat in the national council.[6]

Notwithstanding their scornful denunciations of the anti-

Benton forces as traitors, the Benton Democrats feared the strength of the growing movement, particularly when they viewed it in possible company with the Whig vote. Principle was important, but victory was equally so to the Hards, and they made serious efforts to appease the other branch of their party. When Lewis F. Linn, Benton's colleague in the Senate, died late in 1843, the duty of appointing his successor fell to Governor Thomas Reynolds. Reynolds, a Howard Countian regarded by many as the leader of the Central Clique, unexpectedly appointed David Rice Atchison from the northwestern border county of Platte to the high office. The appointee had very articulately expressed his hostility to the group of politicians with whom Reynolds was identified, and he was suspected of Soft sentiments besides.[7]

Before Atchison ended his senatorial career, devoted followers of Benton would regard the stratagem as an expensive one, and even its immediate dividends were questionable. However, by diluting arguments that the Central Clique selfishly reserved all choice political plums for itself, the move at least increased the willingness of the Softs to attend a Democratic state convention in the spring of 1844. In addition, rumors circulated during the weeks immediately preceding the meeting that a spirit of compromise, especially on the districting issue, prevailed within the Benton camp. As one ardent member of that group put it, the Softs should be given no further pretense for rebellion, for "we want as many votes as possible in the coming elections, & 'prudence is the better part of valor.'"[8]

There was compromise of a sort at the April gathering in Jefferson City, but it was compromise dictated by the Central Clique, without opportunity for bargaining between the two sides. Those who controlled the convention machinery tabled all resolutions pertaining to currency and congressional districting. Their version of concession on these subjects was absolute silence. Two men who had strongly ad-

vocated districting the state received places on the congressional ticket, and instead of nominating ultra-Hard Lieutenant Governor Meredith M. Marmaduke of centrally located
Saline County for governor, the convention conferred the
honor on ex-Congressman John C. Edwards. Edwards was
also from the central part of the state, but he was a moderate
on districting and currency.[9]

The arrangements did not satisfy the Softs. Silence on the
great questions was insufficient; they demanded endorsement of their own position. Nor did the presence of presumably moderate candidates on the ticket still their resentments.
After all, this would not be the first time that men had sacrificed principle on the altar of party harmony or in the interest
of their own political advancement. For instance, the past
record of James B. Bowlin, who was renominated for Congress, indicated a tendency toward a Soft position in regard
to both currency and districting. Once nominated by the 1842
compromise meeting, however, he modified his views; and by
1844 the St. Louisan, at one time somewhat acceptable to
Whigs, was a recognized Hard. Culminating the unpalatable
features of the convention was a ringing endorsement of Benton, committing all who would pose as regular Democrats to
his re-election to the United States Senate.[10]

Even before the convention, Charles H. Allen, a lawyer of
northeast Missouri, had independently announced his candidacy for governor, and less than two months after the
Democratic meeting adjourned there was a full slate of "Independent" nominees in the field. Although the result of no
convention, this ticket nevertheless demonstrated that the
Softs could impose discipline when necessary. By private arrangement the protesting Democrats narrowed the contenders from their ranks to one for each office. The Hards had
controlled the party convention and as a result had priority to
the party name — no worthless commodity in Missouri if the
name happened to be *Democrat*. But the title to party regu-

larity did not carry party control with it, and the Whigs for the first time since 1836 could choose between rival Democratic tickets.[11]

Before the August election Benton's strong stand against Tyler's treaty with the Republic of Texas that provided for immediate annexation briefly clouded the issues. However, currency rather than Texas was Missouri's concern in 1844, and the political lines already drawn held firm. Although many Benton supporters found their leader's position on Texas perplexing and sometimes distasteful, most remained loyal and defended Benton, either on the ground that his stand exemplified political courage or that he opposed only *immediate* annexation, which he felt would cause unnecessary war with Mexico.[12]

One who did not so modulate his criticism was Claiborne Fox Jackson of Fayette. Jackson, who was to lead Missouri's Confederate government in 1861, was the author of resolutions passed by the legislature in 1849 instructing Missouri senators to protect slavery in the territories. This prominent member of the Clique declared in June, 1844, that if elected to the state House of Representatives he "would not vote for Benton or any other man for the United States Senate who was opposed to the immediate annexation of Texas." Nevertheless, the two men had not acted together politically for the last time. As will be shown later, they suppressed their differences sufficiently at the time of the senatorial election in the legislature to arrange a mutually advantageous compromise that endured for some time.[13]

Nor did Whigs change their relationships with Benton in 1844, despite the similarity between his and Henry Clay's reactions to the annexation of Texas. Some Whigs agreed with Benton and said so, but neither the Texas question nor its implications for the slavery controversy were uppermost in Whig thoughts in 1844. Because of his currency views, they continued to regard Benton as their arch political enemy.

Campaigning only for General Assembly seats and local offices in 1844, all Whigs who ran for office stood rigidly on a "Bent-on beating Benton" platform.[14]

Perhaps Benton desired a Whig alliance; but if he did, he was unable to effect it. William H. Russell, Henry Clay's closest personal friend in Missouri, reported to his chieftain that one Colonel Brant, a kinsman of Benton's, "actually imposed upon me the task of furnishing him a list of 15 of my best Whig friends that he might invite them to dine with me at his house — which was done." If the dinner was meant as a proposal, it was certainly a subtle one, for Russell, having attended the affair, yet wondered, "Is it an overture of Benton to join the Whig ranks . . . ?" "If so," he continued, "must we take him . . . or is it best to continue with the Penn party?"[15]

Whether Russell rejected an offer or never received one is unknown, as the records contain no other references to Colonel Brant's dinner party. What is clear is that in 1844 Missouri Whigs collaborated with the Soft, anti-Benton wing of the Democratic party. Since the state was still undistricted, the Whigs again emphasized that the congressional election was illegal and professed lack of interest in the "case of litigation between the descendants of Old Mr. Clique." Whig endorsement of Independent congressional candidates never went beyond counseling Whigs that if they voted at all, they should vote against the convention nominees. Not until the eve of the election did the Whig press urge support for the Independent candidates for governor and lieutenant governor. Although neither Edwards nor Allen was "fit or proper" for the governorship, asserted the St. Louis *Mill Boy*, the state would be safer in the hands of Allen; and therefore it was the duty of Whigs to give him their votes.[16]

Whether their action was directed or merely the spontaneous expression of their preference for the Independents, there is strong evidence from another quarter that many Whigs

did vote in 1844. Their strength went almost unanimously
to the anti-Benton candidates, and it was of major importance to that faction. In 1842, when there was only one set
of congressional nominees, 27,000 voters marked their congressional ballots. Two years later, 63,000 voted. Granted that
a two-way contest would naturally excite more interest, it is
not likely that Democrats alone accounted for the entire difference. A comparison of the congressional returns with the
gubernatorial and presidential statistics for 1844 substantiates
this assertion. In the former race 67,000 votes were cast, and
apparently Whigs who sympathized with the *Mill Boy's*
greater emphasis on this contest accounted for most of the
4,000 who voted for a gubernatorial candidate while ignor-
ing the congressional ballot. The Hard candidates were victorious in both instances, but Governor-elect Edwards defeated his Soft opponent by only 5,000 votes, as contrasted
with the Hard congressional majorities of approximately
8,000.[17]

That some Whigs abstained from going to the polls is indicated by the results in the presidential contest. Normally, the
Whig vote in presidential and state contests was approximately the same, while Democrats, their confidence always
reinforced by the results of the August election, turned out
in fewer numbers. This year 41,000 Democrats voted for
James K. Polk, and 31,000 Whigs voted for Henry Clay. If
Democratic behavior in other presidential election years can
be taken as a guide, approximately 75 per cent of those who
participated in the state election voted in November. This
would mean that almost 50,000 of the over 60,000 voters in
the state elections were Democrats. If the remainder were
Whigs, and if they all voted the Independent ticket, slightly
over 50 per cent of that faction's strength came from the minority party.[18]

There is no evidence that the Democratic split extended to
the presidential election. Although Benton's known prefer-

ence for Van Buren over Polk was cited against him, Benton and his followers in Missouri heartily endorsed Polk, once his nomination was accomplished. Conceivably, a few Democrats boycotted the polls because of distaste for Polk; but if such aversion was present in Missouri, it did not result in Democratic support for Clay. As Benton was anathema to Whigs, so the Whig leader was to Democrats. The national election conformed to national party lines. As important as Democratic unity in creating the situation that contrasted so sharply to the state elections was the Whig party's support of its own candidate, Henry Clay.[19]

The Whigs also maintained their identity in the legislature in the 1840's, just as they had during their pressure-group phase in the 1830's. In local contests they entered their own candidates, except where they found it more profitable to support an anti-Benton candidate. One such instance occurred in the St. Charles area where the by-now venerable George C. Sibley sought to represent his district in the state Senate. Here, Carty Wells, a leading Soft whom many thought should have been the candidate for governor, was the Independent nominee, and practical Whigs found him especially attractive. They were confident both that he could win and that he could be depended upon to refuse to capitulate to the Benton wing after the election.

It is sadly ironical that St. Charles and its neighboring county of Warren should have constituted one of the few districts where the Whigs decided against running their own candidate. There was no more dedicated Whig than Sibley, and aside from their impatience with what they regarded as his political naïveté, his fellow party members apparently thought well of him. He was one of their choices to represent them at the glorious 1844 convention that nominated Henry Clay. Certainly, in 1840 when the Whigs desperately desired to present a complete state ticket, they were more than relieved when the respectable Sibley came forward to shoulder the unwanted burden of the congressional canvass; and on none of the three occasions when Whigs discouraged his running for office did they seek to substitute another Whig in his place. Excessive ambition did not motivate the elderly Presbyterian. Whenever he announced himself as a candidate, it was after all other Whigs had forsaken the field and it appeared to him that Whigs would have to choose between foregoing their suffrage rights and sacrificing their political chastity.

On his return in June from the Whig convention at Baltimore, Sibley discovered that there was no Whig candidate to represent his district in the Senate. Inquiring what the Whig voters would do, he was informed, "O, it has been arranged that the Whigs had better all vote for Mr. Wells, the *soft* Democrat, (if they vote at all), in order to put down Col. Benton, with his clique and currency projects." Sibley, of course, aspired to put down Colonel Benton, too, but to achieve the object by voting for a man who was "ultra-loco" in some respects and who also countenanced his faction's running congressional candidates under the illegal general ticket system was political prostitution of the most venal order.[20]

Sibley's local candidacy became a *cause célèbre* among Whigs in all quarters. From as far away as Springfield, three Whigs jointly addressed a letter to the beleaguered old man, not very politely denouncing his foolish idealism. Before the election Sibley saw that even his close Whig neighbors were succumbing to the advice of the practical politicians, and, though he refused to withdraw, he passively resigned himself to defeat. Ever steadfast in his principles, he rejected outright an opportunity to avenge himself against the callous members of his own party. When representatives of the Hard faction, frenetically interested in defeating the prominent Wells, offered support to Sibley in return for modest concessions, he confided to his diary: "I prefer to be left en-

tirely in the hands of my friends — if they think fit to sacrifice me for an ultra Loco-foco; let them do it; and let *them*
take the responsibility of the defeat, if a defeat awaits them,
as I believe it does."[21]

On election day he did not vote, but remained at Lindenwood, his own home as well as that of the college he and his
wife had founded, and contemplated the dolorous state of
affairs. Again he made an entry in his diary:

> Under the mixed influence of Soft Loco-focoism & Soft Whig-
> gism; the Whig party has been completely thrown into chaos;
> and I fear it well nigh ruined in St. Charles County — not a
> single election has been conducted on Whig principles — The
> Hard Whigs (few indeed in number) and the Hard Locos
> have acted upon the leading principles of the Whig and Demo-
> cratic parties respectively — The Softs, Whigs & Locos, have
> become so mixed and identified, that it is impossible to know
> their distinct view. — I have no doubt but many Whigs — of
> rather weak faith, will be entirely alienated; tho not a single
> soft Loco will be converted to the Whigs — because the Whigs
> have gone over to the Softs & not the Softs to the Whigs — I
> hope and trust that Wells has been defeated.[22]

Besides the indication of Sibley's religious approach to politics provided by his use of *faith* and *converted*, the quotation
contains a realistic analysis of the political situation in 1844.
In both the 1830's and the 1840's Democrats who accepted
support from members of the minority party failed to treat
them as equal partners in the coalition, a primary reason why
even more practical Whig leaders than Sibley in both instances eventually became dissatisfied with the arrangement.

Regarding conditions in his local area, Sibley felt vindicated by Wells's defeat. The margin of the Benton candidate,
a man named P. H. Shelton, was only 49 votes, and it is possible that the remnants of Sibley's own candidacy may have
made that difference. Unfortunately, the returns for this local
election are not accessible, but Sibley's diary reveals that
Shelton won by a plurality rather than by a clear majority.

Perhaps one can blame Sibley for this specific defeat; but one should note also that, as the political purist predicted, St. Charles never again rose up in triumphant Whiggery. Beginning with the presidential election of 1844, St. Charles was distinguished as the only county in the state that had been Whig both in 1836 and 1840 but thenceforth consistently returned Democratic majorities.[23]

The avowed object of Missouri's Whig party in 1844 was the election of men to the General Assembly who would oppose Benton's return to the Senate. In counties where the party thought it could elect a Whig it strove to do so; where circumstances indicated that the presence of a Whig candidate would contribute to the victory of a Benton supporter, Whigs withdrew and attempted to ensure the election of an anti-Benton Democrat. Sibley's district was merely an unsuccessful example of this pragmatic policy.[24]

In the state as a whole, the Whigs had reason to feel that they had made better use of the Democratic cleavage in the contests for control of the legislature than they had in the elections for major offices. Their own total membership in the two houses increased from 33 to 53. Democrats occupied 80 seats, 13 more than necessary to elect a senator, but some of these had been elected as Independents and could be expected to vote against Benton. Exactly how many would be so inclined in the actual voting was open to question, however. Early estimates of relative strength in the General Assembly varied from a comfortable margin for Benton to a majority of eight against him.[25]

When the legislators convened in November, Benton's fate still hung in the balance. Four compromises by his loyal lieutenants purchased enough votes to return the Senator to his post.

First, Claiborne Fox Jackson received the speakership of the House in return for his renewed fidelity. This move not only brought Democrats who had deserted Benton over the

Texas question back into the fold; but, since Jackson was still a decided Hard in his currency views, it manifested "the influence of the Colonel's favorite measures in the House." [26]

A second concession to the Texas dissidents was a promise by the Benton men to support resolutions instructing Missouri senators to vote for annexation. To this promise the Bentonians were not entirely faithful, but the concession served its immediate purpose of ensuring votes for Benton. When the resolutions came to a vote a month later, Benton's friends, joined by Whigs in this instance, insisted that the senators be directed to vote for annexation "at the earliest practicable moment" instead of "immediate" annexation, thus harmonizing the instructions with the position Benton had already taken. One Benton devotee confided to another: "The instructions to our members in Congress are as near no instructions as I could possibly get thru. . . . Nothing but my comital [sic] at a time when I thought Benton's election endangered induced me to go for any instructions." [27]

The third compromise placated those whose resistance to Benton and the Central Clique stemmed from differences on the districting issue. Saving face by claims that they had opposed congressional districting only because the act requiring it constituted a federal encroachment on state rights, the Benton faction now agreed to support such a measure, not out of deference to federal dictation but rather in response to the wishes of the people of Missouri. The legislature created congressional districts, applicable to the 1846 election, a few weeks later. [28]

The fourth appeasement to the anti-Benton forces involved the election of David Rice Atchison for the remainder of Lewis F. Linn's unexpired term. Atchison, known as a champion of districting as well as of immediate annexation and suspected of currency views that differed from Benton's, was popular among the Softs. Benton's friends agreed to vote for the junior Senator's return in exchange for votes for their own candidate. Some Whigs tried to match this appeal, but in vain. Added to his unanimous Democratic endorsement, the Whig votes gave Atchison the prestige of going to Washington with a far more impressive margin of victory than his senior colleague, but they did not bring about their greater aspiration, Benton's defeat.[29]

When Benton's own election came to a vote, the compromises made by his followers proved their worth. Only eight Democrats voted against him, leaving him exactly eight more votes than he needed. The extent of the inroads that Benton's Texas policy had made so far into Whig ranks was illustrated when 2 of the 53 Whigs contributed their votes to his majority. Also demonstrated was the truth of Sibley's observation that Soft-Whig cooperation always meant Whig support for the Softs and never the reverse. The coalition's votes for senator went to a Soft Democrat, even though Whigs furnished by far the greater part of the anti-Benton strength.[30]

CHAPTER 11

WHIG SEPARATENESS

BENTON's re-election to the Senate signified victory for the Hards in the Democrats' internecine struggle. For a short period the Soft, anti-Benton forces appeared to accept the verdict of defeat gracefully. Previously anti-Benton newspapers condoned the legislature's action, and at a series of county rallies Democrats of all shades of opinion gathered to proclaim their restored harmony.[1] However, these protestations of party unity proved deceptive. Internal Democratic dissension soon reasserted itself, and the settlement of other contentions showed again that the fundamental cause of the Soft-Hard split was fiscal in nature.

One of these other issues was territorial expansion. Benton's full cooperation with the Polk Administration once war with Mexico began in 1846 left the Whigs entirely alone in their lack of enthusiasm for the immediate annexation of Texas. The fulfillment of Polk's campaign cry, "Fifty-four forty or fight," had been popular in Missouri, and Democratic opponents of Benton had cited his moderation on the Oregon question against him, too. However, once the treaty with Britain dividing the territory at the 49th parallel was ratified, Missouri Democrats seemed relieved to accept the peaceful solution and became "as mute as mice." From the beginning, the Whigs regarded "the deified line of fifty-four forty" as the "most monstrous of humbugs."[2]

Also removed from polemics was the districting issue, for very soon after Benton's election the legislature at last complied with the federal law and created congressional districts in Missouri.³ There were, nevertheless, both Hard and Soft Democratic tickets in the election of 1846.

Districting did not bring a Whig slate into the field despite the fact that the illegality of the undistricted proceedings was the reason cited by the Whigs for their abstention from the 1842 and 1844 elections. The real reason, of course, for Whig passivity was the Democratic split. Whigs considered making nominations in 1846, but when it became apparent that there would once again be two Democratic tickets, they were content to withdraw in all but one district. Fearful that any sign of Whig activity would augment Democratic solidarity, Whig leaders soon abandoned plans for a state convention. Although they agreed on nominees through private correspondence early in April, they were careful to wait until the end of May, weeks after the Democratic convention, to announce them. Even then Whigs came forth in only two districts, the Third and Fifth, where the Democrats had managed to prevent a duplication of candidates.⁴

The Third District comprised the central Missouri counties where the Central Clique held sway and where Democratic unity was no doubt also fostered by the existence of appreciable Whig strength. Here John G. Miller, a Boonville lawyer who in 1850 finally did find his way to Congress, carried the Whig colors against James S. Green. Green was typical of so many members of the Central Clique who, though they still adhered to Benton in 1846, would stand among his fiercest opponents by 1850. Miller polled about 45 per cent of the vote in this district. His majorities in the Whig counties of Boone and Cooper were offset by the preponderantly Democratic voters from other counties that were carefully included in the district by the Democratic legislature.⁵

Although the Fifth District stretched as far northeast as almost centrally located Pettis County, it was predominantly a southwestern unit. In this area Softism seems to have sprung

mainly from the districting issue, and with that matter settled it appeared that John S. Phelps of Springfield, a Benton
man, would enjoy the support of a united Democratic party.
Before the election, however, John P. Campbell, ancient Soft
who had formerly built his platform on the districting principle, announced that he was an Independent candidate.
Promptly, railroad promoter George R. Smith of Pettis County
withdrew from the race, and, interestingly enough, this Whig
attempted to throw his support to the Hards' candidate,
Phelps. This exceptional Whig behavior is understandable in
the light of Smith's previously displayed insatiable hunger
for federal patronage. None too proud to use his boyhood
acquaintance with Vice-President Richard M. Johnson as a
basis to prevail upon him for federal favor during Van Buren's
Administration, Smith later donned a spurious cloak of Tylerism for similar purposes. Now he had need of a congressional contact to gain what he considered adequate compensation for some mail contracts he had accepted. Phelps served
Smith faithfully, and three years later Mrs. Phelps, her husband "so much fatigued after last nights labor he had to go to
bed," could report to Smith that "The House bill for your relief passed the Senate at eleven o'clock last night. My husband
has been after the Senators from our state since the setting of
Congress." [6]

In St. Louis the plague of nativism revisited the Whigs,
thus early nullifying plans for Whig activity there. In contrast to the situation in 1842 when Democrats had remained
united to capture the normally Whig city from the divided
party, there were two Democratic tickets in the field both in
the spring city election and in the August state and county
contests. The *Missouri Republican* still could not bring itself
to approve nativism, "a mere instrument in the hands of
disappointed men," but with Democrats also divided the
American party enjoyed a degree of success. Although the
Hard candidate for Congress, James B. Bowlin, was re-

elected, the Americans shared the city, county, and state legislative offices with that faction. As the *Republican* was quick to point out, however, the nativists in no case achieved a majority; all of their victories were by pluralities.[7]

The Second District witnessed the easy victory of Hard Democrat John Jameson over Soft Democrat J. S. Brickey. Jameson's home county, Callaway, was predominantly Whig. Since it bordered on the Whig counties of Boone and Audrain, which were in the Third District, Callaway's inclusion in a district composed largely of Democratic counties to the southeast is probably an example of Democratic gerrymandering to vitiate the Whig concentration in central Missouri. Jameson himself was on the fringe of the Central Clique; and Callaway County was on the edge of the area usually designated as its domain, suggesting the possibility that the clique may have endeavored in districting to preserve opportunities to send more than one of its members to Congress.[8] Conceivably, Whigs could have cited unfairness in districting as a reason for their not entering candidates in 1846, just as they had blamed nondistricting earlier. However, if they were dissatisfied with the divisions of the state, they kept their grievance to themselves.

The remaining 1846 congressional contest is of particular interest. In the Fourth District, located principally in rapidly growing northwest Missouri, James H. Birch, the Independent candidate, suffered ignominious defeat at the hands of Virginia-born, Yale-educated Willard Preble Hall. Identity as an Independent, or Soft Democrat, was but a brief interlude in Birch's political career. Besides a period in the early thirties when he was seemingly without political friends of any sort, his political gamut had thus far included dalliances with Jacksonism, Calhounism, Whiteism, Whiggism, and Tylerism; but the parallel his candidacy on the Independent ticket of 1846 affords with the election of 1836 is suggestive. Just as 1836 marked the end of the first Whig pressure-group era, so 1846 terminated the second. In both elections Birch appeared as a congressional candidate on the anti-Benton ticket and ran far behind the other dissident Democrats. When the Whig party became active following both elections, Birch was in each instance one of the very few who sacrificed the Democratic label and crossed the great divide into the land of Whiggery. The Whigs of 1848, as the Whigs of 1838 had done, welcomed him cordially. After all, Birch exerted himself vigorously for whatever cause he was attached to at the moment, and the Whigs could use such diligence.[9]

The results of this second venture in supporting a branch of the Democratic party brought the Whigs fewer successes than their earlier effort at pressure-group politics during the 1830's. Then they had contributed to the election of two bank Democrats to Congress and to Alexander Buckner's election as United States senator. In the gubernatorial races of 1832 and 1836 Democrats who rebelled against regular party leadership missed victory by only slightly more than 1,000 votes. In the 1840's Independents won neither congressional nor state offices. Although these candidates made showings considerably more respectable than the Whigs of 1840 or 1848 did, the races between Hards and Softs were not remarkably close. True, the Whigs saw a legislature more to their liking in 1844 than they were accustomed to, but this did not bring about their great object of defeating Benton. In 1846, with no impending senatorial contest to animate the party, most of the Whig gains were undone.[10]

Two reasons stand out as explanations for the more limited victories in the later era, one originating within the Democratic party and the other within Whig ranks. The arts of party organization and convention politics were considerably more sophisticated among the Benton politicians by 1842 than they were ten years earlier. Never yielding on the central currency issue, they effectively compromised on peripheral matters both in the legislature and in their party conventions, and the use of this skill undoubtedly served to reinforce the fidelity of quasi Softs. Of major importance in reuniting the Jacksonian party in 1836 was Benton's success in convincing Democratic rank-and-file voters that there could be only one genuine variety of Democracy and that dissent from the true doctrine was a form of party treason. This lesson was not lost on the Senator's followers in the 1840's. Their efficient use of the title to party regularity probably was responsible for more than a few voters' remaining loyal.

On their side, Whigs displayed more apathy toward the Softs than their predecessors did toward the bank Democrats of the 1830's. Probably the Sibleys of the party abstained from the polls in both eras, and in each case the press of the minority party stressed that it had no candidates in the field and could only condone one set of nominees as the lesser of two inadequacies. However, whereas the Opposition papers of the thirties ardently advocated that anti-Jacksonians vote in order to defeat all Benton candidates, the later Whig editors reserved such urgency for the contests for legislative seats that would determine the enemy leader's personal political fate.

This difference is accounted for by the fact that more points of issue remained between the Whigs and Softs than had existed between the Opposition and anti-Benton Jacksonians. The distinguishing characteristics of the anti-Jacksonians of the thirties were disapproval of Jackson as a political leader and adherence to the principle of a national bank. On the latter issue the bank Democrats met them fully. The Whigs of the forties still desired the re-establishment of such an institution, but if the Softs coupled such sentiments to their liberal views on state fiscal policy, they did not express themselves publicly.

The Texas policy created another area of disagreement between the two anti-Benton groups. Just as Whigs could not bring themselves to support Benton, even though they approved his early Texas course, so many could not reconcile their distaste for the Softs' position with active support of that faction, in spite of shared currency views. Some, by no means all, Softs carried their anti-Bentonism to the extent of supporting Calhoun's presidential aspirations in 1844, which were anathema to the nationalistic Whigs. Therefore, many Whigs, finding reprehensible characteristics in both Democratic camps, simply did not vote.[11]

These outstanding differences between the Whigs and anti-Benton men go far to explain why the two groups did not take steps to establish a more formal union, to create a new political party. In the thirties, refusal of the bank Democrats to renounce "this Jackson fanaticism" sustained their and the Opposition's separate identities; the greater number of incompatibilities in the forties served the same purpose. Still, a Whig and anti-Benton union would not have been the most promiscuous political party in American history. Something more than conflicting points of view on auxiliary issues is necessary in an explanation of their failure to coalesce.

The aristocratic tinge of the Whig leadership noted in Chapter 6 contributed its share to the continued separateness of the two political elements. Whigs not only held aloof from Independents because of divergent views; they characterized them as "nauseous pills" which must be swallowed. John P. Campbell, anti-Benton editor of the *Ozark Eagle* who twice ran for Congress as an Independent, deserved praise for his resistance to the party dictator, but the "undignified virulence" of the "*ignoramus's*" attacks hardly suited the Whig temperament. Reluctantly endorsing Charles H. Allen in the 1844 gubernatorial contest, a Whig paper declared that, although he was a man of "violent and impetuous feelings, of strong prejudices, very conceited about his own views, very determined in maintaining them, and not overly scrupulous about the means which he employs," Whigs

should support him because he was at least independent of
the despised hard-money faction of the Democratic party.[12]

Allen, whose sobriquet *Horse* perhaps denoted other qualities repellent to the fastidious Whigs, was an eccentric lawyer
and circuit judge of northeastern Missouri. Regarding fist
fights as delightful entertainment, he would adjourn his court
at any time to witness one. His eccentricity may have been
unique, but occupationally he resembled his fellow Independent Democrats. Biographical information about eight of
the nine individuals who ran for major office on that ticket
indicates that all but one, Editor John P. Campbell, were attorneys. While that profession dominated the leadership of
both parties, its ascendancy was considerably less among the
total Democratic party and slightly smaller among the Whigs
than this small sample indicates it was in the Soft Democratic
faction. The anti-Benton candidates unanimously shared two
other common characteristics, both of which, in contradistinc-
tion to their occupations, set them apart from the typical
Whig leader. All of their biographical sketches specifically
mention humble origins and early poverty. Furthermore, none
attended college.[13] Of course, not every Whig leader had been
to college either, and, moreover, the sample of the Softs is
too small to admit of definitive generalization. However,
when one remembers that two thirds of the sixty-six Whig
leaders surveyed in Chapter 6 were college-educated, it is
at least an informed speculation that a major gulf between
Whigs and Democrats who resembled each other politically
was social in nature.

The exceptional Democrats who went to college were for
the most part associated with the Hard faction of that party.
Six of the eleven men who were pro-Benton candidates for
offices subject to state-wide election were college graduates,
including Willard Preble Hall and John S. Phelps, whose alma
maters were the well-known Connecticut colleges, Yale and
Trinity. In addition to the actual candidates, other leaders of

the Hard faction, such as William B. Napton, John F. Ryland, and Frank P. Blair, Jr., were all products of privileged backgrounds.[14] The prevalence of such men in the Benton leadership suggests that the converse of the conjecture at the end of the preceding paragraph is also true: men who socially resembled the Whigs, and yet were not Whigs, belonged to the Democratic wing whose principles were most distant from Whiggery.

In Chapter 6 evidence was presented to show that the purely slaveholding agricultural interest in Missouri was not large enough to dominate either party, but men whose economic pursuits were chiefly of that nature more commonly identified with the Democratic party. In the light of the Benton-anti-Benton struggle of the 1840's, it appears valid to conclude further that they supported the Benton wing of that party, at least during the period so far covered by this study. For one point, much of the Hards' strength lay in the comparatively large slaveholding counties of central Missouri. Since Whigs of that area were not commonly engaged in large-scale agriculture using slaves, those who were must have been either Democrats or neutrals in politics. Carrying this logic one step further, one can reason that since the Central Clique set the tone for most Democrats in central Missouri, the probabilities are that most large slaveholders adhered to that oligarchy and its hard-money, Benton doctrines. As did other political groups in Missouri, the regular Democrats drew most of their leadership from the lawyer class; but unlike their Independent counterparts, the Hards mixed two farmers among their candidates of 1844 and 1846. One of these was Sterling Price, owner of twenty-eight slaves. Among the noncandidates were the farmers John F. Ryland of Lafayette County, who owned sixty-nine slaves, and Meredith M. Marmaduke of Saline County, who owned thirty-three slaves. The lawyer William B. Napton is on record as describing himself and Claiborne Fox Jackson as men "whose entire property consists of large bodies of land & considerable numbers of slaves." [15] Whether the loyalty of these slaveholders to Benton's currency views was contingent on some economic interest related to slave agriculture or merely the result of political opportunism based on Benton's support of the Central Clique is another question. Certainly, they were zealous in their public professions of devotion to the hard-money principle.

Another possible explanation of the prevalence of Hard sentiment in central Missouri is the existence of the effective Whig party there. Perhaps Softism came forth in one-party areas, while Whiggery filled the opposition role where it existed. This functional analysis fits central Missouri nicely, but does not serve well for St. Louis and Marion County. In both of those places the Whig party was strong; so was the Soft faction; and the Hard faction was not negligible. [16]

Leaving consideration of the differences between adherents of the two factions of the Democratic party and returning to reasons for the continued separation of the Whigs and the anti-Benton group, one finds that political dissimilarities and Whig snobbery were not the only factors that kept the two distinct. Democrats as well as Whigs could be exclusive. Naturally, Independents, as all politicians, welcomed additional votes; but they feared that if the Whig vote was openly given, it would alienate precious Democratic support. Hard Democrats hurled charges of Whig-Soft cooperation at their opponents as if they were proof of the nadir of political morality. Apparently, Softs agreed that the Whig label was not to be prized, for they vehemently denied the alleged connection. One Independent went so far as to challenge to a duel a Hard Democrat who had called him a Whig. During a campaign in which the Softs knew they needed Whig support to win, they devoted much of their oratory to asserting that if persons of such ill repute as the Whigs were known to agree with Benton on the Texas issue, then he must surely be rotten to the core.[17]

Realizing the value of the Democratic label, anti-Benton politicians held on to it tenaciously. Whigs could vote for them, but they would be pleased if the Whigs did it quietly. As to ruining their political futures by becoming known as Whigs, never would they consider it. Whigs reciprocated with equal devotion to their own party name. Such men as Birch were welcomed into the Whig organization, but they had to come to the Whigs. In the 1830's Whigs hoped that William H. Ashley would become one of them. When the practical politician refused to renounce his Jacksonism, Whigs were still willing to support him, but not as their own nominee. The conclusion is inescapable that some men who favored an adequate and flexible currency were in the Democratic ranks because that was the sensible place for an ambitious Missouri politician to be.[18]

During the years from 1842 to 1846 Missouri Whigs were attentive to other interests besides actual elections, though without much greater reward. Their successful prevention of extremely severe currency legislation has been noted. However, they were unable to forestall the passage of a modified currency bill late in 1843, which, while outlawing notes under ten dollars, did not prohibit circulation of all "foreign" paper as the earlier bills sought to do. To an extent, the act indirectly served Whig purposes. Its mere existence abetted the continued division of the Democratic party, but at the same time it did not greatly hamper business transactions.[19]

One other event of considerable importance during the early forties was the state constitutional convention of 1845. The Whigs' chief interest in this matter was reapportionment of representation in the lower house of the General Assembly.

Under the original constitution adopted in 1820, every county was entitled to at least one representative, but the total number could never exceed 100. When the legislature increased the number of counties to 96 in 1843, older, more populous counties saw their representation drastically reduced. St. Louis, with four representatives, and young Platte with two, were the only counties entitled to more than one seat in the House of Representatives. Yet, the difference in population between Boone and Caldwell counties, for example, was almost 13,000.[20] New, undeveloped counties tended to be Democratic, and Whigs voted against their creation, calling the increase of counties the "rotten borough system." However, what Whigs really opposed was the injudicious clause in the constitution. The Democratic legislatures were not unduly hasty in creating new counties; rather, Missouri's population grew at an astonishingly rapid rate between 1835 and 1845.[21]

As soon as the Democratic disputants became irreconcilable, members of that party also agitated for reapportionment, and a constitutional convention became a certainty. Some writers have regarded the apportionment controversy as an integral part of the Hard-Soft altercation, but the divisions on this issue were more strictly geographical. Softs of thinly populated southwest Missouri were not favorably disposed to reapportionment, but Softs of St. Louis and rapidly growing northwest Missouri were. Leaders of the Central Clique were satisfied with the existing arrangements as long as new counties sent Benton men to the capital at Jefferson City. When sparsely populated areas, largely motivated by a desire to see congressional districts created, gave signs of opposing Old Bullion, the clique's opposition to reapportionment melted. Whigs were apparently united in favoring reapportionment, but most Whigs resided in counties that stood to gain by a change in the constitutional provision.[22]

The constitutional convention of 1845 wrote clauses that in

large measure rectified the representational inequalities. Other issues intruded, however, and the voters rejected the new document a year later.

The predecessors of the Whigs had championed life tenure for judges in the early thirties, before they had known the state would be so permanently in the enemy's hands. Seeing a Democratic instead of an independent judiciary result from their labors, they were now amenable to altering the life tenure provision, especially if it would add to the new constitution's voter appeal.[23]

What the Whigs were not prepared for was the adoption by the convention of an ultra-Hard article on banks and corporations that called for abolition even of the conservative Bank of Missouri and for seriously curtailing corporation privileges that could be granted by the legislature. Thus far Whigs had not encountered serious hostility to their corporate aspirations, except when they happened to bear on banking or fiscal matters, and this article, which forever precluded the principle of limited liability, alarmed them.[24]

Dismayed, the *Missouri Republican* nevertheless urged Whigs to vote in favor of the proposed basic law. The apportionment adjustments, it stated, would further the election of men to the General Assembly who opposed such actions as the corporation clause and currency bills, a necessity if the state were ever to be redeemed under any constitution. Probably the Whigs found this too uncertain compensation for the presence of the odious article in the proposed constitution. In any event, the objectors to the corporation section and those in thinly settled sections who were not pleased by the clause relating to representation voted in sufficient numbers to defeat the efforts of the convention, and Missouri continued to operate under her outmoded 1820 constitution.[25]

The years from 1842 to 1846 were not felicitous for the Whig party in Missouri, even though a divided Democratic party seemingly created an auspicious political climate. However, James O. Broadhead, a young Whig of Pike County who had not long previously come to Missouri from Virginia, found some consolations in membership in the minority party of his adopted state. Referring to plans by Democratic members of the legislature "to get up some Hallelujah resolutions, lauding President Polk — the Mexican War etc etc," Broadhead portrayed Whig attitudes during the dismal period:

> They can't pass of course without some grumbling on the part of the Whigs — for although we are few in number, we have the glorious privilege of grumbling — a privilege "inestimable to us and troublesome to democrats only" — Few as we are, so far we have been able to manage the democrats pretty well — by resorting to various devices — sometimes patting them on the back and praising them up — then by throwing firebrands into their camp — arraying them against each other — and when they get each other by the ears — by alternately abusing and encouraging as you would in a dog fight — we keep them in an eternal snarl and sometimes carry off the bone — if we do not we at least have some sport at their expense — We have had one right, royal dog fight during the session between McBay and the Governor about state bonds, special agencies & personal privileges etc — to the no small amusement of the Whigs, who would have been glad enough to have swallowed themselves — if the combatants could have succeeded in prostrating each other, or in convincing their own party that they were as bad as they represented each other to be, and as the Whigs knew they were even before the fight commenced.[26]

CHAPTER 12

TAYLORISM IN MISSOURI

ATTENTION was called earlier to the differentiation commonly made by political scientists between political parties and political interest, or pressure groups. Both seek to influence governmental policy; but interest, or pressure, groups are more "issue oriented" than parties. The main concern of parties is to fill political offices. According to these distinctions, the Whigs of Missouri infrequently acted as a political party during the years covered in the preceding chapters. Instead of presenting their own nominees for political offices, they usually, in the manner of a pressure group, supported other candidates who were willing to bend in their direction.[1]

Although they were consistently active in presidential elections and never entirely withdrew from contests for seats in the state legislature, the pressure-group approach was characteristic of Missouri Whigs in congressional and gubernatorial elections from 1832 to 1836 and again from 1842 to 1846. Following the elections of 1846, the Whigs entered their longest continuous period as a bona fide political party, and, as usual, the Whig course was determined by conditions within the Democratic party. Although Whigs miscalculated in 1842, both in 1832 and 1842 they assumed a passive role in order to take advantage of Democratic factionalism. After 1846, as after 1836, a reunified Democratic party rendered continuation of pressure-group tactics futile.

A number of circumstances explain the majority party's resumption of a monolithic character. Texas and Oregon no longer constituted divisive issues. The solution of the Oregon problem, satisfactory to all, was noted in the preceding chapter. Also remarked there was Benton's endorsement of the Polk Administration's Mexico-Texas policy, once war began. In 1846 David Wilmot first submitted his famous proviso to Congress as an amendment to a bill appropriating money for the acquisition of Mexican territory. The Wilmot Proviso, forever outlawing slavery in any territory so acquired, was to rear its head frequently in Missouri's Democratic party after 1848. Benton consistently voted against it, however, and as yet, few Missourians openly demanded that their senators go to the other extreme of supporting John C. Calhoun's resolutions, which absolutely denied the power of Congress to interfere with slavery in any territory.[2]

Since the Texas and Oregon issues were not the fundamental causes of the Democratic split, however, the healing of the party's divisions cannot be credited primarily to their disappearance. More directly dulling the edges of the basic currency conflict were actions of the legislature and Governor following the 1846 elections. Although the act outlawing notes under ten dollars remained law, the General Assembly's session of 1846–1847 granted more corporation charters than any session in the preceding ten years. Among the new ventures authorized were a number of insurance companies, a type of business previously suspect. The decisive defeat of an individual liability amendment that an Osage County representative attempted to attach to one charter further demonstrated the weakening of Hard antibusiness sentiments. Of the Democratic representatives from once ultra-Hard central Missouri, only Claiborne Fox Jackson supported the amendment.[3]

The Governor of the state also shared the legislature's relaxed antibusiness attitude. John C. Edwards was a product of the abortive efforts for compromise at the Democratic convention of 1844. When Edwards, with his reputation for sentiments in favor of districting and of paper money, was nominated at that gathering, he was denounced by Softs as a man who would sacrifice his principles for preferment from the Hard leaders. During his early years in office, Edwards fulfilled this description, for he established a reputation as a Hard, Benton governor. However, as his term neared its conclusion, Edwards not only countenanced the aforementioned incorporating activity but even advocated a liberal general incorporation law.[4]

The leading authority on Missouri's pre-Civil War economic history has shown that general incorporation was not "a defeat for old-fashioned Bentonian-Jacksonian Democracy." Certainly, as James Neal Primm states, the Hard, Benton faction had enough strength in the legislature to defeat both the general law and the numerous charters granted just prior to its passage. They could have read Governor Edwards out of the party had they felt his proposal smacked of treason. Not only had Jacksonians elsewhere favored such legislation, but Governor Edwards couched his own recommendation in good Jacksonian rhetoric, "The same privileges to all — the same restrictions upon all."[5]

Equal treatment, however, was not what Softs and Whigs asked from the legislature in relation to their business endeavors. In essence, their complaint was that the Hards, seldom interested in business themselves, thwarted, with equal treatment for all, all sensible efforts in that direction. Whigs would still find fault with Democratic attitudes toward business and investment, but clearly the softening of the Hard wing of the Democratic party toward corporate enterprise made that party a more comfortable place for Democrats who resented Benton's attitudes toward currency and business. The lenient attitude of the Hards toward corporations after 1846, while not representing a defeat for them, was a significant shift from their earlier attitude as exemplified, for instance, by the harsh anticorporation clause they had fostered in the state constitution proposed in 1845.

The corporation law was not actually passed until early in

1849 when the new legislature convened. However, it was
the outgrowth of Edwards' earlier recommendation and the
legislature's generous chartering policy and therefore is properly included in this discussion as the culmination of the
shift in Hard attitudes. The press was noticeably silent on the
matter, and Primm feels that this silence indicates it was not
a hotly contested issue. Such an interpretation still permits
the view that the Softs were relieved when the Hards relaxed their doctrines.[6]

Not the least of the reasons for the Softs' reassimilation into
the ranks of the regular Democracy was their consistent record of defeat. The failure of the Independent candidates to
achieve success in both 1844 and 1846 must have caused
them to reconsider the possibilities of controlling the Hards'
excesses from within the same party. Also, the death in 1846
of Shadrick Penn, leading editor of the Soft press, contributed
to Democratic reunification. It deprived the Softs of a vigorous leader, removed from the scene the man who had most
vituperatively attacked Benton, and paved the way toward
merging the *Reporter*, Penn's paper, with the *Missourian*, the
Benton organ in St. Louis. The resultant larger press was appropriately dubbed *"The Union."*[7]

Possibly, the Whigs would have remained passive if they
had seen prospects of a continuation of the Democratic
schism. Sensing that they would not be able to choose between Democratic contenders in 1848, Whigs were faced, as
they had been ten years earlier, with the alternatives of re-
activating their own organization or of abandoning the state
by default to its Democratic masters. They chose the former
course, and the presence of a Whig ticket thereby became
both effect and cause of Democratic unity. With a common
enemy in the field, dissident Democrats were less inclined to
depart from party regularity.

Democratic unity was not the only reason for Whig organization in 1848. Some leaders naturally chafed at the subordi-

nate, voters-only roles assigned them by the Softs and were anxious to have again party councils of their own to dominate. Such desires were stimulated by a surge of optimism resulting from events related to the Mexican War.

Missouri Whigs, as Whigs throughout the nation, had disapproved of that war. Although Whigs in other areas have been credited with a clairvoyant foreknowledge of the sectional controversies that war with Mexico and the consequent territorial acquisitions would arouse, Missourians did not voice objections of this nature. Their opposition, no doubt motivated to some extent by a partisan desire to find fault with the Tyler and Polk administrations, was confined to denouncing the war as unjust and unnecessary. It was unjust and dishonorable because the stronger United States had deliberately provoked the weaker Mexico in order to satisfy the territorial ambitions of opportunistic politicians. It was unnecessary because Mexico, if not insulted and goaded, would soon peaceably relinquish her untenable position in Texas anyway.[8]

Once war broke out, Missouri Whigs, again in company with their brethren elsewhere, continued to lament the Polk Administration's taking the country into the conflict, but they also professed the motto, "Our Country right or wrong." Since there were no Whigs from the state in Congress, the Missouri branch of the party had no record of opposition or support for war measures. However, the Whig press proudly claimed that members of the party numbered prominently among the Army volunteers from Missouri.[9]

While it is impossible to determine the politics of the numerous Missourians who enthusiastically volunteered for war service, there is no doubt as to the Whiggery of Missouri's most famous war hero. This was Alexander Doniphan, a Clay County lawyer. Doniphan had seen service in 1838 when he had commanded a brigade of the state militia against the Mormons, the despised sect that western Missourians re-

fused to tolerate in their midst. At that time the tall soldier-
lawyer of aristocratic Virginia lineage had demonstrated his
independence of character when he refused to obey a gubernatorial order to execute the Mormon leader Joseph Smith.[10]
In 1847 the whole country was singing hosannas to Colonel
Doniphan for his victories at El Brazito and the Sacramento,
battles he had won at the expense of only one American life.
Zachary Taylor had already distinguished himself also, and
Whigs looked increasingly to him to carry their colors in the
coming presidential canvass.[11]

Members of the party in Missouri, particularly those
accustomed to eying the main chance, calculated that a combination of Doniphan, who had a reputation for powerful
oratory as well as for military exploits, and Taylor would be
irresistible. Even in an overwhelmingly Democratic state
such as theirs, Whigs could win on a ticket headed by such
popular personalities if they would do two things. They must
avoid committing themselves to Whig doctrines proven to be
unpopular in previous elections. When questioned on the tariff or on the national bank issue, Whigs, decreed John Wilson,
should "on all occasions shout, shout for Taylor Buena Vista
& Sacramento & Doniphan for governor & my word for it we
shall carry this state." For victory it was further necessary
that Whigs organize "to the smallest office." Wilson, one of
the very few outside St. Louis who expressed sympathy for
the Native American movement during the 1840's, was no
middle-of-the-roader on the subject of organization. In years
when he deemed it profitable to support a branch of the
Democratic party, he urged his fellow Whigs to go under-
ground completely. Now in 1848, the year of Whig resur-
gence, he implored, "Organize — organize — make that organization *Broad* enough while it seems a Taylor meeting to
take in a state organization — Govnr, Lt. Gov, Congress . . .
so there is an efficient & immediate organization — Let us
make all the noise we can."[12]

Most Missouri Whigs agreed with Wilson, both in regard to strategy and in regard to candidates. One who did not concur on the latter point, however, was Alexander Doniphan who, reminiscent of earlier Whig favorites, preferred to attend to his neglected law practice rather than to launch an active political career. When the Whigs assembled at their state convention in April, 1848, they nominated instead James S. Rollins of Boone County. Like most Whig nominations, this one was by acclamation.[13]

There had been other aspirants, but their claims were sifted long before the delegates assembled at Boonville. For example, John Wilson notified Abiel Leonard that his brother Robert Wilson was willing to accept the nomination, although he would not be anybody's rival for it. Wilson preferred his brother, of course, but personal preference was not the decisive factor with this practical politician. Rollins he regarded as the better electioneer, and, therefore, Rollins was his candidate if he was willing to run.[14] There was also a movement in behalf of the politician-artist George Caleb Bingham. However, more than a month before the convention it was abandoned in favor of acclamation for Rollins. Although disappointed, Bingham graciously accepted Rollins' nomination as the man "to take the track against the next *donkey* that the Locos may put forward for governor."[15]

These examples indicate that the unanimity ascribed by the Whig press to the Whig conventions of 1839 and 1848 was authentic.[16] The Whig party was large enough to contain a number of politically ambitious men, but at the same time it was small enough to make its members aware that they must act harmoniously if they would entertain any hopes of victory. Furthermore, in contrast to the situation within the heterogeneous Democratic organization, the rivalries within the Whig party were confined to those based on ambition and did not include any based on conflicting principles. Discussion of the dissension within Missouri's Whig party over the relative merits of Henry Clay and Zachary Taylor will follow. Here, it is pertinent to mention that this difference merely represented an extension of the familiar dialogue between pure and opportunistic Whiggery. When the subject was a gubernatorial nominee, all Missouri Whigs could accommodate themselves to any man who was widely known, possessed a reputation as an effective orator, and was recognized as a Whig. In Missouri, the third requisite axiomatically established the politician as a champion of the national bank and of aggressive action by the state in behalf of business and investment interests. Doniphan's fame and oratorical prowess were both more compelling than Rollins'. When he withdrew, the Whigs simply turned to the man among the willing who was most impressive in these particulars.

The pretensions of Edward Bates, Abiel Leonard, Henry S. Geyer, or John F. Darby were stronger had they cared to press them, but Rollins was not without claims on his party. As a resident of Whiggish Boone County, election to the legislature was an easy matter for him. Nevertheless, the fact that by 1848, when he was only thirty-six years old, he had been willing to serve three terms indicates that he put his devotion to Whiggery into practice more often than many of his party allies. In 1839 he proved his adroitness at political maneuver by winning for his county the location of the state university, in the face of strong claims put forth by neighboring Democratic counties.[17]

Although the highest place on the Whig ticket was in some demand in 1848, the nomination for lieutenant governor very nearly went begging. The convention conferred the honor on David Dawson Mitchell of St. Louis, manager of the Missouri and California Overland Mail and Transportation Company. Immediately, rumors circulated that Mitchell was more interested in a nomination to Congress, which involved a far less arduous canvass in the now districted state. He failed to receive such preferment from his district convention, but nevertheless he resigned his candidacy. Unwilling to contend for the second post themselves, St. Louis leaders Edward Bates and sometime mayor John F. Darby approached Jesse H. McIlvain, heretofore unknown in politics. McIlvain declined, not because of want of zeal, he said, but because his stump presence was so woefully inadequate. Finally, quaintly named Littleberry Hendricks of Springfield agreed to undertake the canvass. A reserved, diminutive lawyer of more humble origins than many Whig leaders, Hendricks years before had begun to "doubt the sufficiency of the virtue & intelligence of the people to sustain the government." A Democratic contemporary considered him the leading Whig from his part of the state. However, as the same contemporary pointed out, when one's part of the state was southwest Missouri, that was not saying a great deal.[18]

Nevertheless, the Whigs had candidates who were willing to campaign far more energetically than those of 1840 had done. Then only John B. Clark, candidate for governor, had conducted a full-scale campaign. In 1848 Rollins covered even more ground than Clark had, and Hendricks was equally active. There were congressional candidates in all five districts, all of whom campaigned vigorously.[19]

Without heroic Doniphan at their head, the Whigs could not concentrate their oratory as exclusively on military exploits as John Wilson had advocated. They did direct attention to Taylor's war record when possible, but the Whig platform remained basically economic. There was a significant shift in emphasis from the past, however.

Whereas a national bank had always been the Whig *summum bonum* before, in 1848 the party stressed the need for internal improvements — internal improvements by anybody: the national government, the state government, and "liberally incorporated companies." Such an appeal might have been more effective than the bank issue had not the Democratic party also adopted internal improvements as its principal is-

sue. Austin King, Rollins' Democratic opponent for governor
and also a Boone Countian, was equally vociferous in his
advocacy of internal improvements, qualifying his endorsement only with opposition to creating a *large* debt for the
purpose. James S. Green, Democratic candidate for re-election to Congress in central Missouri's Third District, had been
a moving force behind the generous charter granted the still
unbuilt Hannibal and St. Joseph Railroad. If his constituents
were on the verge of an internal improvements mania, as
events in the succeeding decade indicated most Missourians
were, why should they prefer his opponent John Wilson, who,
though he strained his lungs shouting "internal improvements," answered to the tainted name of Whig? [20]

After the election Whig editors complained that Democrats had appropriated an issue from them. Snarled Palmyra's
Missouri Whig:

> But what is all this, ye hypocrites, but good, old, long-tried,
> much abused, but solid and sterling Whig doctrine? What is it,
> ye miserable drivellers, but the principles you have fought
> against and kept down by baseborn and low-flung calumnia-
> tions of the best men in the State for twenty-five years? What
> has become of the idea that Congress has no power to make
> internal improvements? Is not all Missouri Locofocodom on
> the tiptoe of anxiety to show how devout they are in spirit to
> make a road a mile wide and 2,500 miles in length. . . . Mis-
> souri Locofocos have become the advocates of internal im-
> provement, in the state: the advocates of such improvement
> by Congress; the advocates of the most stupendous work of
> the kind ever known! What is it a Locofoco cannot do? What is
> it he will not say or unsay, to keep on the strong side?
> Nothing! [21]

The editor's bitterness was not justified, for, in truth, Whigs
more radically than Democrats had shifted to a position "on
the strong side." The Whigs had always favored internal improvements, and everyone had assumed that they did so. But
throughout their previous history they had been content to

suppress the issue in favor of their more cherished object, a national bank. Until 1848, Whig pronouncements in favor of internal improvements were buried in generalized endorsements of the American System or were mere echoes of their opponents' "of a truly national character" hedging device.[22] In the years immediately preceding the 1848 election, the Whigs had not been stumping the state for internal improvements. Rather, they had been estivating in their caves, crawling out only to cast unenthusiastic votes for Soft candidates. Their emphasis on internal improvements in 1848 was actually an elongation of their attempt to revamp the popular image of Whiggery through its association with idolized military heroes. Noting that the legislature, chiefly through its liberalized corporation policy, had taken several well-received steps in the direction of internal improvements, Whigs sensed that internal improvements could be a clarion call to Missouri voters. In a letter to George R. Smith, written before Doniphan's reluctance was known, realist John Wilson put the matter clearly.

> That we ought to make the race on old "Rough and Ready," and internal improvements of the State as our only watchword is to me entirely evident. The masses of our State, I feel sure, are in favor of both. Like it was in 1828, everybody knew all about General Jackson; so now more than everybody knows all about General Taylor. On the other hand the low stage of the Missouri river for two years, the high freight, not to say impossibility of sending produce to market at all, has at once brought all minds to consider the importance of internal improvements. There is now a general fever in favor of such projects. It is true, different parts of the State ask different improvements; and all taken together they would amount to more than could be made at short notice. But it will be a great oversight in our friends if they do not take vigorous hold of this feeling, and if added to Taylor and Doniphan, we shall surprise ourselves in the final result.[23]

Certainly, it was presumptuous of Missouri Whigs to think that normally Democratic Missouri voters would prefer them because they belatedly dusted off an old principle. A Missourian who wanted internal improvements now felt that he could have them through the party he had traditionally supported. Furthermore, those who were attentive to the campaign could observe that the Whigs were still very much the same as they had always been. Try as they would, Whigs could not eliminate the national bank issue from their political vocabularies. Rollins pronounced the question "obsolete and decided" in a speech at remote Bloomington, but in the same breath he gleefully predicted that within a few years ruin and disaster would engulf the land. Then, he asserted, the country would see the need for re-establishing a national bank.[24]

The election returns told the tale of a party that Missouri voters refused to believe represented their interests. Despite a more vigorous campaign than Whigs had ever waged, despite their concentration on the most popular issue they could find, Rollins and Hendricks received only 41 per cent of the total vote cast. A famous Kentucky Whig and close friend of Rollins attempted to console the defeated candidate. After urging his friend not to despair over the people's rebuff, Cassius Marcellus Clay concluded with an unusually candid, if self-flattering, statement of the Whig philosophy:

> For it is greater to be recorded among the great whig party than first among democrats. What if we remain in a minority — We are yet the great intellectual wealthy *conservative* party of the nation — the *balance wheel* without which true liberty and democracy would speedily end in anarchy or despotisms.[25]

All five Whig congressional candidates lost. Although the crest of Whig leadership was not represented among them, neither had the field been left to nonentities. In all but one instance the Whig candidates for Congress were well-known men, both within their party and within their communities. In the eastern First District, which included St. Louis, respected but unknown John D. Cook, a participant in the 1820 constitutional convention, lost to incumbent James B. Bowlin by almost 4,000 votes. The nativistic proclivities of St. Louis Whigs were intensified when Democrats marched to victory both in the city and county elections. This had never happened before, except when the St. Louis Whigs were divided among themselves; and rural Whigs joined their city cousins in proclaiming the German element responsible for the disaster.[26]

Gilchrist Porter, a prominent lawyer of Pike County, fared best among the Whigs who aspired to represent Missouri in Washington. In the Second (central-southeastern) District he polled almost 45 per cent of the vote, losing by less than 2,000 votes. John Wilson, who had in large measure set the tone of the campaign, lost by only a slightly larger margin in the centrally located Third District. At the other extreme were James Winston of Benton County, Whig candidate for governor in 1852, and Edward M. Samuels, Clay County merchant who had associated himself with George C. Sibley in the state-wide congressional canvass of 1840. In the two western districts these men each trailed their successful opponents by over 6,000 votes.[27]

The two houses of the newly elected legislature contained a total of 35 Whigs and 98 Democrats. Fortunately, Missourians who hungered for internal improvements would not need to rely for their accomplishment on the party that claimed a monopoly on their advocacy. The defeat was dismal on all fronts, and Whigs could only moan, "We give it up. . . . The dark pall of locofocoism hangs over Missouri."[28]

The presidential election in November brought no relief. Although ten thousand Democrats who had voted in August stayed away from the polls in November, apparently none, as in states farther south, crossed the line to vote for Taylor. Indeed there is no evidence that this stay-at-home vote was either for Taylor or against Lewis Cass, the Democratic presidential nominee. Probably it was simply a product of renewed Democratic confidence after the party's easy victories in the state elections. The fact that Taylor's vote was almost exactly the same as that received by Rollins and Hendricks indicates that Whigs gave him their united support.[29]

Most Missouri Whigs had been enthusiastic about Taylor's candidacy; some had merely acquiesced in it. Few had abandoned their almost filial piety toward Henry Clay in 1848, but many of his most ardent admirers imitated Clay's close Kentucky associate, John J. Crittenden, who pressed the more auspicious candidacy of the Mexican War hero. As a resident of that state confided to Rollins almost two years before the election, "I certainly agree with you in thinking it preposterous to run Clay for the purple again, and so do a large majority of the Whigs here. While the Whigs of Ky. would prefer seeing Clay president to any living man, they do not wish the cause jeopardized by his nomination."[30]

The attitude of Missouri Whigs toward the presidential nomination of 1848 reveals that the state was less preoccupied with slavery issues than other areas of the nation were. Northern Whigs were dubious about Taylor's availability because he was a Louisiana planter and large slaveholder as well as a general. Southern Whigs, increasingly aware of antislavery sentiment in the North, esteemed Taylor for that same reason. Missouri Whigs, however, preferred Taylor solely because he appeared a likely winner. "Clay is undobtly [sic] the choice of the Whig leaders . . . ," wrote a Democrat who had observed an early Taylor demonstration in St. Louis. "If there is a probability of success Clay will be the man. Otherwise the shout will be for Taylor."[31]

Such flexibility was not characteristic of all Missouri Whigs. The session of the state convention devoted to instructing delegates to the Whigs' national meeting was not so serene as the one concerned with state nominations. It was only after lengthy debate that, according to the Democratic press, reached a feverish pitch that a resolution instructing the delegates to vote for Taylor passed by a vote of 191 to 80. Harmony-minded Whigs accepted this decision, however, and the rigid Clay branch of the party made itself heard only once again.[32] This occurred at the Philadelphia convention in June, when one of the seven Missouri delegates, William H. Russell, refused to follow the instructions.

As the youngest member of the Kentucky legislature in 1806, Transylvania-trained Russell had cast the decisive vote in favor of Clay's first election to the United States Senate. The two had developed a close personal relationship, and Russell professed that he admired Clay "above all living men." Admitting that this advocacy of his "second father" violated party instructions, Russell asserted that Clay was the preference of Missouri's "true Whigs." His fellow Missouri delegates questioned his right to remain in the convention with such independent attitudes, but remain he did; and Missouri's vote divided, 6 for Taylor, 1 for Clay, throughout the four ballots. Ironically, this devotion to Clay later caused some to suspect the quality of Russell's Whiggery. In order to qualify for patronage, he found it necessary to give assurances that though he was "terribly shocked when he [Clay] was made to give way . . . nothing on earth could ever have converted me into a Loco-Foco."[33]

The Russell incident emphasizes that by the time of the national convention most Missouri Whigs were on the Taylor bandwagon.[34] This contrasted with the situation in 1840 when the entire delegation held fast to Clay over William Henry Harrison, and the difference showed in the campaigns.

Following their defeats in August of 1840, Whigs exerted little energy in behalf of Harrison. The Missouri party put on its most enthusiastic show for Clay in 1844, but there was also considerable Whig campaigning between the state and presidential defeats in 1848. Although, as usual, the highly

placed party members outside the state ignored hopelessly
Democratic Missouri, the most prominent Whigs within Missouri were more willing to serve the party than they had been
on other occasions. Abiel Leonard bestirred himself to speak
at a barbecue in his home town of Fayette. In keeping with
his previously displayed distaste for the stump, however, this
Coriolanus reneged on his promised speeches at Columbia
and Lexington. Vainly hoping to benefit by Taylor's military
reputation, Edward Bates presided over several rallies for
the General. Exhausted and disheartened as they must have
been, the defeated candidates for state offices recited Taylor's exploits at reportedly well-attended rallies throughout
the state. Perhaps the party remembered *Missouri Republican*
editor A. B. Chambers' warning of 1842 that Whigs who retired in the face of adversity could expect few favors from
the national party when it came into power. In any event,
once tidings of Taylor's victory spread to Missouri, the Whigs
of the state entered into a patronage scramble of unprecedented dimensions.[35]

CHAPTER 13

PATRONAGE DISAPPOINTMENTS

THE Whig party in Missouri had patronage ambitions of a grand order following the election of a Whig President in 1848. Having no successes on which to base their claims, the Whigs of the Democratic state asserted that their failures entitled them to preferential treatment from the Taylor Administration. There were 33,000 Missouri Whigs, and this large body of citizens was without representation in government, reasoned St. Louis' *Missouri Republican*. Therefore, Missouri deserved the highest favor in the President's gift, a place in his Cabinet. Soon the newspaper narrowed its choice to Edward Bates, and a concentrated St. Louis effort was under way.[1]

However, the St. Louis Whigs had neglected to obtain clearance from their country affiliates. Even before the *Republican* put forth the claims of Bates, John C. Richardson, a young but prominent lawyer of Boonville in Cooper County, informed Abiel Leonard, "The Ball is rolling." Richardson was no more specific than the friends of Bates as to which Cabinet post was sought, but already, in Leonard's behalf, he had written friends in all parts of the state, communicated with national leaders to whom he was a stranger, and taken steps to have Leonard endorsed by the handful of Whigs in the legislature.[2]

When he read the pronunciamento in the *Republican*, Richardson was unperturbed. James S. Rollins would be in the legislature as a hold-over senator, and having borne the Whig flag so defiantly in the August canvass, he could expect to exercise considerable influence among the other Whigs there. Richardson conferred with him and came away with his hearty concurrence in the plans to advance Abiel Leonard's candidacy. Like Rollins, Richardson was a native of Kentucky who had studied at Transylvania College. To Leonard, he wrote:

> Whilst I would not detract from the just claims of Mr. Bates for any office his friends may see fit to designate him for, *we* desire the appointment of a gentleman who lives in the *right place*, who looks beyond the limits of a city, who is of the people — and among them, and is in sympathy and interest with the great body of the suffering, working, Whig party.[3]

Leonard, consistently unwilling to struggle for elective office, was no more inclined to expose himself in an intraparty contest for appointive favor. Richardson had to reassure the venerated lawyer that the movement was understood to originate entirely with his friends. "You have no agency in the affair, and all responsibility may be imparted to us," he assured Leonard and continued:

> If you are called to the cabinet *we* desire that it shall not be charged to the activity of a faction or a "clique" . . . [but] as a compliment to one of its [Whig party's] most distinguished members. . . . We commenced this affair before we knew of the movement which has since been indicated by Mr. B.'s friends and I can see no reason why we should now desist. . . . I have no idea that a single man out of St. Louis has been conferred with on that subject.[4]

What thus appeared to be the germ of an unprecedented city-country quarrel in Missouri's Whig party suddenly turned into a wrangle in which geographical or any other lines were impossible to decipher. When the Whig legislators caucused, Rollins refused to "open his oracular lips" in support of Leonard, and the legislative recommendation went to Bates. According to Richardson, "bargain, intrigue, and chicanery" between Rollins and the indefatigable James H. Birch defeated Leonard. In order to arrange an appointment for Birch to the state supreme court, Rollins had agreed to use his influence to moderate the Taylor removal policy toward certain Democratic officeholders, Richardson asserted. Then, that St. Louis Whigs might overlook this treachery, he had not opposed the pretensions of their favorite. Exactly what Rollins' compensation for Birch's appointment was to be, Richardson failed to make clear. These heated allegations constitute the total evidence of a Birch-Rollins conspiracy, and it is by no means certain that there was any connection at all between Birch's enigmatic appointment and the Whig patronage strife. It is clear, however, that Abiel Leonard and his admirers felt that Rollins had used against them his influence over the Whig legislators.[5]

Even the influence of the legislative caucus cannot be taken for granted. The General Assembly contained only 34 Whigs in 1849, but Whig officeholders were a rarity at all political levels in Missouri. In any event, Missouri Whigs seeking appointments assumed that a recommendation from the Whig legislators would carry weight in Washington. Naturally, it is impossible to attribute any decisions by President Taylor or members of his Cabinet to advice from the Whigs of the Missouri legislature, though events point to the conclusion that legislative recommendations were potent enough to diminish the force of recommendations from other Missouri sources. If Taylor or his advisers were moved by the arguments for a Missouri Cabinet appointment, they very likely were overwhelmed by the conflicting testimonies of Bates's and Leonard's partisans. Leonard, fearing as much, finally tried to yield to Bates. He instructed an underling to inform John J. Crittenden, whose guiding role in Taylor's nomination was expected to furnish him considerable influence over appointments, that he was "unwilling to jeopardize the claims of the Whigs of Missouri for such an appointment by division and want of concert in action." Either this disclaimer came too late or the claims of Missouri Whigs were weak in the first place, for there were no Whigs from Missouri in the Taylor Cabinet.[6]

It is ironical that, aside from St. Louis' local schism over Native Americanism, Missouri Whiggery's most serious rupture before 1850 should have centered upon Edward Bates and Abiel Leonard. Both had refused to serve their party when it asked them to do so. Their fidelity to Whiggery was unimpeachable, yet their devotion to the cause never impelled them to undertake arduous canvasses in its behalf. Nor did they customarily exert themselves to give the party direction or to stimulate its organization. Following his defeat in the congressional race of 1828, Bates had suffered himself to be elected to the General Assembly for a few terms, but by 1836 he had all but retired from politics. He had not even attended the first Whig convention in 1839. Leonard chronically refused to stir the lethargic, but potentially strong, Whig group in Howard County. It was of such men as Leonard that the hard-driving John Wilson once complained, "those whose position and capacity entitle them to lead are too exclusively engaged in their own affairs." In justice to both Leonard and Bates, it should be noted that neither made an exception to his behavior when the Cabinet position was at stake. Each avoided an active role in the designs for his own elevation.[7]

Whether or not they deserved such esteem, there is no question that Abiel Leonard, Edward Bates, and, to a lesser extent, Henry S. Geyer, occupied the pinnacles of prestige and influence within the Whig ranks. All three were recognized by contemporaries, Whig and Democrat alike, as outstanding practitioners before the Missouri bar, and perhaps the explanation for their prestige lies outside the political sphere.[8] It may have stemmed from professional deference, accorded by a Whig leadership preponderantly composed of other lawyers. Conceivably, such deference was alloyed by the desire of younger men of the profession to ingratiate themselves with those able to direct clients their way and otherwise affect their advancement.

In addition, Missouri Whigs possibly felt that only these expert legalists and accomplished orators were sufficiently sophisticated to impress men of national prominence who were in a position to grant important favors. Early in his career, when he represented territorial Missouri as a delegate to Congress, Bates himself furnished an example of how oversensitive Missourians could be in the presence of erudite Easterners. During his lifetime he issued only one challenge to a duel, and the recipient was a South Carolinian who had cast aspersions on the intellectual refinements of Missourians. In 1847 Bates served as president of the Chicago Rivers and Harbors Convention, which coupled to his very early career did entitle him to more serious consideration for a Cabinet post than Leonard. Describing Bates's Chicago presidential address, John Darby reminds one of the small-town editor boasting of the local boy's success in the great metropolis. Wrote Darby, "Men of genius, of distinction, and cultivated talents were there, and they were astonished to hear a man of such splendid eloquence and elegant elocution and force of delivery among Western delegates." [9]

If a western-frontier inferiority complex can explain why Missouri Whigs sought to advance Bates and Leonard instead of those willing to sacrifice for the party, it may also bear on the reluctance of Whigs at all levels to campaign for office. What happened to a man's motivation to serve his party diligently when the tangible plaudits always went to Bates, Leonard, and Geyer? It is pure conjecture, but not beyond the realm of possibility that James S. Rollins, unashamed of his own cultural attainments, was piqued when the influential Leonard made no move to encourage Whigs to seek a reward for their standard-bearer. Rollins had steadfastly campaigned for his party, even after his own defeat in August. Yet no one suggested that he direct his aspirations beyond completion

of his term in the state senate. From Bates he had no reason
to expect special attention, but Rollins' relations with Leonard had been close. When Leonard ignored him, he reciprocated in kind.[10]

Neither the patronage scramble nor the patronage haggle
was confined to the celestial heights the friends of Bates and
Leonard had in mind for their favorites. To balance their
failures at the polls, Missouri Whigs felt they should have at
least one appointment "of the bureau grade." John G. Miller,
Richardson's fellow lawyer in Boonville and the lone Whig
candidate for Congress in 1846, received a legislative recommendation for such an office, but he complained that it was
weakened when the legislators also endorsed another man
for a position of equal rank. The Rollins-dominated caucus
asserted there were enough offices in Washington to supply
Missourians with three or four bureau appointments. To Miller this was a tactic to weaken his claims.[11]

Richardson hoped for the office of United States Marshal,
but he failed to gain even a neutral recommendation from
the Whig caucus. Bitterly he lamented, "The same *disguised*
influence which gave to *Mr. Bates* the recommendation,
which neutralized the recommendation of Miller by giving
Allen a similar one, which helped and advised a corrupt
Locofoco Governor to make Jim Birch a judge of the Supreme
Court, defeated me."[12]

Leonard was deluged with requests for his aid and influence in obtaining appointments of lower rank. Some of these
came from Whigs who had suffered personal economic reversals, such as Thomas Campbell of Boonville who, having
"failed in business," sought support for himself and his family. A St. Louisan begged directly to Thomas Ewing, Secretary of the Interior, for "any" federal job because losses he
had suffered in a St. Louis fire rendered his situation desper-
ate. Only a few minor jobseekers might be classified as ca-
reerists in the appointive service.[13] An example from this

small category was William B. Farmer of Springfield. President Harrison appointed him postmaster there in 1841, but President Polk removed him in 1845. Without regular employment in the interim, he desired to supervise Springfield's mail once again. A medical doctor frankly declared his wish to supplement the income from his practice with a land-office clerk's salary. Actual past service to the Whig party does not appear to have been a salient characteristic of the applicants for minor offices in 1849. Indeed, their letters to Leonard and to other prominent Whigs contain almost no references to work in local campaigns; and if any of them ever served a term in the legislature or attended a state convention, they did not cite such party activities in support of their claims.

Besides the applicants themselves, men of middle prominence, such as James Winston, a candidate for Congress, and Littleberry Hendricks, a candidate for the office of lieutenant governor, wrote Leonard in behalf of their neighbors. Since nothing could be done through "that damned Whig caucus at Jefferson City," wrote Winston, it was necessary that Leonard override them and write directly to Whigs prominent on the national scene. Leonard's friends had written to the same leaders, telling them of the Howard Countian's high position in Missouri, and now Leonard was to use the influence supposedly thus generated in their behalf. He complied in volume, indicating that he shared the dissatisfaction with the caucus Whigs.[14]

Operating more independently was John Wilson. After Taylor's nomination, Wilson had made the General's acquaintance while on business in New Orleans and had received an invitation to visit him at his plantation near Baton Rouge. Boasted Wilson, "He opened his whole mind on all subjects to me; there was not anything that he could think of as connected with his duties as President that he did not speak about." Having encountered no scruples in exploiting

Taylor's military record in the hope of political profit, Wilson now desired to take advantage of his acquaintance with the President-elect. Immediately after the new year, Wilson wrote letters to at least nine Missouri Whigs pointing out that Taylor had no way of knowing his standing in Missouri. To remedy this circumstance, he suggested that

> if the Whigs of Missouri should think me worthy, and will at once — right now — fully endorse me as of good character, pretty good capacity, and entirely acceptable to the Whigs of Missouri, recommending me at large as fit for anything, if they can say so, speaking of me for no specific office; and if our Whig members in the legislature will join to do this — all this, and my present start with him, will put me in a position to do much for my friends, and perhaps something for myself.[15]

The astute Wilson knew what he was about. By approaching neither the friends of Leonard nor the members of the legislature directly, he steered clear of the factional fight, and he went to Washington with both a legislative recommendation and a personal one from Leonard besides what he had mustered in other quarters. His reward came in the form of the superintendency of the Salt Lake Indian Agency, located in the newly acquired Utah Territory. Eventually Wilson moved on to San Francisco, and Missouri Whiggery was without its most practical-minded mentor.[16]

Wilson would probably have preferred an office of higher rank, but he nevertheless fared better in the matter of patronage than his fellow Missourians. In fact, the circumstances surrounding the office he received were symptomatic of the Washington attitude toward Missouri's patronage aspirations. The new Salt Lake Indian Agency was created only after the one at Council Bluffs, Iowa, much nearer to Missouri, had been abandoned. "Come out and tell Mr. Ewing," John G. Miller urged Abiel Leonard, "that Missouri will not be content with an agency in the Rocky Mts. & one other upon our frontier — [Leavenworth, in what is now the state of Kansas]. The Democracy did better than that." Missouri Whigs filled a number of postmasterships and land office sinecures within the state, but there were no appointments of the bureau grade and not many of the clerical in the nation's capital.[17]

The Whig patronage debacle is instructive from another point of view. Following neither William Henry Harrison's election in 1840 nor Zachary Taylor's in 1848 was there any significant purpose attached to the efforts by Missouri Whigs to gain appointive favor. Granting that it was unreasonable to expect politicians to seek office chiefly for the purpose of improving the federal service, it is nevertheless noteworthy that Missourians who asked for appointments always cited their claims and never their qualifications. The Leonard Collection contains numerous letters pertaining to patronage, and an appreciable amount of that type of correspondence is scattered throughout the extant papers of other Whig leaders. While there are frequent references to applicants' consistent Whiggery and high character and occasional ones to their need of employment, there are none to special abilities pertaining to particular positions. The ambiguous designs to obtain unspecified Cabinet posts and appointments of the "bureau grade" are illustrative of this catholic approach to patronage. Only Whigs of the lesser orders who sought the local postmastership or a clerical position in a nearby land agency ever applied for a particular office.[18]

If it is too idealistic to suggest that Whigs might have desired to better their country's bureaucracy through patronage, perhaps one could expect attempts to improve their own party's situation. This was not the case, however. It is true that the supporters of both Leonard and Bates emphasized that Missouri Whigs deserved some form of representation in government, but they did not elucidate what benefits would redound to the party from this representation. Presumably, they had further patronage in mind. Certainly, John Wilson implied as much when he pointed out that his own elevation would "put me in a position to do much for my friends." [19] The evidence indicates that such patronage was only to be awarded to the already faithful and, further, that promises of renewed or increased zeal for Whiggery were not to be exacted in return. Again referring to the patronage letters in the available manuscript collections, one notes that they were exclusively testimonial in nature. Whether one wrote in his own behalf or in behalf of a friend, consideration of the desired appointment's possible effect on voter behavior, campaign contributions, or press coverage of Whig activities was consistently absent.

Nor did national leaders attempt to influence the uses made of patronage. If John J. Crittenden, Secretary of the Interior Thomas Ewing, or Taylor himself even replied to Missourians who wrote them about appointments, the addressees did not preserve the letters. Not only did they withhold their guidance, but the powerful men also displayed their indifference to hopelessly Democratic Missouri by slighting her. At one point, John G. Miller thought he would receive an appointment as Commissioner of Indian Affairs, but, in June, Secretary Ewing informed him that Taylor had determined that Kentucky deserved the office. Resorting to the Missouri party's argument that defeat at the polls entitled it to privilege at the trough, Miller complained to Leonard:

> It seems to me that if there had been any great desire upon the part of the President to give Missouri any thing that the appointments we sought might have been made without conflicting with the claims of Kentucky — Surely she did not particularly need a representative at Washington, in addition to her Senators & Representatives.[20]

Other unkind cuts came when the Administration awarded desirable offices to men unknown to the local leadership. When this happened in the case of the United States Marshal for the Missouri District, A. B. Chambers, who had so often used the columns of the *Republican* to goad Missouri Whigs to campaign, rose up in wrath. Writing to Thomas Ewing, he protested:

> The [Whigs of Missouri] have always contended without the hope or prospect of success in their own state. But the certainty of defeat and the great majority against them did not deter them from the conflict. Now if it is to be understood that the working men, those who have borne the heat and burthen of the day are to be thrown aside . . . there will be no more rallying, no more contests in this quarter.[21]

It is, of course, possible that national Whig leaders would not have been particularly dismayed to see these threats carried out. As Chambers stated, Whig defeat in Missouri had become axiomatic. This being the case, it made sense to use federal offices there as rewards to the faithful in doubtful states rather than as incentives to a local party without prospect of victory.

At least Chambers, unlike the other Missouri Whigs, saw a connection between patronage and party strength. However, the most expedient suggestion regarding the use of federal patronage came from a Democratic lawyer and editor, Abel Rathbone Corbin. This St. Louisan, who had acted with the anti-Benton wing of his party, was not concerned with converting Missouri into a Whig state, but at least he had a refreshing plan for increasing the voice of Missouri Whigs in the party's smoke-filled rooms. Cautioning John F. Darby that "while my experience *may* prove of very great service to you in this matter, . . . yet my *known* support could do you *no good*," Corbin advised Darby to cultivate his acquaintance with Crittenden. As a young man Darby had read law in the office of the powerful Kentuckian. Darby should have little trouble in gaining the St. Louis postmastership, said Corbin, if he cited in the proper quarters his two terms as mayor of St. Louis and several more as representative of that city in the state legislature. Thus, being "in contact with the Whigs of Missouri and Illinois through the post masters of each neighborhood," it was not too much to expect that Darby could deliver the votes of both states in a national convention to Crittenden, or to another if he preferred.[22]

Darby either did not apply or else was rejected, and the office went to Archibald Gamble. No mean lawyer in his own right, Gamble's brother, Hamilton Rowan Gamble, stood next behind Leonard, Geyer, and Bates at the Missouri bar. The Gamble brothers shared the distinguished triumvirate's distaste for the risks of politics, and there is no evidence that Archibald thought of his office as an opportunity either to promote Whiggery in Missouri or to groom himself for the role of kingmaker at the 1852 Whig convention.[23]

The election of 1848 and the patronage disappointments that followed it appropriately terminated Missouri Whiggery's most dismal decade. Consistent, overwhelming defeat had characterized the party's record since its first real organization in 1839. Even when the Whigs retired from 1842 to 1846 they had been unable to cast victory to the branch of the Democratic party they preferred. New forces were at work, however, and these were far more powerful than the economic considerations that had thus far dictated Missouri political alignments. The first years of the 1850's would see Missouri Whigs in unaccustomed high places.

Chapter 14

PLURALITY PARTY

EVEN while the Whigs of Missouri carried on their feuds over patronage, the groundwork was laid for a redistribution of political strength which, just two years after the routs of 1848, gave Missouri three Whig congressmen and its first Whig senator. The Whigs did not themselves recast Missouri's political mold. Rather, the movements that so improved the party's fortunes originated in the Democratic party. Taylor's Administration began with the status of slavery unsettled in the lands acquired from Mexico, and a group of Democratic politicians seized upon that issue and used it to tear their party asunder. They created a chasm beside which the split of 1842–1846 appeared in retrospect as a mere crevice.

Prior to Taylor's election, sectional controversy played an unimportant role in Missouri politics. Just as *Communist, Papist,* or *appeaser* have spelled political ruin in other places and in other times, so both *abolitionist* and *nullifier* became politically fatal labels in Missouri. Either party would have been pleased to have attached one of those designations to the other, but such accusations were so far removed from reality that they never adhered. Political competition between Whigs and Democrats or between Democrats and Democrats always reverted to its economic basis, with an admixture of charges of corruption, inefficiency, and demagoguery. South Carolina's nullification effort in the early 1830's met virtually no response in Missouri. When the *Missouri Intelligencer,* an anti-Jackson paper, characterized Democratic Governor Daniel Dunklin as a nullifier, it offered no evidence in support of its charge. Undoubtedly, it was embarrassing to Whigs when their opponents informed Missourians that 3,786 of the 4,079 abolition petitions presented to Congress before 1840 were sponsored by Whigs, but neither this propensity of Whigs from other states nor Whig descriptions of Van Buren as the "free Negro candidate" proved decisive in Missouri politics.[1]

True, some Missourians sympathized with Calhoun's presidential aspirations in 1844. This, however, was a natural alliance between the national and local opponents of Thomas Hart Benton. His Washington tormentors may have derived their position from sectional considerations, but Benton's opponents in Missouri objected to his currency views. The Wilmot Proviso was anathema to all Missourians during the campaign of 1848. Each side sought to convict the other of sympathy with that proposal, but the issue never really shifted from internal improvements. Beginning in 1849, however, a politician's views on slavery became the primary determinant of his political success.

Soon after the new legislature convened, it passed the Jackson Resolutions, a set of dicta sponsored by a former Benton supporter and Central Clique leader, Claiborne Fox Jackson of Fayette. These resolutions denied Congress the power to interfere with the existence of slavery in the territories and further argued that Northern antislavery aggressions relieved the South from obligations to the long-established principles of the Missouri Compromise. Most importantly, they instructed Missouri's senators to act in conformity with these sentiments.[2] As a Democrat who sided with Jackson in the subsequent struggle reported, the resolutions were designed "not [for] . . . any practical effect they were likely to have, but to head Benton."[3]

Benton had repurchased Jackson's loyalty in 1844 with the speakership of the state House of Representatives. Now taking what following he could with him, Jackson broke away again and united with the Soft Democrats, whose anti-Bentonism surged forth anew as another opportunity to unseat the party leader in 1850 rapidly approached. Together the new political bedfellows passed these anti-Benton resolutions in what had been regarded at the time of the August elections as a Benton legislature.

Explanations of important events that depend on the existence of a clandestine conspiracy are often suspect in historians' circles and rightly so. Certainly, the Jackson Resolutions relied on the national crisis for their development, and it is unlikely that the issue of slavery in the territories would not soon have evoked a response of some description in Missouri. However, the spontaneity of the Missouri reaction was abetted and shaped by a plot against Benton. Not only was the alliance that produced the Jackson Resolutions a strange one of parties that had consistently opposed each other on other matters; but the Whigs, at any rate, were aware of the designs months before they were effected. "It has been stated in private circles," announced the *Missouri Republican* a month before the legislature convened, "that an effort will be made at the coming session of the legislature to instruct Col. Benton out of his seat in the Senate of the United States." Slavery rather than currency was to be the focal point of the new onslaught, foretold the Whig journal.[4]

By forcing Benton into an even more open stand on slavery in the territories than he had hitherto taken, the resolutions quickly thinned the ranks of those still loyal to the Senator. Benton sent word that he would return to Missouri in the summer to make a "great Appeal" directly to the people of the state, and men who had stood by him reserved judgment until he clarified his position. George Penn, candidate for president of the Bank of Missouri whom the Softs and Whigs defeated in 1843, was not consulted about the intended dethronement of the veteran Senator. His first reaction to the resolutions was opposition, but soon he wrote another loyal Bentonite, Meredith M. Marmaduke, that if Benton did not renounce "free-soilism," he would be unable to support him. In July, when it was clear that Benton's appeal was a request to the voters to release him from the resolutions that required him "to promote disunion" and to pledge "the state to cooperate with other states in eventual civil war" Penn announced that he was duty bound to join the anti-Benton camp.[5]

John J. Lowry, former confrere of Jackson in the Central Clique, regarded his party's disruption as a scheme to elevate Jackson to Benton's seat in the Senate, a prospect not at all to Lowry's liking. Yet, when Benton's reaction to the Jackson Resolutions became known, Lowry sadly parted from him. He commented, "From all this I infer that he [Benton] is a Wilmot-Provisoist . . . he abandons the South & the West! I mourn over him as one of Democracy's champions, & a great mind in perfect error. Well, with heartfelt emotion I now leave him."[6]

The Whigs, too, had to choose a path to follow in Missouri's new political maze. In the legislature they had consistently and unitedly opposed the Jackson Resolutions, urging instead proposals introduced by George Caleb Bingham. The Bingham Resolutions affirmed that Congress had the power to legislate on slavery in the territories, but they added the qualification that Congress would be unwise to use that power. Although these views resembled Benton's more nearly than those of his Democratic enemies, the dominant Whig attitudes toward the Democratic "family quarrel" combined neutrality with an opportunistic watchfulness for the greatest advantage to the Whig party.[7]

Charles Daniel Drake, the energetic director of Henry Clay's Missouri campaign, exemplified the self-interested approach of the Whigs to the crisis created by the Jackson Resolutions. When he learned that Benton planned a trip to Missouri "for the purpose of knocking in the head the curs that have been sneakingly trying to head him in reference to his re-election," Drake advised:

I hope the Whigs will let him alone. He is leaning away from Locofocoism very considerably, & the Whigs should treat him as kindly as consistent with their devotion to their party & to their principles. If he is let alone by the Whigs, particularly on the subject of the Wilmot Proviso, he will upset Missouri Democracy & leave it in absolute destruction. Deal with him, therefore, wisely and gingerly.[8]

Drake was not asking kindness either for a troubled old man or for a potential political ally. He was reminding his correspondent that Democrats tended to unify in response to Whig action. Severe censure of Benton by Whigs could conceivably modulate the denunciations hurled at him by his own party; Whig praise of Benton might alienate so many of his followers that the Democratic party would effectually reunite. Drake, in common with a host of other Missouri Whigs, hoped that his party would, after the 1850 elections, hold the balance of power between the wings of an irrevocably divided Democratic party. "If the Whigs keep aloof from both the factions . . . ," counseled the watchful Edward Bates, "it need surprise no one if a *Whig Senator* should succeed Colonel Benton."[9]

Thus the Whigs set their course for the campaign of 1850. The party would acknowledge no alliances with either wing of the Democratic party, but would put forth its own candidates for all offices, standing firmly on the platform provided by the Bingham Resolutions. Of course, not all Whigs fully complied with this active neutralism. As a Whig newspaper observed, the *Old Issues* were unimportant in this campaign, and it was the common ground shared by Whigs in regard to the old issues, particularly the national bank question, that had so far sustained Missouri Whiggery's remarkable degree of unity. Whig opinions about slavery's extension were not so unanimous.[10] All members of the party in the legislature had opposed the Jackson Resolution, but Whig representation

there was pitifully small. Furthermore, as Benton's appeal
progressed, it infused new heat into the slavery issue.

Some Whigs began to doubt both the feasibility and the
desirability of their party's moderate "Congress has the power
but must not use it," stand. Noting the apparent favor of the
anti-Bentons in western Missouri, a Whig with Carolina con-
nections wrote, "Thank God . . . Missouri is true to the
South." He could not bring himself to look upon the Democratic strife with indifference, as merely a war in the opposite
party from which the Whigs might benefit.[11]

Mixed with strong personal feelings held by some Whigs
on the slavery issue was their inability to resist the tempta-
tions for their own advancement that a divided Democratic
party offered. Some felt restricted as Whigs. Both of these
motives appear to have guided John B. Clark, who joined
Claiborne Fox Jackson on a state-rights ticket for Howard
County's representatives to the legislature. Still professing devotion to the Whig party, Clark boldly denied that Congress
possessed any power whatsoever over slavery in territories
and contended that an alliance between the Whig party and
the anti-Benton faction was so natural as to be inevitable.
Privately, Clark, who had been his party's candidate for
governor in 1840, let it be known that he had grown weary
of consulting Abiel Leonard at every turn of his political
career.[12]

Leonard and his Howard County coterie disapproved of
Clark's action and hastily put a regular Whig ticket into the
field. Sober second thought, however, convinced them that
this might further divide the Whig party, rendering it too
weak to furnish John G. Miller a plurality in the three-cornered congressional election. One Whig suggested that Leonard himself should take the field. With Howard County's most
prominent Whig running against him, Clark could no longer
sustain his pretense of Whiggery, and he would be forced

from the party, taking no one with him. Not surprisingly, Leonard refused to carry his anti-Clarkism to such an extreme. The Whigs of Howard County, instead, acquiesced in Clark's candidacy, hoping either that his uncontested victory would entitle him to little esteem in the anti-Benton ranks or that after the election he might turn out to be still a Whig after all.[13]

The visibility of the internal breach within Howard County's Whig party was exceptional in 1850. That Whigs and Democrats did form other interparty alliances of varying degrees of covertness is beyond question, although Whig separateness was more the rule. The Whigs admitted arrangements with anti-Benton forces in a few counties where more than one General Assembly seat was at stake and it appeared doubtful that the Whigs could win either. These joint enterprises did not take the same form as in Howard County, where Clark and Jackson regarded themselves as members of the same slate. Rather, as in St. Charles County, the Whigs and the anti-Benton group each nominated only one candidate. The Whig stood firmly against the Jackson Resolutions, and the anti-Benton contender occupied the reverse position.[14] In the Second Congressional District an alliance between Whigs and Benton forces resulted in the election of Whig Gilchrist Porter. Only in this district did the Benton forces fail to enter a candidate, and only there did a Whig candidate for Congress achieve a majority victory.[15]

In the main, the Whigs relied on the duplication of Democratic candidates to give them plurality victories. The Whig recapture of the St. Louis delegation to the legislature, for instance, cannot be attributed to fusion with either branch of the Democratic party. In that area of free-soil, Benton strength, the Whigs and Anti-Bentons together could have had a majority, but the Whigs preserved their independence and settled for victories based on only 4,000 of the 8,500 votes cast. Plurality triumphs went to the Whig congressional candidates in the eastern First District and the central Third District also. As an earlier student of this period of Missouri Whiggery has noted, the party achieved the unprecedented feat of electing three congressmen; yet its total vote was almost exactly the same, both numerically and proportionately, as two years earlier when defeat was the fate of all five Whig candidates.[16]

The Whigs made profitable use of the Democratic split in the election of 1850. Not only could they point to Missouri's first Whig congressman, they could also look forward to a legislature that would include 64 Whigs, an increase of 29 over the previous session. This was not a majority, but if Whigs remained united, it was a larger bloc of votes than either Democratic faction could command.[17] Hopes for a Whig senator from Missouri did not appear fanciful.

Although threatened at times between the election and the convening of the legislature in December, Whig unity endured. Henry S. Geyer emerged as the Whig candidate for senator, and, after faithfully supporting him through 40 ballots, his party saw him elected. Not all Whigs were entirely happy with the methods used to achieve the result. Geyer's legal prestige matched even that of Edward Bates, and his Whiggery was ancient and unquestioned. Before Jacksonian issues cast their shadows over Missouri politics, he served as speaker of the Missouri House of Representatives, though by 1851 he had long shunned electoral contests. It was not Geyer's lack of recent party sacrifice that caused chagrin within Whig ranks, however. The Senator-elect was the most prominent Whig whose inclinations were more in the direction of anti-Bentonism than Bentonism, and such sentiments were crucial in his election. In particular, Abiel Leonard's devoted protégés in the central part of the state charged "intrigue" between a St. Louis Whig clique and the anti-Benton forces.

Indeed there was intrigue, although all St. Louis Whigs

did not participate in it, and all rural Whigs did not condemn it. An old letter in which Geyer denied the power of Congress to legislate on slavery in the territories was resurrected immediately after the August elections, and anti-Benton newspapers in St. Louis soon announced that Geyer was acceptable to their faction. When the city's two Whig newspapers, the *Missouri Republican* and the *Intelligencer*, failed either to refute the letter or to disavow Geyer, Leonard's friends were convinced of conspiracy.[18]

Some weeks later, however, the *Republican* did publish an article by Geyer in which he repudiated any sympathy with the Jackson Resolutions and affirmed his belief in congressional power over slavery in the territories. The compromise measures of 1850 became law in September, and the *Republican* heartily endorsed them in a strongly unionist editorial, further quieting fears among moderate Whigs that their party would be made an instrument of nullification to bring about Geyer's election. Leonard's promoters, at his imperative, now joined the rest of the party in support of Geyer.[19]

Thus, the Whigs entered the balloting in the most favorable position they could possibly have arranged for themselves. The party did not have a majority. If its members were to entertain any hopes of winning the senatorship, they must preserve their own unity and at the same time appeal to at least part of one of the warring Democratic factions. If Geyer had failed to modify his views on congressional power and the Jackson Resolutions, Leonard or someone else would have opposed him; and the Whig party would not have been united. Any open union with the Benton faction would have been as disruptive to Whig unity as one with the anti-Benton faction. The only policy that offered any prospect of success to the Whigs was the one Geyer's managers pursued. In August Geyer's public position on slavery was identical to that of the Anti-Bentons, but later he and his followers modified this similarity enough to pacify Whigs who particularly opposed that branch of the Democratic party. However, they did not do so until they had established a foundation for negotiation between the Whigs and the Anti-Bentons.

James S. Rollins made an effort to effect exactly the same relationship with Benton that the Geyer managers achieved with the Anti-Benton Democrats. He informed Benton that he knew that Whigs would aid the Benton men in the legislature toward repealing the insulting Jackson Resolutions. However, Rollins also told Benton in positive terms that it would be "the duty as well as the policy of the Whigs to elect one of their own men" as senator. Only if that became clearly impossible did Rollins offer any hope — and he was careful not to promise it then — of Whig support for Benton's re-election.[20]

Alliance with Benton forces was precluded from the beginning, however, by the commitment of that faction to return Benton to the Senate. Throughout the 40 ballots, Benton's 55 supporters in the legislature remained immovable. On the other hand, the anti-Bentonites were committed only to the defeat of Benton, and, while they disliked seeing the high post go to a Whig, as long as Benton did not get it they could claim partial victory. The anti-Benton forces withdrew their public support from Geyer at once after he recanted his views on congressional power over slavery. For 39 ballots all but a few sporadic wanderers withheld their votes from him. Yet, they could not avoid being aware that the Whig candidate was at least equivocal on the question of congressional power and that he had been leisurely indeed in denying his alleged affinity for anti-Benton principles.[21]

Nightly anti-Benton legislators conferred with Benton leaders, always to be told that compromise must begin with Benton's reinstatement. Some timorous Whigs feared that if their party held too long to its own candidate the Democrats might reunite, but the wisdom of those who saw that the belligerents were beyond reconciliation prevailed. At last the

Anti-Bentons abandoned hope of capitulation from either Whig or Benton forces. Then, the Whigs' promises of support for offices in the legislature's appointive power, particularly in the management of the Bank of Missouri and its branches, added to the enigmatic reputation established by Henry S. Geyer, enabled the Anti-Bentons to release enough votes to the Whig candidate to give him a bare majority.[22]

Immediately following this great triumph, factional jealousy was renewed within the Whig party. Rollins, apparently writing Leonard for the first time since the two men had taken different sides in the patronage haggle of 1848, prudishly informed the venerated lawyer that the Whig party was in a "h–ll of a fix" and that he was certain that a noxious bargain had been struck with the Anties. To Edward Bates the victory was "barren." Samuel T. Glover, one of the St. Louis lawyers most devoted to Leonard, predicted "there is a war of extermination to be made on us." It was not too soon, thought Glover, for the "True Whigs" to think of a new party platform, one "that the Benton men will be glad to stand on."[23]

Obviously, there were divergent sectional views within the Whig party. However, rivalry over party leadership was as important as political principles in explaining the Whig dissension in the face of unprecedented victory. All of those who complained of the circumstances surrounding Geyer's election lamented the loss of the bank offices to the Anties as much as they did the seeming approval of Southern doctrines. Rollins, for instance, was embarrassed that a friend of his whom he had led to expect the presidency of the branch at Fayette had not received the office. Glover expressed surprise that Edward Bates now joined the Leonard clique in denouncing the Geyer forces. He attributed Bates's action, not to his views on the extension of slavery, but to his resentments over the distribution of offices and over insults that one Geyer follower had expressed to his good friend and former law student, James O. Broadhead.[24]

The Geyer forces simply consummated the hopes and plans acknowledged by all Whigs ever since the Jackson Resolutions had split the majority party two years previously. Neither Leonard, Rollins, Bates, nor anyone else who complained about the manner of the victory ever advocated sacrificing the election of a Whig Senator to preserve political purity. True, they would have considered their reputations less soiled had the Whigs' succor come from the Benton wing, but they had been totally unable to offer the Whigs that alternative.

The patronage fiasco of 1848 and the controversy over the election of a senator in 1850–1851 revealed more than divergent points of view within the Whig party in Missouri. The two incidents also showed that Whigs could battle among themselves as vehemently as the members of any political party when they had something for which to battle. Missouri Whigs still did not clamor to go before the people in elective contests as Democrats had done, even in their united periods. The election of 1852 would find the party once again searching frantically for willing candidates for governor and lieutenant governor. In 1848, however, the Whigs thought they had a quantity of federal patronage available to them, and in 1850 they had both a seat in the United States Senate and part of the state patronage at their disposal. All wanted to have a hand in the distribution of these prizes.

The most serious flaw in the Geyer strategy was forcing the Anti-Bentons to come to the Whigs in the election of speaker of the House of Representatives. The office went to Nathaniel W. Watkins, wealthy lawyer of Cape Girardeau, whom the Whigs had endeavored to induce to run for Congress both in 1838 and 1840.[25] Watkins' election required Anti-Benton assistance, and it is interesting that "Benton" Whigs voiced no complaints about the nature of this victory. Their dissatisfaction became apparent only when they had no voice in the distribution of favors after Geyer's election.

Even those who had no doctrinal qualms about cooperation with the Anti-Bentons admitted that they would have been wiser to have yielded to the Anti-Bentons on this early vote, thus making it easier for them to come to the Whigs in the senatorial election and reducing their claims on the Whigs in return for such support. Nevertheless, the Whigs who had promoted Geyer's election deserved more praise than blame from their party. As one St. Louis representative, William McPherson, pointed out, nearly all the Whig members of the General Assembly were serving their first terms, and even those who assumed the leadership lacked experience. Leading the plurality party had fallen primarily to St. Louis' two Whig editors, A. B. Chambers of the *Republican* and Joseph B. Crockett of the *Intelligencer*. The latter, according to McPherson, was too much of an alarmist to be really effective, and Chambers, though possessed of considerable ability, was "too anxious to be known as the prime mover." Other sections of the state offered no better alternatives. Watkins, the speaker-elect, was too provincial to impress St. Louis Whigs, and the central part of the state had not sent its best men to the legislature. If one took these factors into consideration together with the additional complication that most Whigs personally preferred Edward Bates to Geyer, McPherson felt that

> . . . under all these circumstances to see the Whigs stick together for eleven days amidst all the scenes and the many ingenious efforts made by men of both factions of the democrats to distract them . . . & still no one faltered but fought to the last giving a full vote thirty seven times out of forty & never more than two missing on any ballot [thus] they are entitled to some credit and all should be excused for any little faults you may have discovered.[26]

Those who had arranged the cooperation with the Anties had no more desire to destroy the newly powerful Whig party than did those who preferred mutual understanding with Benton Democrats. Crockett was not insensitive to the "considerable umbrage" his fruitful maneuvers had caused within his party, and immediately after Geyer's election he made plans to restore Whig unity by introducing in the legislature resolutions "which will satisfy all [Whig] parties except Clark and Young." Samuel Young was a Boone County Whig, who, along with John B. Clark had associated himself with a state-rights Whig ticket. Sounding very much like Rollins or Leonard, Crockett declared that Clark and Young were so opposed to the mass of Whigs, it would be just as well "to bring it out in the open and settle it."[27]

Crockett introduced the resolutions, and though they did not satisfy the dictum of Rollins and Glover that "one resolution . . . declaring the power of Congress to govern territories . . . would put us right side up," they did serve to restore Whig unity. From the position taken in the Bingham Resolutions of 1849, that Congress possessed power over slavery in the territories but should not use that power, the Whigs shifted to a repudiation of the power question as having no importance either for practical affairs or as a test of Whig orthodoxy. Deserting Clark, Young used the occasion to reinstate himself in Whig favor by sponsoring a resolution that characterized secession as from "the original warehouse of hell."[28]

The Whigs took no steps to repeal the Jackson Resolutions. Those with Bentonian tendencies were content to rest on the unanimous opposition to the instructions at the time of their adoption. Not only did it seem unwise to risk new divisions among the Whigs in an attempt to rescind them in 1851, but repeal might be a potent bait to hold out to Benton forces in a later contest.[29]

Regardless of the incompleteness of the Anti-Benton renunciation, Whig unity was restored. Even James O. Broadhead, the only Missourian who had yet gone so far as to characterize himself as a "Free-Soil Whig," wrote, "We have triumphed." With a determination not to be diverted by abstract argument the Whigs set out to take further advantage of the division among the Democrats in the forthcoming 1852 elections. Nevertheless, the internal distrust and rivalry that had appeared as soon as the Whig machine became politically powerful remained with the party after 1851.[30]

CHAPTER 15

SOUTHERN WHIGGERY

MISSOURI's Whig party, its harmony uneasily restored, looked forward to facile triumphs over the divided Democrats in 1852, but events within the Democratic camp soon modi-fied this optimism. While "Benton" Whigs worried lest "poli-ticians of the Calhoun school" should have influence in their 1852 nomination convention, Democrats took note of Henry S. Geyer's election as Senator and wondered whether some sort of expedient union, mutually advantageous to both Democratic factions, might not be effected. In November, 1851, Benton returned from Washington, "full of mischief and malevolence," and this "proposed union on the spoils prin-ciple" was temporarily in doubt. However, the Democrats carried out their plans. In April the two factions convened at Jefferson City to nominate a frankly mixed ticket. Sterling Price, one of the old Central Clique leaders whose political attitudes had shifted from Bentonism to anti-Bentonism, was the convention's choice for governor. Wilson Brown, a minor but loyal follower of Benton, was nominated for the office of lieutenant governor.[1]

With only one Democratic ticket in the field, the value of Whig nominations depreciated immediately. The party re-verted to its familiar character, and once again the Whigs had to search for willing candidates. The Whig mood as their 1852 convention approached was aptly conveyed by one cyni-cal party member who wrote, "Under the present aspect of affairs, wouldn't it be as well to let Watkins get beaten as anyone else?" Nathaniel W. Watkins of Cape Girardeau had been elected speaker of the state House of Representatives in 1850. Although respected for his legal abilities, he was dismissed by most Whigs as "too provincial" to fill the prominent role that a few loyal friends in his party thought he deserved.[2]

The Whig convention nominated for governor Mexican War hero Alexander Doniphan, who did not attend the meeting. Doniphan would not suffer himself to be thus used, however, and without "even an encouraging and polite letter, in return for the high honor of a nomination!" he refused to carry the Whig colors. In desperation the Central Committee turned to the convention's choice for lieutenant governor, James Winston of Springfield, one of the unsuccessful candidates for Congress in 1850. Winston agreed to run if the wealthier members of the party would give him financial assistance. Though a few Whigs wondered whether the "unadorned, unrefined, and unpolished" Winston was sufficiently sophisticated to represent their distinguished party, he received campaign contributions and canvassed the state with a thoroughness almost matching that displayed by James S. Rollins four years earlier.[3]

Before the Democratic union took place, Rollins himself was an active contender for the nomination, and to make himself acceptable to all shades of opinion within his party he worked hard to establish the fact that no special rapport existed between himself and the now-fallen Benton. Seeking to attach what it called "States Rights" Whigs to its own party, an anti-Benton newspaper, *The Metropolitan* of Jefferson City, published a version of a letter Rollins had written to Benton before the senatorial election. According to *The Metropolitan*'s transcription of the letter it had "found," Rollins unconditionally offered the controversial Benton Whig support in his bid for re-election. The paper distorted Rollins' overtures, for he had written only two letters to Benton and had gone no further than to suggest that if the Whigs were utterly unable to elect a Whig senator, "I have thought . . .

you would be preferred by them to any one of the opposite faction who have been waging this war upon you."[4]

Indeed, Rollins' first letter to Old Bullion, which he wrote shortly after the Senator spoke at Columbia during his 1849 appeal, was prompted by his interest in the state university rather than in the senatorial election. This institution was located in Columbia where Rollins lived; he was instrumental in arranging its location there in 1839; and his interest in both its policies and its welfare had continued. In 1849 Rollins appealed to Benton to use his personal influence in behalf of the university's president, John Hiram Lathrop, a New Yorker known to be unsympathetic to slavery. Because of his views on the peculiar institution, Southern-minded politicians sought to remove him from office. Although Rollins buttressed his request for Benton's aid in this matter with high praise of Benton's earlier stands on Texas and Oregon and a description of his Columbia speech as "beautiful and appropriate," the Columbian also pointed out that "Born and reared in the vicinity of Ashland, and taught to revere the name of Henry Clay from my earliest infancy . . . I am a Whig true & steadfast."[5]

Whigs such as Joseph Crockett and A. B. Chambers, both of whom found Benton less palatable than his opponents, were willing to let the accusations against Rollins go unnoticed in the interest of party harmony. It was certain, though, that they would oppose the gubernatorial nomination, which at that date still appeared valuable, going to a man so pungently tainted with Bentonism. In fact, there were almost no Whigs so pro-Benton that they were likely to approve a nominee who had actually been willing to give, not even sell, the Whig vote to the ancient enemy.

Rollins worked hard to refute the allegations. He wrote Benton, asking him to deny the reports, and Benton complied in a letter that he authorized Rollins to publish. Affirming that he had received only two letters from Rollins in his life, Benton went on to state positively that there had been no offer of collaboration. Rollins, in common with "all Whigs . . . who spoke or wrote to me on the subject," had merely declared that Benton was, in his opinion, preferable to an Anti-Benton if the Whigs could not elect a member of their own party. In case Rollins entertained any private hopes that Benton was willing to meet him more than half way, the veteran Democratic leader disenchanted him with these concluding remarks: "And, Sir, I now reciprocate the compliment, and say to you, that *if the democracy cannot elect a democratic governor next summer I shall be glad to see you elected.* . . . I am dear Sir, your friend and well wisher in every thing except beting [*sic*] a democrat for governor of Missouri." [6]

Rollins used this letter to good effect in a series of newspaper articles. That he emerged the favorite of the Whig party is by no means certain, but he at least began the year 1852 in good standing. When the Democratic union became a reality, however, the nomination lost its attractiveness to Rollins as decisively as it did to other Whigs. If the candidacy again meant sacrifice instead of opportunity, someone else would have to make the offering. [7]

At their convention the Whigs adopted a platform favoring extensive internal improvements by the state and national governments, upward tariff revision, and the Compromise of 1850 as the final settlement of slavery controversies. Their campaign, however, consisted of efforts to shatter the fragile Democratic union. After all, it certainly was a "flagitious amalgamation," and Winston was not unjustified when he labeled all Democrats "a damned set of knaves after having such a quarrel to unite, without saying anything, or settling anything in relation to the questions which they said were of such paramount importance." [8]

Hoping to force debate of the divisive issue, Whig leaders prepared a circular distinctly advocating repeal of the Jackson Resolutions but at the same time strenuously denouncing "abolitionism, freesoilism and every other ism except Whiggism." Repeal, declared strategist Rollins, was actually unimportant; but Benton had made it the issue between the two Democratic factions. Perspicuously illustrating the combination of expediency and principle in the Whig approach to the flaming slavery issue, he continued, "This is *the* question about which the Democracy have been so much disturbed, and we ought to touch it just far enough to get the state for the Whigs, and no further. . . ."[9] The circular, in the form of a public letter from Winston to George Caleb Bingham, caused some clashes in the Democratic ranks, but the majority party gave its united support to Sterling Price, who won by a customary Democratic margin.[10]

In the congressional races the Whigs lost two of the seats they had won in 1850, but they were again victorious in the centrally located Third District. There incumbent John G. Miller defeated James S. Green, who had earlier been one of Benton's staunchest supporters. Now that slavery had replaced currency as the source of strife within the Democratic party, Green opposed his former leader and, indeed, rivalled Claiborne Fox Jackson for the anti-Benton leadership. Whigs knew that Benton, not especially pleased about the compromise convention anyway, "would almost as soon die, without the hope of a resurrection as see Green elected," and they took steps to profit from the displaced Senator's animosity toward the Democratic candidate. To ensure a Whig victory leaders of the party felt that two Democratic candidates were necessary. When no Benton man could be found willing to enter a race in which he was certain to take third place, Whigs resorted to what would surely have been the crassest political maneuver in Missouri annals had it been realized.

The Whig plan was to induce an unidentified "old Ugly" to enter the lists by promising him a desirable Indian agency appointment immediately after the election. Arrangements for the appointment were the responsibility of none other than Congressman John G. Miller, the presumed beneficiary of the spurious candidacy.

Old Ugly was too ill even to accept a comfortable sinecure, and he would not be "resurrected." Luckily, the Benton voters concluded they "would prefer 2 like Miller to one like Green," and in spite of "foul undercurrents" emanating from the Green camp, Miller won by 400 votes. Unable to effect similar arrangements in the Second and Fifth districts, the Whigs saw their candidates defeated by the tenuously united Democratic party.[11]

In the western Fourth District Whig Mordecai Oliver, a lawyer who had migrated to Missouri from Kentucky ten years earlier, won a plurality victory over Austin A. King and James M. Birch. King was governor of the state, having defeated Rollins in 1848, and while still in office he moved from Boone County to Buchanan County. Fearing the "imprudent actions of men of both wings" of his party, he regarded Birch as too extreme in his anti-Benton views and ran as an Independent. Birch was the son of the flexible James H. Birch, who now also identified with the anti-Benton faction as much as his position on the state supreme court permitted.[12]

The only other three-cornered congressional contest was in the eastern First District, where Benton himself ran against Whig Samuel Caruthers, one of the few Missouri-born politicians of the period, and anti-Benton Lewis V. Bogy, son of the Whig candidate for lieutenant governor in 1840. Benton, with the estimable oratorical and editorial assistance of Frank Blair, Jr., and B. Gratz Brown, surpassed Caruthers to win by a slim plurality. Just as Bogy and John B. Clark were examples of Whigs who had deserted their party for open affiliation with the Anti-Bentons, Brown is an early example of a Whig crossing into the Benton camp. When visiting his cousins the Blairs at Silver Springs, Maryland, in 1847, Brown had assured his immediate family that there was no danger to his own firm Whiggery in the Democratic household. Nevertheless, almost from the moment of Brown's arrival in St. Louis from Kentucky in 1849, Benton received the support of this young graduate of both Transylvania and Yale colleges. When, in 1849, the Benton forces established the *Missouri Democrat* to aid their cause in St. Louis, Brown became its brilliant and effective editor.[13]

Diverse reactions to Benton's success illustrated that while all who remained Whigs still wished for their own party's triumph over all Democrats, they differed sharply over which Democratic faction was the less offensive. A Bogy victory quite plainly would have been less displeasing to the *Missouri Republican*. In contrast, James S. Rollins regretted the defeat of Caruthers, a "whole souled Whig," but thought the Benton victory was the next best result. Benton, he wrote, "is too old to do us great harm, but young enough to do us much good, and to kill the nullifiers yet. That's the use we have for him."[14]

Although divided on how best to take advantage of the Democratic rupture in 1852, Missouri Whigs agreed on their party's presidential nomination. Millard Fillmore, who had become President upon Zachary Taylor's death in 1850, enjoyed the unanimous approbation of the Missouri branch of his party. Unlike his predecessors in the White House, Fillmore had been attentive to leading Missouri Whigs. Since he did not sweep away the Taylor appointees to federal jobs, the new President dispensed relatively little patronage; but when he did fill Missouri places he consulted with Whigs in the state. To Edward Bates he offered a post in his Cabinet. Though Bates characteristically refused, on grounds of personal financial necessity, he and his friends could not help but note that Fillmore showed more awareness of Missouri than either Harrison or Tyler.[15]

Also endearing to the Whigs of Missouri was Fillmore's contribution to the Compromise of 1850. He had removed the obstacles his predecessor had placed in the path of the compromise measures, and since their passage he had remained firmly committed to them. In the view of Missouri Whigs, a strong stand for the compromise offered their party's best hope of success in 1852.[16]

Fillmore's rival for the Whig nomination was General Winfield Scott, who had been unable to attach the same glamour to himself that Taylor did during the Mexican War. Lack of popular appeal was not the main objection Missouri Whigs had to Scott, however. The General was "fishy" in his stand on the Compromise of 1850. Not only his refusal to unequivocally favor the compromise, but also the support he received from Horace Greeley, William H. Seward, "and other abolitionists" made him suspect in all Missouri Whig circles.[17]

The undivided approval of Missouri Whigs for Fillmore and the Compromise of 1850 tells much about the party's status in 1852. For one thing, the Whigs behaved very much like members of a political party. Their preference for Fillmore was dictated more by the belief that only he could carry necessary Southern states than it was by purblind worship of the Compromise of 1850. Congressman John G. Miller, for example, professed great respect for Scott but preferred Fillmore because "with him I should have strong hopes of success and my conviction is that if we cannot succeed with him, we cannot with any other."[18]

Expediency was not the only characteristic of Missouri Whiggery in 1852, however. There is no reason to doubt that the Compromise of 1850 was the ground truly preferred by all Missouri Whigs, except those who had actually renounced

the party. In 1852 no Whig was on record as favoring either
the Wilmot Proviso or its counterpole, the Calhoun Resolutions of 1847. The area of agreement within the Whig party
in Missouri was wide enough to cover matters of internal
party policy, but Whigs could hope to control their state only
through combination with one branch of the Democratic
party, a contingency for which their common ground was not
sufficiently broad. While they all preferred a middle course,
Whigs differed sharply over which direction to deviate in,
when some deviation was necessary.

The events that caused serious discord within Missouri's
Whig party furnish support for this conclusion. In popular
elections alliance with either branch of the Democratic party
was seldom profitable. The Whigs either strove for a plurality
victory or, if the Democrats united as they did in 1852, resigned themselves to defeat. It was in the legislature, where a
majority was required to elect a senator or a speaker, that
Whig factionalism became apparent. The most serious breach
within the Whig party before 1852 occurred at the time of
Henry S. Geyer's election in 1851. Between the senatorial
contests of 1851 and 1854 the Whigs unitedly occupied their
moderate ground, and none were particularly uncomfortable.

Fillmore, of course, did not receive the Whig nomination
in 1852. Missouri's delegates supported him unanimously for
24 ballots before they began to break ranks and join the
Scott band wagon. Nominated at last on the 50th ballot, Scott
remained silent on the Compromise of 1850. Nevertheless,
since the Whig platform endorsed the compromise, Missouri's Whig press supported the nominee.[19]

Quite clearly, though, even the belated acceptance of Scott
by Whigs in Missouri was unenthusiastic. A few Scott Clubs
appeared, but they were lethargic affairs compared to earlier
organizations for Clay and Taylor. In the state campaign, references to Scott were noticeably absent. After the August

elections interest in the presidential contest evaporated, and no one seemed greatly disturbed when Missouri and the nation chose Franklin Pierce. Commented the *Missouri Statesman* as the election approached, "Were a stranger to our institutions to pass through Missouri at this time and read no newspapers in his travels he would scarcely learn that one week from next Tuesday the people of the United States will elect the highest officer known to our Constitution." [20] Regular readers of the *Statesman* would have been scarcely more informed than the hypothetical stranger.

In contrast to earlier years, the vote for the Whig presidential candidate was appreciably smaller than that for governor; Winston's vote exceeded Scott's by 3,000. In 1848 Rollins polled only 600 more votes than Taylor.[21] Also, for the first time the Whig party in Missouri neatly fitted into a Southern pattern in 1852. Missouri Whiggery's obliviousness to the sectional considerations surrounding Taylor's nomination in 1848 has already been mentioned. Prior to that year, the Missouri party, if it had a sectional aspect at all, was Northeastern-Western in its outlook. Although recent scholarship indicates that most Southern Whigs willingly favored a national bank, it remains true that what Whig opposition there was to such an institution was primarily Southern. Missouri Whigs, however, matched Whigs anywhere in their unanimous devotion to the national bank principle. The party was Western in its refusal to notice plans, even when they were put forth by Henry Clay, which seemed to threaten easy access of settlers to public lands.[22]

Throughout the lower South, Whigs opposed Scott's nomination, seemingly acquiesced in it immediately after its accomplishment, and then gave a very soporific performance in the campaign and election. Embittered Pennsylvania Whigs could rightly include Missouri in their complaints that Southern states had exacted endorsement of the Compromise

of 1850 from the national convention and then had refused to
sustain the party's candidate.[23]

However, there were important differences between the
South and Missouri, not the least of which was Missouri's
strife-torn Democratic party. While the Whig party in most
southern states all but disappeared after the election of 1852,
the Missouri Whigs held tenaciously to their identity in order
to profit once again from their plurality situation.[24]

CHAPTER 16

UNITED WHIGGERY

SHORTLY after the results of the 1852 state elections were known, the newly elected General Assembly met in special session. In June Congress had granted a handsome parcel of public lands for the benefit of Missouri railroads, and the Governor called the legislators together that they might indicate their willingness to be the federal government's beneficiary and to adopt measures for the disposition of the grant.[1]

The matter was attended to with ease. Much as Whigs relished the role of rail champion, neither branch of the Democratic party would permit them a monopoly in the field. Democrats who remembered their party's ancient scruples against federal appropriations for internal improvements within states rationalized them away by differentiating between grants of land and grants of money. During the 1850's Whigs more than once suggested to each other that if their party could present itself as the foremost advocate of internal improvements, "niggerism would be thrust aside," and Missouri, freed from sectional controversies, would march forward under Whig hegemony.[2]

But slavery polemics did not yield their pivotal place in Missouri politics, partially because Missouri politicians were too united on economic matters to make issues of them. From 1848 on, the Whigs refused to mark themselves as the national bank party, and they joined the two Democratic factions in regarding the Bank of Missouri, with its myriad of officers, mainly as an important element for political bargaining. There were no party lines in regard to either federal or state aid for railroads. The railroad legislation introduced at the special session passed without significant dissent from any of the three factions.[3]

By virtue of their wealth and investment capacity, Whigs did assume a disproportionate share of the leadership in Missouri's railroad movement, but the opposition they encountered was not from opponents of railroads. Rather, rival promoters and sections challenged each other. For instance, James S. Rollins and two wealthy St. Louis Democrats, Thomas E. Tutt and Thomas T. January, corresponded extensively in the 1850's about the North Missouri Railroad, of which they were all directors. Their fear was not that the legislature would fail to grant state aid, but rather that it might make such aid conditional on the railroad's construction over the "Southern Route" as opposed to the "Ridge Route" where the directors' lands lay. Similarly, George R. Smith contended for the "Inland Route" instead of the "River Route" for the Pacific Railroad. Smith's biographer reproduces eight letters in a chapter entitled "The Struggle for the Pacific Railroad," and significantly the words *Whig, Democrat,* or *Loco Foco* do not appear in any of them.[4]

More exciting than the debate over railroad legislation in the special session was the contest over organization of the legislative body. In the August elections the united Democrats reduced the total Whig membership to 51, which, though more impressive than Whig strength during the 1840's, did not give the party the position it held in the preceding session.[5] Because of the Democrats' problematical union during the election, the relative strength of the Democratic factions was at first ambiguous. However, if any expected Democratic unity to persist beyond the necessities of the election, they were soon undeceived, for the party promptly fragmented in the election of a speaker of the House of Representatives. After the factional lines were redrawn, the Whigs ranked numerically between the Benton and anti-Benton forces.

The *Missouri Republican*'s editor, A. B. Chambers, attempted to negotiate with the anti-Benton faction, but, fortunately for Whig unity, the Anties spurned his offer to deliver Whig support for the speakership to a relatively unknown and moderate member of their faction in return for election of Whigs to certain clerkships and bank offices. The Anties were determined to place their leader, Claiborne Fox Jackson, in the speaker's chair. Neither expecting nor desiring his party to go this far, Chambers acquiesced in Whig cooperation with the Benton party. At one point the Whigs considered preventing any organization of the legislature at all, intending instead "publicly to cram down the Locofoco throat the amazing but destructive lie of the late canvass, that the democracy of Missouri are united — a lie which beat our state ticket by some 12,000 votes." However, after three days of balloting, the Whigs deserted their own candidate and aided in electing a Benton speaker. Whigs of the Benton stripe rejoiced over having saved their party from a "sell-out" to the anti-Benton faction, and, forgetting that the Anties had once made possible the election of a Whig senator, noted with pride how much better the Benton forces treated Whigs in the matter of bank offices than the Anties had two years earlier.[6]

Encouraged by the seemingly pleasant relations between the Whigs and his own political organization, Benton's protégé, Frank Blair, Jr., sought to rescind the Benton-insulting Jackson Resolutions. However, only a few of the Whigs who leaned furthest in Benton's direction were inclined to give him such a decisive victory and risk eliminating the all-pervading divisive force of the Democratic party. The *Missouri Statesman*, which usually deplored any sign of alliance with the Anti-Bentons, now discovered that the Jackson Resolutions were a bagatelle about which Whig opinions might vary widely. "If they [Whigs] . . . are against the Resolutions," counseled the *Statesman*, "they will vote to repeal them; if not, not — and that's the end of it." Blair's motion was tabled, and though a number found it inconvenient to be present at that day's session, only ten Whigs actually voted to continue the discussion.[7]

Whig unity to profit from Democratic disunity remained party policy until 1854. Missouri gained two congressional representatives as a result of the Census of 1850, and special elections took place in 1853 to fill the additional seats.[8]

Central Missouri Whiggery entered into open alliance with the Benton faction to accomplish the election of young, relatively unknown James J. Lindley in the Third District. Lindley, an Ohio-born lawyer who had settled in Chariton County in 1846, was not the first choice of his party. Whigs of the region would not realize that Abiel Leonard simply was not interested in entering doubtful electoral contests, and once again they pressed him to accept the candidacy. When Leonard refused, the leaders determined that J. P. Vaughan, a Glasgow physician, should conduct the canvass. Vaughan admired Leonard; indeed, he thought Leonard was the only Whig with a prospect of victory. However, he could see no reason why he should perform a task which the party sachem found too onerous. Declaring that he had no interest in a political career and occasionally took interest in politics only as a form of recreation, Vaughan did not accept what "others have determined." "Leonard is the man and no one else," said Vaughan. If the man who enjoyed his party's highest esteem was unwilling to sacrifice himself for the cause, the Glasgow doctor saw no reason why he should either.[9]

Lindley's claims were put forth by his neighbors in the northeastern part of the district, and when the party managers discovered that he was "completely sound on all questions important to us as Whigs or Gentlemen," they willingly countenanced his candidacy. The Benton party, unable to produce a candidate of its own in this district where its standing was so low, agreed to support Lindley. His opponent was Claiborne Fox Jackson, who, with James S. Green, was the object of the Bentonites' greatest enmity. Blair requested Rollins to supply campaign copy to the Benton newspapers, and the Benton press campaigned for a Whig more openly and more actively than it ever had before. That such support was imperative to Whig success in this district became apparent when Lindley was elected by only 44 votes.[10]

In the other new district, composed of counties immediately south of St. Louis and surrounding counties, no Democratic allies were wanted by the Whigs. There, one third of the total vote cast was sufficient to give Samuel Caruthers, whom Benton had defeated a year earlier, a plurality victory over three Democratic candidates.

Perhaps the circumstances in the Seventh District contest furnish evidence that Benton's arrogance as much as his principles caused dissension among his followers. Not only was there an Anti-Benton candidate in the field, there were also two professed Bentonites. Both agreed with the leader on slavery issues. Only one, however, recognized the right of Benton, Blair, and B. Gratz Brown to appoint candidates.[11]

A Benton paper's assertion that "Mr. Caruthers was elected . . . by the division in the Democratic ranks, and not on his own popularity or that of the principles he espoused," was correct.[12] The editor should have added, though, that Caruthers also profited from Whig harmony. Unlike central Missouri, where John B. Clark's complete severance with the Whig party left a relatively homogeneous "Benton" Whig leadership, Whiggery in St. Louis and its adjacent areas contained elements that entertained widely divergent views as to the respective merits of the two Democratic factions. At one extreme was A. S. Mitchell, editor of the *Evening News*, a paper founded for the express purpose of counteracting those who had entered into the "disreputable coalition" with Anties to elect Henry S. Geyer. The other pole was best exemplified by George W. Goode, a graduate of the University of Virginia who moved to Missouri after his participation in a duel disqualified him from holding civil office in Virginia. Goode was "most uncompromising in his adherence to slavery" and "looked upon every man who did not concur with him on that subject as an abolitionist."[13]

Certainly, there was ample provocation for internal friction in a party that included these two men, as well as representatives of almost every point of view on the line between them. Caruthers was much closer to Mitchell than to Goode, but no Whig protests were voiced when he was selected by the district convention to carry the party colors. Nor did St. Louisans allow themselves to be diverted by discussion of the morality of the avowed Whig-Benton reciprocity which was occurring in central Missouri. Instead, St. Louis Whigs sheathed their differences to take advantage of the multiplicity of Democratic candidates.

The debates in Congress during the winter and spring of 1854 have been noted as marking the final disruption of the national Whig party. Within Missouri, however, they furnished the Whigs one more opportunity to affirm their unity. With the two congressmen elected in 1853, there were four Missouri Whigs in the House of Representatives and one in the Senate when Congress considered Stephen A. Douglas' fateful measure, which substituted squatter sovereignty for the Missouri Compromise as the device for determining slavery's status in a territory. All the Missouri Whigs voted for the bill, and in doing so they accurately reflected the sentiments of their Whig constituents.[14]

The uniformity of Whig opinion was not entirely spontaneous. There were those in Missouri who, in common with a portion of the Whig party in states farther south, felt that repeal of the Missouri Compromise would only inflame the slavery controversy to the detriment of the institution and those who held it dear.[15] At least one Missouri Whig opposed the bill for the same reason that Thomas Hart Benton did,

namely, that it lent itself to the designs of a slave-power conspiracy. Writing from Philadelphia where he was making
arrangements for the engraving of "County Election," his
painting which so condescendingly portrays the yeomanry of
Missouri at the polls, George Caleb Bingham noted with
pleasure at the beginning of the year that only the *Missouri
Republican* among the state's Whig newspapers unequivocally favored the bill.

By April, however, Bingham was disillusioned, and he
moved toward Bentonism as the first step in his journey toward affiliation with the embryonic Republican party. From
Philadelphia he wrote to James S. Rollins:

> I fear that you are all at least half committed in favor of
> Douglas's Nebraska bill. Old Bullion turns out to be the only
> man of full stature in our entire Congressional delegation, and
> if I resided in his district I would take great pleasure in voting
> for him in opposition to any Whig who sacrifices right to
> expediency.[16]

Bingham assumed that Rollins' views were similar to his
own, but had he been in closer touch with Missouri politics
he would have known such was not the case. When the bill
was first introduced, Rollins did write to "our Congressional
friends . . . to stand by the Missouri Compromise!" Abiel
Leonard at first advised the Missouri representatives to attempt to table the measure, but by March Congressman John
G. Miller could write to Rollins, "the principle recognized by
the bill is the correct one. . . . I am gratified to know that
the course determined upon by the Whig delegation from
Mo. is so fully endorsed by you, & Mr. Leonard & other
friends." The *Missouri Republican* correctly reported that
every Whig newspaper in the state now endorsed the Kansas-
Nebraska bill. At a widely attended Whig meeting in Columbia, Rollins was instrumental in the adoption of resolutions
pledging all Whig General Assembly candidates in 1854 to
support no man for senator who did not accept the Kansas-

Nebraska principle, whether it became law or not. Bingham left the Whig party unaccompanied in 1854.[17]

In effect, the Benton wing of the Missouri Whig party had yielded to the rest of the party in the interest of harmony for the forthcoming election. Democrats, who had expectantly noted the split "brewing in the Whig camp" were disappointed in their hopes.[18] Certainly, such men as Rollins and Leonard were helped in their shift on the Kansas-Nebraska bill by their desire to believe what came to be the Missouri Whig defense of the measure, that it was merely an extension of the Compromise of 1850 and that it would contribute to nonagitation of the slavery question. However, it is significant that they did not come to this view until it became evident that holding fast to the Missouri Compromise would leave them with no party of their own and would force them into open alliance with Benton.

That the Whig party teetered on the brink of disruption during the winter of 1854 is shown by letters of William T. Wood, a prominent Whig of western Missouri, to Rollins and Leonard. After Rollins' leadership at the Whig meeting in Columbia, Wood informed him:

> There is no longer the slightest danger of division in the Whig ranks, all may stand upon the platform you have adopted — opposition to the principle of the Wilmot proviso, approval of the principles of the compromise measures of 1850, unbending non-intervention by Congress and the right of the people of the state and territories to determine the character of their own domestic and local institutions and with all over approval of the Nebraska bill.

Soon Wood wrote Leonard that he was satisfied that he had been misinformed about Leonard's views regarding the Kansas-Nebraska bill and that in view of satisfactory assurances he had received from Rollins also, he saw no reason why the Whig party in Missouri could not battle in unison during the coming elections.[19] Benton's difference with the anti-Benton congressmen from Missouri over the Kansas-Nebraska Bill and the impending 1854 senatorial election presaged a fierce Democratic cleavage in the 1854 elections. Under such conditions the Whig party was too pregnant with potentialities of success to permit its abandonment over an internal difference of principle.

Chapter 17

WHIG FINALE

MISSOURI Whigs suppressed their own internal differences in 1854 because they expected even more disunity within the Democratic party in the August elections. They correctly foretold the majority party's situation. There was no compromise convention in 1854, and the Democrats' division reached to every level of the political campaign. "Union and Harmony!" and "No entangling alliances!" shouted the Whigs.[1]

This alleged absence of arrangements with either Democratic faction would not bear close scrutiny. In the eastern Seventh District, where they were without hope of electing a candidate of their own, the Anties gave their votes to Samuel Caruthers, enabling him to win a majority over the Benton aspirant for Congress. Privately, Samuel T. Glover observed that the *Missouri Republican* was "dumb and deaf" to the depredations of the Anties and acutely attuned to the wrongdoings of Benton's followers. The *Republican* could in turn have noted that in behalf of James J. Lindley, Whig candidate for re-election in the Third District, Leonard and others furnished a Benton Democrat with transportation and an expense account in order that he might ride through the area persuading Benton voters to support Lindley.[2]

Beyond question, all the ingredients were present for another Whig quarrel over which Democratic faction was the more noxious. Few of the frictions surfaced before the election, however. In Boone County a Whig nominee for the General Assembly metamorphosed into a State-rights candidate, and in Lincoln County an effort to join Whigs and Anti-Bentons into a similar party met with moderate success. Whig newspapers denounced such defalcations, if they noticed them at all.[3] With "Union and Harmony" the main body of the Whig party marched together, so that it might take advantage of the spoils that the Democratic split tantalizingly assured.

The election results demonstrated what a plurality party could do if it kept its own house in order. Polling only 43.2 per cent of the vote cast in the seven congressional races, the Whigs were victorious in six of them. In three they could claim majority victories. Besides the Third and Seventh districts, where Lindley and Caruthers received aid from different species of Democrats, the Whig incumbent Gilchrist Porter triumphed in the new Second District, which, dominated by Boone, Callaway, and Montgomery counties, was Missouri's first safe Whig district. In three districts a plethora of Democratic candidates dealt victory to the Whigs. Mordecai Oliver and John G. Miller were both returned to Washington, and Luther M. Kennett defeated Benton and a future governor, Trusten Polk, in the predominantly St. Louis First District. Brother of Ferdinand Kennett, whom the Whigs and Softs had combined to install as president of the Bank of Missouri in 1843, the new St. Louis congressman was one of the very few Democrats to associate himself with the Whig party as a result of slavery issues in politics. Disturbed by what he considered radicalism in St. Louis, Kennett had been the Whig candidate for mayor in 1851 and 1852, and he was successful both years in his fight against "the combined influence of Abolitionism, Free-Soilism, Socialism, Red Republicanism, Communism, Infidelity, and all the isms combined." Only in the Sixth District, located in almost Whigless southwest Missouri, did the Democrats elect a congressman in 1854.[4]

The Whigs could look forward to a legislature where they would command 60 votes, if all members elected as Whigs remained faithful. While not a majority, this was a greater proportion of the 160 members than either Democratic faction claimed, and hopes for the election of another Whig senator did not appear too fanciful. However, clashes in the Whig caucuses held in December when the legislature convened doomed the party's senatorial aspirations. Intraparty differences, so adroitly suppressed during the campaign, would not repose at this crucial juncture. Assertions by the Whig press that there were no "Benton Whigs" or "Atchison Whigs" in the party's legislative delegation failed to smother the dissension within Missouri Whiggery.[5] The party did not have a majority. Its motive for prolonging its existence after the Kansas-Nebraska Act had been to gain power and offices, and now the most important office, United States senator, was at stake. To win it for one of their own, the Whigs would have to conciliate at least part of one of the Democratic factions.

In caucus the Whigs attempted to settle their own differences by dividing the spoils. For speaker of the House of Representatives they nominated William Newland of Ralls County, one of the last to join his party in approving the Kansas-Nebraska Act and known to be acceptable to the Benton Democrats. Whigs with anti-Benton tendencies carried off the grand prize when the caucus selected Alexander Doniphan to be the Whig contender for the senatorial seat. Doniphan's course in the months before the legislature convened resembled that of Henry S. Geyer four years earlier. In regard to the constitutional power of Congress over slavery in the territories he had run a "hare & hound course," but in December he privately assured Whigs that, though he heartily approved of the repeal of the Missouri Compromise, he did concede to Congress the legal right to pass such legislation.[6]

This internal Whig compromise was abetted by the nonavailability of those Benton Whigs with sufficient stature to entitle them to serious consideration for the high post. Edward Bates had accepted election as Judge of the St. Louis Land Court in 1853, and when approached he informed his party that he was not interested in becoming senator. Furthermore, Missouri already had one Whig senator from St. Louis. Some rural Whigs voiced "objections arising out of his proximity to Geyer," and the St. Louis Whig delegation in the legislature, including such men as Joseph B. Crockett and George W. Goode, made no effort to offset provincial prejudices.[7]

Abiel Leonard also accepted a judicial post rather than contend for the senatorship. In 1850 the legislature had passed amendments to the state constitution providing for the popular election of Missouri's judges. Ironically, this belated extension of Jacksonian democracy worked out very well for the Whigs. Judges were elected at special elections in which the voters took little interest, and endorsement from the bar, where Whigs were better represented than in the state at large, was sufficient to guarantee election. During the 1830's the minority party regularly collaborated with dissident Jacksonians to prevent the passage of similar amendments. That, however, was before Whigs realized that in Missouri an appointive judiciary would mean one permanently in the custody of Democratic governors, and by the middle forties it was the Whigs who occupied the position in favor of judicial election. When they held the balance of power in the 1850 legislative session, they once again joined forces with recalcitrant Democrats, this time to pass the amendments. Bates and Hamilton Rowan Gamble had both profited by the new mode. Now Leonard, after ascertaining that lawyers of all parties favored him and that he would not have to "engage in a party scramble or electioneering," agreed to be an unopposed candidate for the state supreme court in the election scheduled for January, 1855.[8]

When the results of the August elections indicated that the Whigs might have the high office within their gift, the group of young lawyers so devoted to Leonard as usual pressed his claims. James S. Rollins was among those who did so, but two other young attorneys, Samuel Glover and John C. Richardson, soon became suspicious that Rollins was more interested in promoting his own fortunes than Leonard's. Since his campaign for governor in 1848, the defeated candidate had enjoyed considerable prestige in Missouri Whig circles; and when party members made senatorial calculations, his name was frequently mentioned. Glover and Richardson warned Leonard that while Rollins "praises you to the skies," yet "he allows himself to be flattered and all the time is electioneering for himself." [9]

These charges appear unfounded, and one suspects that Glover and Richardson, who had recently formed a law partnership, either were still nursing old wounds from the patronage fiasco of 1848 or that they resented seeing a man of their own vintage and, until recently, of no greater fame, surpassing them in the realm of politics.[10] Rollins' own correspondence indicates that he consistently advocated the election of "the Veteran Whig of Boonslick." Leonard, ever unwilling to take a political risk, was slow to declare whether he preferred the supreme court or the Senate position, and when he finally decided in favor of the former, Rollins urged him to reconsider because he was the only "orthodox Whig" who could command the undivided support of the party. In response to a Whig of western Missouri who wrote that, since "Bates is out of the ring, and Leonard soon will be" Rollins was his first choice for senator, Rollins replied with a rebuke and pointed out that Leonard was not yet in judicial robes.[11]

Rollins was ambitious, but at this point in his career he aspired no higher than to be the alternative to Leonard, should the noted lawyer refuse to run or for some other reason become unacceptable to the legislators at Jefferson City. Indeed, the younger man had reason to feel that Leonard, if he did not want the office himself, would look upon his claims with favor. Although the patronage debacle of 1848 separated the two men temporarily, since the passage of the Jackson Resolutions they had been politically close. Their positions in regard to the slavery controversy were identical, and they had joined hands to preserve the Whig party with a minimum of sacrifice to anti-Benton principles.

Leonard refused to allow his party to use his name, but he did not withdraw in favor of Rollins. Glover had declared that he wanted Rollins defeated for senator "and if it can be done I will come up to Jefferson to do it." Evidently Leonard also felt that Rollins' defeat took precedence over the future of the Whig party and the curbing of its "Anti" faction. Sensing that the Whig nomination for senator would go by default to Doniphan, and consequently the Whig appeal would be to the Anti-Bentons, a frantic Jefferson City lieutenant of Leonard pleaded for clearance to push Rollins. "To Rollins I know your objection," wrote Joe Davis, another Howard County lawyer, "but he is gaining and is on the right side."[12] Permission was not forthcoming, however, and Rollins' name never came before the joint session.

Reticence and rivalry within the leadership of one wing of the Whig party paved the way for negotiation within the Whig caucus. Their only aspirant's claims canceled by his own ally, Benton Whigs were content to accept the speakership for themselves and allow the "nullifying" Whigs to furnish the senatorial nominee. This compromise proved lethal to the Whig party in Missouri.

After only token ballots for their own candidate, Benton legislators joined Whigs in electing William Newland as speaker of the House.[13] The senatorial contest deadlocked, however. In purchasing each other, the Whigs had reserved no capital to spend in the Democratic marketplace. The parties in the legislature had three items with which to bargain: the speakership, the senatorship, and the offices in the Bank of Missouri. When the Whigs spent the speakership on themselves they created obligations to the Benton forces. The candidacy of Doniphan was designed to appeal to the Anties, but supporting him would bring them no profit if the Whigs already had commitments to the Bentonites. Knowing they could not receive favors from the Whig party, the Anties pursued the wise policy of stalemating the election, hoping that the Whig party would sunder and Whig individuals would come to the Anties.

Rollins had received indirect assurances that Benton was willing to grant the Whigs the speakership, the senatorship, the bank offices, and even cooperation in achieving more liberal banking legislation with "no bargain, no quid pro quo" in return except that Whigs not corrupt themselves "by intrigue with the nullifiers & by sacrificing eminent & honored Whigs who wished to be Senator."[14] It is questionable whether Benton's control over his followers was so absolute that they would have been content without some reward. However, that question became academic as soon as the Whigs violated Benton's one condition by nominating Doniphan.

The legislature balloted forty-one times for senator in 1854, all three factions remaining rigid throughout the proceedings. Suggestions, even demands, came forth that Rollins be substituted as the Whig nominee, and at least one Benton man let it be known that he would shift his vote to Rollins.[15] Probably the Whigs themselves would have refused to unite on Rollins. He had enemies within his own camp, and memories of *The Metropolitan's* exposé in 1851 of his correspondence with Benton naturally recurred to anti-Benton Whigs in 1854. Abiel Leonard's name might conceivably have been a different matter. If Leonard instead of Doniphan had been selected in the Whig caucus, the plurality party would have been in the same situation it was in 1851 when it placed Henry S. Geyer in the United States Senate. In 1851 the Geyer managers bargained with only one branch of the Democratic party. They controlled the Whigs in the legislature by bringing forth a Whig of such high standing that even those members of his party who disagreed with him on slavery issues held their protests until after he was elected. Leonard's views on slavery were different from Geyer's, and his appeal would have been to the Benton wing of the Democratic party instead of to the anti-Benton faction as Geyer's had been. However, both he and Geyer combined high standing within the Whig party with palatability to one Democratic branch. Leonard did not permit his name to be used. Nor did he permit Rollins to find out if he had attained sufficient stature to command the loyalty of Whigs who disagreed with him.

Before the balloting ended, tempers grew short, and in debate on the floor Whigs publicly aired their divisions in caucus. Rollins and Goode exchanged the epithets "free-soiler" and "nullifier" in speeches that won high acclaim, but in effect spelled the death of Missouri's Whig party. The "Whig Phalanx" held for a few more ballots, but only adjournment of the joint session, without the election of a senator, averted open abandonment of all pretense of Whig unity.[16] Before the first General Assembly session ended in March, the legislators turned to the election of bank officers, and by that time there was no recognizable Whig party. The "natural combination of the political elements now in a state of fusion" which George Caleb Bingham had looked for as early as 1851 had taken place. Not only did Whigs divide their support between the Democratic factions, they vied with each other in actually nominating their new allies.[17]

On November 30, after the legislature had reconvened, 27 of the 60 who had looked upon themselves as Whigs at the beginning of the first session attended a Whig caucus. Resolutions recommending that the Whig party hold a state convention in April passed by a vote of 15 to 12.[18] Not surprisingly, the convention never took place. Missouri had seen its last Whig ticket.

The House of Representatives defeated a motion to go into joint session with the Senate, and the legislature adjourned on December 13 without electing a senator.[19] There was never a Whig party in the legislature again.

A favorite theme of current political historiography is that Whiggery somehow "persisted" after the actual party no longer existed. Studies written from this point of view note that after 1855 former Whigs frequently acted together under different political labels and that some members of the defunct party continued to call themselves Whigs.[20] For Missouri, the generalizations about persistent Whiggery do not serve. Of course, all Whigs did not retire from politics in 1855; and, therefore, Missouri's later political history affords instances of cooperation among individuals who had been members of the party. It is a vain search, however, for a political organization composed exclusively of Whigs. Equally fruitless is a search for a time when all former Whigs pursued the same course.

Examples abound of men who had acted with the Whig party referring to themselves as Whigs after 1855, but they represent a combination of nostalgia and efforts to clothe political activities of the moment in the whitest cloth. Just as Whigs and Democrats, nullifiers and unionists, all characterized themselves as Republicans and Jeffersonians following the realignment of parties after 1824, so former Whigs of different varieties clung to their old political label, now clad in the respectability of the past. The variety of political decisions attributed to pure Whig philosophy in 1856 illustrates the point. That year the *Missouri Republican* endorsed Democrat James Buchanan for the Presidency because that was the true ground for "old-line Whigs." James O. Broadhead, however, discovered that "the beauty, . . . the crowning glory" of the American party was that it was "no less conservative than the old Whig party." "Indeed," Broadhead wrote Rollins, "it has placed itself on the platform that you and I have always occupied." Exceptional among the former Whigs of Missouri, but providing a sample of yet another direction taken by Whigs after 1855, was George Caleb Bingham, who discovered in 1856 that the true Whig ground was now "clear over to the black republicans."[21]

Some men did not substitute a new political affiliation for Whiggery, and these might be considered the remnant of the Whig party. However, they are logically regarded as one more fragment of the old group that had acted together as Whigs. Until the end of the Civil War, Missouri politicians calculated the effect of "the old-line Whig vote," but it was a group of independent voters they were reckoning with instead of a political party.

One who continued to classify himself a Whig frankly recognized that the label connoted only a political philosophy and not a political party. Congressman Gilchrist Porter found both the new American party and the Democrats unacceptable and decided to remain a member of the Whig party "if there be such a party." If not, then Porter felt "at liberty to go where I choose."[22]

There were five other Missourians elected to Congress as Whigs, and the dispersion of this delegation mirrored the party's condition. John G. Miller died in office, without revealing any intentions for his political future. At the end of the term, James T. Lindley moved to Iowa. Never a candidate for office again, he declared no new allegiances. Luther Martin Kennett found a temporary home in the American party, while Mordecai Oliver, Samuel Caruthers, and Senator Henry S. Geyer followed the *Republican* into the Democratic party.[23]

The affiliations of 1856 were transitory indeed, but the Whigs of Missouri did not regroup in later years. The election of 1860 found Edward Bates an enrolled Republican, having unsuccessfully contended for that party's presidential nomination. Although a contingent of prominent Whigs joined Bates, more accepted the leadership of Columbia's *Missouri Statesman* in supporting the Constitutional Union ticket. On the other hand, the *Missouri Republican* effectively aided the candidacy of Stephen Douglas and the Northern branch of the Democratic party.[24] After the Civil War Missouri continued to see former Whigs prominent in her political wars, but again they were on different sides. Charles Daniel Drake, who masterminded Henry Clay's Missouri campaign in 1844, led the Radical Republican movement. Among his leading opponents was former Whig James S. Rollins, working closely with Thomas Hart Benton's chief manager, Francis P. Blair, Jr.[25]

The Whig party in Missouri had its Alpha and Omega. It began after the election of 1824, when some of Henry Clay's supporters joined with John Quincy Adams' few Missouri followers. It ended when the General Assembly failed to elect a senator in 1855, and its members took divergent political paths. In its first years, the Whig party did not answer to the Whig label, but the situation then was not comparable to that which existed after 1855 when no clearly discernible group of Whigs existed in the state. The Whig party was composed of essentially the same men who had acted together from 1825 to 1838. There is no continuity between the membership of the Whig party and any political group after 1855.

NOTES

CHAPTER 1

1. *Missouri Republican* (St. Louis), November 7, 1839; *Western Emigrant* (Boonville), October 24, 1839.

2. V. O. Key, Jr., *Politics, Parties, and Pressure Groups*, 88–92; Angus Campbell, Gerald Gorin, and Warren E. Miller, *The Voter Decides*, 83–90; William Nisbet Chambers, *Political Parties in a New Nation, The American Experience, 1776–1809*, 45–48; William Nisbet Chambers, "Party Development and Party Action: The American Origins," *History and Theory: Studies in the Philosophy of History*, 3, No. 1 (1963), 108–10.

3. *Missouri Republican*, September 7, November 25, December 8, 1837; *Missouri Intelligencer* (Columbia), July 18, 1835. On rare occasions the Democrats used the word *Whig* derisively, just as the Whig press in the 1840's used a term to describe Democrats that they themselves shunned, *Loco Foco*. For examples, see *Jeffersonian Republican* (Jefferson City), July 2, 1836; *Farmers and Mechanics Advocate* (St. Louis), February 7, 1835.

4. Edward Dobyn Memoir (Missouri Historical Society, St. Louis), 14–17; *Missouri Intelligencer*, December 11, 1830; *Missouri Republican*, December 21, 1830; George R. Pitts to Meredith M. Marmaduke, Marmaduke Collection (State Historical Society of Missouri, Columbia).

5. John F. Darby, *Personal Recollections*, 270; John F. Darby to Board of Aldermen of the City of St. Louis, May 26, 1837, Darby Papers (Missouri Historical Society, St. Louis); *Missouri Republican*, June 15 and 16, 1837.

6. Printed circular of the St. Louis Whig Committee of Correspondence, January, 1838, Abiel Leonard Manuscript Collection (State Historical Society of Missouri, Columbia); *Missouri Republican*, April 5, 1838.

7. E. Malcolm Carroll, *Origins of the Whig Party*, 125–26.

8. Horace Greeley, ed., *Whig Almanac and Politicians Register for 1838*, 3. Examples of similar accounts of the origins of the Whig party are Glyndon G. Van Deusen, *The Jacksonian Era, 1828–1848*, 96–98; Wilfred E. Binkley, *American Parties, Their Natural History*, 157–60; Charles A. Beard, *The American Party Battle*, 68; D. W. Brogan, *Politics in America*, 42; Herbert Agar, *The Price of Union*, 287–89.

9. Dixon Ryan Fox, *The Decline of Aristocracy in the Politics of New York*, 366–68; Lee Benson, *The Concept of Jacksonian Democracy, New York as a Test Case*, 60–62; Henry R. Mueller, *The Whig Party in Pennsylvania*, Columbia University Studies in History, Economics and Public Law, CI, 16–18, 54–55; Arthur B. Darling, "Jacksonian Democracy in Massachusetts, 1821–1848," *American Historical Review*, 29 (January, 1924), 274–79. On Whiggery and Anti-Masonry in Massachusetts, see Charles McCarthy, *The Anti-Masonic Party*, American Historical Association Annual Report, 1902, I, 525.

10. Henry Harrison Simms, *The Rise of the Whigs in Virginia, 1824–1840*, 63–86; Herbert Dale Pegg, "The Whig Party in North Carolina, 1834–1861," (unpublished Ph.D. dissertation, University of North Carolina, 1932), 8–22; William S. Hoffman, *Andrew Jackson and North Carolina Politics*, in The James Sprunt Studies in History and Political Science, XL, 72–73, 118; Carolyn Andrews Wallace, "David Lowry Swain, The First Whig Governor of North Carolina," J. Carlyle Sitterson, ed., *Studies in Southern History in Memory of Albert Ray Newsome, 1894–1951*, The James Sprunt Studies in History and Political Science, XLII, 82–84; James E. Winston, "The Mississippi Whigs and the Tariff, 1834–1844," *Mississippi Valley Historical Review*, 22 (1935), 505.

11. Clement Eaton, *Henry Clay and the Art of American Politics*, 112–14; Albert D. Kirwan, *John J. Crittenden, The Struggle for the Union*, 96–97; William E. Connelly and E. Merton Coulter, *History of Kentucky*, II, 709–10; David L. Smiley, *Lion of White Hall, The Life of Cassius M. Clay*, 34–36.

12. Francis P. Weisenburger, *The Passing of the Frontier, 1825–1850*, 272–97; McCarthy, *The Anti-Masonic Party*, 530.

13. Powell Moore, "The Revolt Against Jackson in Tennessee 1835–1836," *Journal of Southern History*, 2 (August, 1936), 335–59; Thomas Perkins Abernethy, *From Frontier to Plantation in Tennessee, A Study in Frontier Democracy*, 301–2; Charles Grier Sellers, Jr., *James K. Polk, Jacksonian, 1795–1843*, 302–3, 340–47.

14. Charles Manfred Thompson, *The Illinois Whigs Before 1846*, University of Illinois Studies in the Social Sciences, IV, 59–61; Theodore Calvin Pease, *Illinois Election Returns, 1818–1848*, Collections of the Illinois State Historical Library, XVIII, xxxii–xxxiv, xli.

15. Pease, *Illinois Election Returns, 1818–1848*, 80, 104; Samuel R. Gammon, Jr., *The Presidential Campaign of 1832*, Johns Hopkins University Studies in Historical and Political Science, XL, 170; W. Dean Burnham, *Presidential Ballots, 1836–1892*, 368, 570; Charles O. Paullin, *Atlas of the Historical Geography of the United States*, 97, plate 104A; Thompson, *Illinois Whigs*, 53–56.

16. Paul Murray, *The Whig Party in Georgia, 1825–1853*, The James Sprunt Studies in History and Political Science, XXIX, 88–94, 190.

17. Frederic Arthur Culmer, *A New History of Missouri*, 240–42; John Miller to Daniel Dunklin, August 27, 1832, Daniel Dunklin Collection (Western Historical Manuscripts Collection, University of Missouri, Columbia, Missouri); Arthur Loyd Collins, "The Anti-Masonic Movement in Early Missouri," *Missouri Historical Review*, 39 (October, 1944), 45–52.

18. Editorial from *St. Charles Clarion*, quoted in *Western Emigrant*, April 25, 1839.

19. Chambers, *Political Parties in a New Nation*, 47–48.

CHAPTER 2

1. *Journal of the Senate of the State of Missouri at the Third General Assembly*, 43.

2. *Missouri Intelligencer* (Franklin), March 29, April 12, 1825; David Barton to Rufus Easton, February 16, 1825, Rufus Easton Papers (Missouri Historical Society, St. Louis); John Scott to Doctor L. Watkins, August 2,

1827, Henry Clay Papers (Library of Congress); Charles Francis Adams, ed., *Memoirs of John Quincy Adams, Comprising Portions of His Diary from 1795–1848*, VI, 473; Elbert R. Smith, *Magnificent Missourian, The Life of Thomas Hart Benton*, 94–95; William Nisbet Chambers, *Old Bullion Benton, Senator from the New West, Thomas Hart Benton, 1782–1858*, 128–30.

3. *Missouri Intelligencer*, April 28, June 29, July 19, 1826; John S. Savage, *Our Living Representative Men*, 35–38.

4. John B. C. Lucas, ed., *Letters of Honorable J. B. C. Lucas from 1815 to 1836*, 77–83; *Missouri Advocate* (St. Louis), quoted in *Niles Weekly Register*, 37 (September 2, 1826), 4–5.

5. Edward Bates to Hamilton R. Gamble, April 1, 1828, Gamble Papers (Missouri Historical Society, St. Louis); John R. Grisham to M. M. Marmaduke, April 4, 1828, Marmaduke Collection; John O'Fallon to Thomas A. Smith, June 12, 1828, Thomas A. Smith Collection (State Historical Society of Missouri, Columbia); *Missouri Intelligencer* (Fayette), June 11, 1828; Marvin Cain, "Edward Bates, The Rise of a Western Politician, 1814–1842," (unpublished Master's thesis, University of Missouri, 1957), 64.

6. John O'Fallon to Thomas A. Smith, June 2, 1828, Smith Collection; *Missouri Republican*, July 29, September 15, 1828.

7. Printed circular from Nathaniel W. Watkins to the Voters of Cape Girardeau County, June 28, 1828, in Political Papers (Missouri Historical Society, St. Louis); *Missouri Intelligencer*, August 1, 1828; *Journal of the House of Representatives of the State of Missouri at the Fifth General Assembly*, 1. (On this page the accredited members of the newly elected General Assembly are listed. Neither Watkins nor Wilson appears.)

8. *Missouri Republican*, July 22, 1828; *Missouri Intelligencer*, June 27, 1828; Floyd Calvin Shoemaker, *Missouri and Missourians, Land of Contrasts and People of Achievements*, I, 411. There was no Adams candidate for governor in 1828.

9. *Missouri Republican*, November 29, 1827, March 4, 11, 1828; *Missouri Intelligencer*, March 7, 1828; Edward Bates to Henry Clay, October 6, 1828, Henry Clay Papers; Lauses Tate to John Tate, September 15, 1828, Tate Family Papers (Western Historical Manuscripts Collection, University of Missouri, Columbia).

10. *Missouri Republican*, November 18, 1825.

11. *Missouri Republican*, November 25, 1828.

12. Thomas Hart Benton, *Thirty Years View; or, A History of the Working of the American Government for Thirty Years, from 1820 to 1850*, I, 47–48; Letter from Benton to Scott, February 8, 1825, in *Niles Weekly Register*, 36 (March 26, 1825), 51.

13. Richard P. McCormick, "New Perspectives on Jacksonian Politics," *American Historical Review*, 65 (January, 1960), 288–301; Chilton Williamson, *American Suffrage from Property to Democracy, 1760–1860*, 210. The issues of the *Missouri Republican* for September 16, 1824, and September 6, 1828, provide election returns for the two years.

14. *Missouri Advocate*, quoted in *Niles Weekly Register*, 37 (September 2, 1826), 4–5; *Missouri Intelligencer* (Franklin), April 5, December 23, 1825; Hardage Lane to Thomas A. Smith, Smith Collection.

15. *Missouri Republican*, November 29, 1827, March 18, 1828; *Missouri*

Intelligencer, December 7, 1827; Leota M. Newhard, "The Beginnings of the Whig Party in Missouri, 1824–1840," (unpublished Master's thesis, University of Missouri, 1932), 17–18.

16. *Missouri Intelligencer,* June 5, 1828; Cain, "Rise of a Western Politician," 58–59; Chambers, *Old Bullion Benton,* 137–39.

17. *Adams Memoirs,* VII, 194, VI, 473; Finis Ewing to Henry Clay, August 6, 1825, Henry Clay Papers; Henry A. Wise, *Seven Decades of the Union,* 82–85.

18. *Niles Weekly Register,* 37 (June 17, 1826), 283, Thomas Hart Benton to Finis Ewing, February 14, 1828, Thomas Hart Benton to William C. Lane, January 2, 1827, Benton Papers (Missouri Historical Society, St. Louis); Hattie M. Anderson, "Frontier Economic Problems in Missouri, 1815–1828, Part II," *Missouri Historical Review,* 34 (January, 1940), 189–94; Chambers, *Old Bullion Benton,* 136–37; Perry M. McCandless, "Thomas H. Benton, His Source of Political Strength in Missouri from 1815 to 1838," (unpublished Ph. D. dissertation, University of Missouri, 1953), 129–48; *Register of Debates in Congress,* 20th Congress, 483–88.

19. See William E. Foley, "The Political Philosophy of David Barton," *Missouri Historical Review,* 58 (April, 1964), 283–86, for a sympathetic analysis of Barton's land views. Foley stoutly maintains that Barton was as democratic as Benton and was the victim of misunderstanding.

20. A recent study of the origins of the Jacksonian party in Maryland found its sources neither in state nor national issues, but "rather in the needs of able politicians who found themselves politically dispossessed." I feel that a parallel study for Missouri would give more emphasis to reactions to national issues. Expediency may or may not have dictated the reactions. See Mark H. Haller, "The Rise of the Jackson Party in Maryland, 1820–1829," *Journal of Southern History,* 27 (August, 1962), 325.

21. For the view that the Adams party in Eastern states was philosophically opposed to party activity and organizationally incompetent, see Robert V. Remini, *The Election of Andrew Jackson,* 121–50.

CHAPTER 3

1. *Journal of the House of Representatives of the State of Missouri at the Fifth General Assembly,* 131–39; *Journal of the Senate of the State of Missouri at the Fifth General Assembly,* 57–59.

2. *Missouri Republican,* June 22, July 6, July 27, August 10, 1830; *Missouri Intelligencer* (Columbia), July 24, 1830. Lane, a congressional aspirant whom Benton rejected in favor of Spencer Pettis in 1828, eventually did leave the Jackson party and openly identified with its opposition. This was the action of an individual whose relations with Thomas Hart Benton had become intolerable; it did not signify the coalition of a segment of the Jackson party with the pre-Whigs.

3. *Missouri Republican,* August 10, 1830; *Western Monitor* (Fayette), August 11, 1830.

4. Thomas Hart Benton to Finis Ewing, August 22, 1830, Benton Papers; *Journal of the House of Representatives of the State of Missouri at the Sixth General Assembly,* 65.

5. *Missouri Republican,* December 7, 1830; *Missouri Intelligencer,* December 11, 1830; Edward Dobyn Memoir, 14–17.

6. *House Journal, Sixth General Assembly,* 77–80.

7. *Niles Weekly Register,* 39 (January 8, 1831), 334. The characterization of politicians of Buckner's stripe as "counterfeit Jacksonians" occurs in John Miller to Daniel Dunklin, September 16, 1832, Dunklin Collection.

8. *St. Louis Beacon,* March 24, June 2, 1831; *Missouri Republican,* May 31, 1831; J. C. Edwards to Daniel Dunklin, May 16, 1831, Daniel Dunklin to Charles Keemle, June 28, 1831, Dunklin Collection; *Laws of the State of Missouri Passed at the First Session of the Fifth General Assembly, 1828–1829,* 44.

9. Daniel Dunklin to Charles Keemle, June 28, 1831, Dunklin Collection.

10. Edward Bates to Leonard, April 4, 1831; John Stapp to Leonard, May 8, 1831; Rufus Easton to Leonard, May 8, 1831; John Wilson to Leonard, May 10, 1831; A. S. McGirk to Leonard, May 25, 1831; petition signed by twenty citizens of Lafayette County, June 5, 1831, Leonard Collection.

11. Edward Bates to Abiel Leonard, April 4, 1831; C. H. Veeder to Leonard, April 20, 1831, Leonard Collection.

12. *Missouri Republican,* July 5, 1831; *St. Louis Beacon,* July 14, 1831; David S. Lamme to Abiel Leonard, July 9, 1831; L. C. Wood to Abiel Leonard, June 23, 1831, Leonard Collection.

13. *St. Louis Beacon,* July 21, 1831; *Missouri Intelligencer,* July 30, 1831; *Jeffersonian Republican,* September 17, 1831. Pettis received 8,905 votes, Barton, 5,227.

14. Dobyn Memoir, 27; John F. Darby, *Personal Recollections,* 189–92; *St. Louis Beacon,* July 28, September 1, 1831; John Wilson to Hamilton Rowan Gamble, August 5, 1831, Gamble Papers; Benjamin H. Reeves to Abiel Leonard, August 3, 1831, Leonard Collection; *Missouri Intelligencer,* September 12, 1831.

15. *Missouri Republican,* September 6, 1831; *Missouri Intelligencer,* September 3, 1831.

16. *Missouri Republican,* November 29, 1827; *Missouri Intelligencer,* March 21, 1828.

17. *Missouri Republican,* May 3, 1831, complained that most Jacksonians were "on fence" in regard to this subject. See also announcements of Democratic candidacies in *Missouri Intelligencer,* October 1, 1831; *St. Louis Beacon,* October 13, 1831; *Jeffersonian Republican,* June 18, 1831. For Jackson's veto message, see James D. Richardson, ed., *A Compilation of the Messages and Papers of the Presidents 1789–1902,* III, 1050–52.

18. William Nisbet Chambers, *Old Bullion Benton: Senator from the New West,* 171–75; *Register of Debates in Congress, 21st Congress,* II, 4850–75.

19. Edward Bates to Abiel Leonard, April 4, 1831, Leonard Collection; *Jeffersonian Republican,* June 18, 1831; *Missouri Republican,* May 3, 1831.

20. *Missouri Republican,* September 6, 1831; *Missouri Intelligencer,* September 17, 1831.

21. *Missouri Republican,* September 27, 1831.

22. Richard P. McCormick, *The Second American Party System: Party Formation in the Jacksonian Era,* was published too late to permit extensive comparison with the findings presented here. McCormick, more than the

present writer, accepts the statements of pre-Whigs that they were neutrals in politics and also gives credence to Benton charges that some who called themselves Jackson Democrats were not actually of that faith. My study of Missouri party formation tends to support McCormick's central thesis that party alignments in the Jacksonian era derived from presidential alignments. McCormick regards Missouri as an exception to his thesis, however, at least until 1836. See McCormick, *Party Formation*, 13, 304–10.

CHAPTER 4

1. V. O. Key, Jr., *Public Opinion and American Democracy*, 500–501; Gaylon L. Caldwell, *American Government Today*, 99; Clinton Rossiter, *Parties and Politics in America*, 29–32.

2. James Aull to George C. Sibley, August 22, 1831, Sibley Papers (Missouri Historical Society, St. Louis); *St. Louis Beacon*, October 6, 1831; *Missouri Intelligencer*, October 1, 1831.

3. *Missouri Republican*, November 8, 1831. The vote was Ashley 4,931, Wells 4,811. *Jeffersonian Republican*, November 26, 1831; *Missouri Intelligencer*, October 8, 1831.

4. *St. Louis Beacon*, August 30, 1832; *Missouri Republican*, November 8, 1831, September 5, 1835; *Missouri Intelligencer*, September 14, 1833; *Missouri Argus* (St. Louis), September 23, 1836; *Biographical Directory of the American Congress, 1774–1961*, 263. The directory incorrectly classifies Bull as a bona fide Whig during his congressional term.

5. W. V. N. Bay, *Reminiscences of the Bench and Bar of Missouri*, 436–39; Louis Charles Krauthoff, "The Supreme Court of Missouri," in *The Green Bag*, 173–74; Walter Williams, ed., *A History of Northwest Missouri*, I, 111; *Missouri Argus*, June 12, 1833; *Missouri Intelligencer*, June 18, 1835; William T. Wood to Abiel Leonard, August 1, 1835, Leonard Collection. The distaste for Birch was strongest in the central part of the state. In St. Louis the *Missouri Republican* at first disapproved of the candidacy, but very shortly before the election did give Birch an unenthusiastic nod. July 11, July 30, 1835. See also William H. Lyon, *The Pioneer Editor in Missouri, 1808–1860*, 20, 69–70.

6. *Missouri Republican*, July 30, 1836; *Jeffersonian Republican*, January 16, July 2, 1836; *Missouri Argus*, September 23, 1836.

7. Samuel Smith to Nicholas Biddle, December 17, 1831, in Reginald McGrane, ed., *The Correspondence of Nicholas Biddle Dealing with National Affairs — 1807–1844*, 143; William Nisbet Chambers, *Old Bullion Benton: Senator from the New West*, 183–84; Thomas Hart Benton, *Thirty Years View, or, A History of the Working of the American Government for Thirty Years, from 1820 to 1850*, I, 398.

8. A. G. Harrison to Daniel Dunklin, July 13, 1834; Daniel Dunklin to F. H. Martin, August 21, 1834, Dunklin Collection; Sinclair Kirtley to John F. Darby, August 12, 1834, Darby Papers; *Argus*, August 5, 1836.

9. *Journal of the House of Representatives of the State of Missouri at the Eighth General Assembly*, 58–65.

10. James Neal Primm, *Economic Policy in the Development of a Western State, Missouri, 1820–1860*, 22–26; *Laws of the State of Missouri Passed at the First Session of the Ninth General Assembly, 1836–1847*, 11–24; *Mis-*

souri Republican, June 28, July 30, 1836; M. Ferguson to Abiel Leonard, January 27, 1835, Leonard Collection. Ashley also conformed to the new view. In 1836 he informed voters that the only change in his political creed was that he then favored a "well regulated state bank." Political circular of William H. Ashley, June 16, 1836, Ashley Papers (Missouri Historical Society, St. Louis).

11. *Missouri Intelligencer,* January 29, 1831; *Journal of the National Republican Convention which Assembled in the City of Baltimore, December 12, 1831,* 6; Frederic Arthur Culmer, *A New History of Missouri,* 245; *Missouri Republican,* May 3, November 13, 1831; *Jeffersonian Republican,* September 21, 1831. For comments on the lack of exertion by Clay supporters, see *Missouri Intelligencer,* November 17, 1832; *Missouri Republican,* November 13, 1832.

12. December 16, 1832, Van Buren Papers (Library of Congress).

13. Powell Moore, "The Revolt against Jackson in Tennessee, 1835–1836," *Journal of Southern History,* 2 (August, 1936), 346–47; *Missouri Argus,* September 11, 1835; *Farmers and Mechanics Advocate* (St. Louis), February 7, 1835.

14. *Missouri Intelligencer,* August 29, October 3, 1835; *Missouri Republican,* February 13, November 24, 1835, September 1, 10, 23, 1836; B. H. Reeves to John J. Crittenden, January 13, 1836, Crittenden Papers (Library of Congress).

15. Henry Clay to William S. Woods, July 16, 1835, Miscellaneous Manuscripts Collection (State Historical Society of Missouri, Columbia); Henry Clay to Henry Russell, July 18, 1835, Rollins Collection (State Historical Society of Missouri, Columbia).

16. *Missouri Republican,* December 2, 1836. The vote was 10,995 for the Van Buren electors to 7,227 for the Harrison-White electors. No result of Harrison vs. White write-ins ever appeared.

17. Thomas Hart Benton to Finis Ewing, November 21, 1831, Benton Papers; Chambers, *Old Bullion Benton,* 178–80, 187.

18. *Jeffersonian Republican,* July 2, 1836.

19. *Missouri Intelligencer,* July 13, 1833; *Missouri Republican,* July 19, 1833.

20. *Missouri Republican,* June 12, 1832; *Missouri Intelligencer,* July 20, 1833; William T. Wood to Abiel Leonard, November 5, 1835, Leonard Collection.

21. August 24, 1832, Sibley Papers. For biographical information on Sibley, see Lucinda de Leftwich Templin, "Two Illustrious Pioneers in the Education of Women in Missouri; Major George C. Sibley and Mary Eaton Sibley," *Missouri Historical Review,* 21 (April, 1927), 420–37; on Wilson, see Howard L. Conard, ed., *Encyclopedia of the History of Missouri, A Compendium of History and Biography for Ready Reference,* VI, 484.

22. *Missouri Republican,* September 10, 1832.

23. In 1832 an obscure Colonel Smith received 314 votes in the race for governor. *St. Louis Beacon,* August 10, 1832. Sibley, as a candidate for Congress, received 392 votes in 1833. *Missouri Intelligencer,* September 14, 1833.

24. *Jeffersonian Republican,* July 2, 1836. Writing in the 1870's, Edward Dobyn asserted that Ashley finally joined the "Federal party," but the contemporary evidence indicates that he only acted with it. Dobyn Memoir. For

biographical sketch of Buckner, see Louis Houck, *Memorial Sketches of Pioneers and Early Residents of Southeast Missouri*, 19–33.

25. March 31, 1832, Dunklin Collection.

26. Dunklin to Alexander Buckner, May 26, 1832; Dunklin to [unknown], June 1, 1832, Alexander Buckner to Dunklin, May 3, June 16, 1832, Dunklin Collection.

27. Edward Bates to Abiel Leonard, April 4, 1831, C. H. Veeder to Leonard, April 20, 1831, Weston F. Birch to Leonard, January 20, 1832, Leonard Collection; Arthur C. Cole, *The Whig Party in the South*, 39–44; Paul Murray, *The Whig Party in Georgia, 1825–1833*, 64–66; Henry Harrison Simms, *The Rise of the Whigs in Virginia, 1824–1840*, 97, 107–9; James Roger Sharp, "Governor Daniel Dunklin's Jacksonian Democracy in Missouri, 1832–1836," *Missouri Historical Review*, 56 (April, 1962), 221–24; Richard N. Current, *Daniel Webster and the Rise of National Conservatism*, 79.

28. Weston F. Birch to Abiel Leonard, December 22, 1831, January 20, 1832, Edward Bates to Leonard, April 4, 1831, Gary Bynum to Leonard, August 2, 1832, Leonard Collection.

29. *Jeffersonian Republican*, June 29, 1833; *Missouri Republican*, July 11, 1835, June 30, 1836; F. H. Martin to Daniel Dunklin, November 14, 1835, Dunklin Collection; William T. Wood to Abiel Leonard, August 1, 1835, Leonard Collection. Quotation is from *Palmyra Courier*, Palmyra, Missouri, August 17, 1833, clipping in Van Buren Papers.

30. William Henry Lyon, *The Pioneer Editor in Missouri*, 65–66, 69–70. Ashley received 13,057 votes, Birch 10,007, and the White-Harrison electors 7,227. Fewer participated in the later presidential election. *Missouri Argus*, September 23, 1836; *Missouri Republican*, December 2, 1836.

31. The political imbalance in Missouri was widely taken for granted by the mid-thirties. Discussing political strategies that would profit his party in the 1836 election, a Tennessee Jacksonian dismissed Missouri as a state "where no additional strength is wanted." John Catron to Andrew Jackson, March 21, 1835, in John Spencer Bassett, ed., *The Correspondence of Andrew Jackson*, V, 330.

32. Perry M. McCandless, "Thomas H. Benton, His Source of Political Strength in Missouri from 1815 to 1838," 129–48.

33. See Sharp, "Dunklin's Jacksonian Democracy," 218–20.

CHAPTER 5

1. *Missouri Republican*, St. Louis, September 7, 1837.

2. *Ibid.*

3. William Nisbet Chambers, *Old Bullion Benton: Senator from the New West*, 230–32.

4. William N. Campbell to Abiel Leonard, May 1, 1838, Leonard Collection.

5. Dorothy B. Dorsey, "The Panic and Depression of 1837–1843 in Missouri," *Missouri Historical Review*, 30 (October, 1935), 132, 135–39.

6. *Missouri Argus*, December 2, 1837; *Missouri Republican*, November 25, December 8, 1837.

7. *Missouri Republican*, January 22, 1838; *Jeffersonian Republican*, Feb-

ruary 10, 1838; Benjamin H. Reeves to Abiel Leonard, June 6, 1838, Leonard Collection.

8. *Missouri Republican*, January 22, January 26, 1838; Circular of the St. Louis Whig Committee of Correspondence, January, 1838, Leonard Collection.

9. *Missouri Republican*, April 5, 7, 14, 1838; *Missouri Argus*, April 5, 1838; John F. Darby, *Personal Recollections*, 398.

10. W. V. N. Bay, *Reminiscences of the Bench and Bar of Missouri*, 474–78; *Missouri Republican*, April 20, 1838; Frederic L. Billon, *Annals of St. Louis in Its Territorial Days from 1804 to 1821*, 363–64.

11. *Missouri Republican*, April 20, 1838.

12. *Missouri Republican*, June 13, 1837; Nathaniel Pope to Beverly Allen, September 19, 1837, Isaac Sturgeon Papers (Missouri Historical Society, St. Louis); Glyndon G. Van Deusen, *The Jacksonian Era, 1828–1848*, 127–29; Arthur Charles Cole, *The Whig Party in the South*, 51–52.

13. *Jeffersonian Republican*, March 31, 1838; *Missouri Republican*, May 10, May 24, 1838.

14. Beverly Allen to Abiel Leonard, July 23, 1838, Leonard Collection; N. Paschall to Rollins, June 7, 1838, Rollins Collection. See also William M. Campbell to Abiel Leonard, May 1, 1838, Leonard Collection.

15. Albert G. Harrison to Daniel Dunklin, March 3, 1838, Dunklin Collection. For biographical sketch of Harrison, see Bay, *Bench and Bar of Missouri*, 65–66. For election returns, see Floyd Calvin Shoemaker, *Missouri and Missourians, Land of Contrasts and People of Achievements*, I, 412.

16. *Ibid.*

17. Frederic Arthur Culmer, "Abiel Leonard," *Missouri Historical Review*, 27 (January, 1933), 113; James S. Rollins to Abiel Leonard, November 23, 1838, Leonard Collection.

18. Linn's political biographer offers only the Senator's popularity as an explanation for this novelty in Missouri history. There is no evidence that the Opposition received any plums in exchange. Linn's record in Congress was one of amenability to Benton's proposals, though there is evidence that the two senators were not always compatible. Perhaps the event is best explained as coincident with a low point in pre-Whig morale, when the group came near abandoning its seemingly futile cause. James Robert Hartley, "The Political Career of Lewis Fields Linn," (unpublished Master's thesis, University of Missouri, 1951), 49–50. For evidence of incompatibility between the two senators, see William E. Parrish, *David Rice Atchison of Missouri, Border Politician*, University of Missouri Studies, XXXIV, 228–29; Elizabeth A. R. Linn to David Rice Atchison, February 19, 1844, David Rice Atchison Papers (Western Historical Manuscripts Collection, University of Missouri, Columbia).

19. *Western Emigrant*, April 25, 1839.

20. For accounts of enthusiasm and county organization in various parts of the state, see *Missouri Whig and General Advertiser* (Palmyra), August 10, October 12, 1839; *Western Emigrant*, May 9, September 19, 1839. For Leonard's role, see circular pertaining to the establishment of the *Boon's Lick Times*, December, 1839; James H. Birch to Abiel Leonard, December 17, 1839, Leonard Collection. Quotation is from *Missouri Whig and General Advertiser*, August 10, 1839.

21. *Missouri Republican*, November 7, 1839; *Western Emigrant*, November 21, 1839; *Missouri Whig and General Advertiser*, November 16, 1839.
22. This slogan was used in a circular pertaining to the establishment of the *Boon's Lick Times*, December, 1839, Leonard Collection.
23. Quoted from *St. Charles Clarion*, in *Western Emigrant*, April 25, 1839.
24. To John F. Darby, January 11, 1839, Darby Papers.

CHAPTER 6

1. Jonas Viles, "Sections and Sectionalism in a Border State," *Mississippi Valley Historical Review*, 21 (June, 1934), 3, 14–16.
2. U. B. Phillips, "The Southern Whigs, 1834–1854," in Guy Stanton Ford, ed., *Essays in American History, Dedicated to Frederick Jackson Turner* (New York, 1910), 203–29; Arthur C. Cole, *The Whig Party in the South*, 71–74.
3. Charles G. Sellers, Jr., "Who Were the Southern Whigs?" *American Historical Review*, 59 (January, 1954), 341–44.
4. Phillips and Cole both treated Missouri as a Southern state. Besides their usual explanation of Southern Whiggery's nationalism, the two added that in Missouri the presence of a hemp interest created a group within the Whig party which had a bona fide interest in tariff protection. Phillips, "The Southern Whigs," 214; Cole, *Whig Party in the South*, 97. Actually, the hemp interest in Missouri was not extensive, and, furthermore, Democrats supported protection for that product. James Neal Primm, *Economic Policy in the Development of a Western State*, 119. Viles went beyond Phillips and Cole in emphasizing divergent interests of St. Louis and rural Whigs.
5. Sellers, "Who Were the Southern Whigs?" 343; Grady McWhiney, "Were the Whigs a Class Party in Alabama?" *Journal of Southern History*, 23 (November, 1957), 511.
6. McWhitney, "Were the Whigs a Class Party in Alabama?" 510–22; Thomas B. Alexander, *et al.*, "Who Were the Alabama Whigs?" *Alabama Review*, 16 (January, 1963), 5–19; Lee Benson, *The Concept of Jacksonian Democracy, New York as a Test Case*, 64–85; Glyndon G. Van Deusen, "Some Aspects of Whig Thought and Theory in the Jacksonian Period," *American Historical Review*, 63 (January, 1958), 318–21; Marvin Meyers, *The Jacksonian Persuasion, Politics and Belief*, 8–9. For a moderate rejection of the middle-class norm thesis, see Herbert J. Doherty, Jr., *The Whigs of Florida, 1845–1854*, 71–72. John Higham, "Beyond Consensus: The Historian as Moral Critic," *American Historical Review*, 67 (April, 1962), 609–25, questions the philosophical assumptions which he feels underlie the current "antipathy to formal ideologies and clearly defined categories."
7. *Jefferson Inquirer* (Jefferson City), April 1, 1848; *Missouri Statesman* (Columbia), April 14, 1848, August 30, 1850; *Western Emigrant*, November 21, 1839; *Missouri Republican*, March 11, 1828; *Missouri Argus*, May 6, July 27, 1839; *Jeffersonian Republican*, October 12, 19, 1839; *Journal of the House of Representatives of the State of Missouri, Tenth General Assembly*, 21–22.
8. Microfilm copies of the original white and slave schedules of the Seventh Census of the United States (1850) (State Historical Society of Missouri, Columbia). The counties selected, with their dominant political tendencies

indicated by initials, were Boone (W), Callaway (W), Cape Girardeau (D), Cole (D), Cooper (W), Greene (D), Jackson (D), Howard (D), Marion (W), Pettis (D). As the text will reveal, these counties varied in age, average wealth, and percentage of Negro population as well as political preference. While it would have been desirable to have included St. Louis, the magnitude of the census returns for that county rendered the endeavor unprofitable. The population of St. Louis County in 1850 was 105,000.

9. The census also gave the individual's age in 1850, a factor which merits at least mention in a note because of occasional characterizations of the Whig party as a society of the aged resisting changes by younger men. (See, for example, Doherty, *Whigs of Florida*, 71–72; Henry R. Mueller, *The Whig Party in Pennsylvania*, 246.) In Missouri, age does not appear to have been a significant factor in political affiliation. The average age of the Democrats who attended their party's 1848 convention was forty-six; of the comparable Whigs, forty-four.

10. The term *planter* did not occur in the portion of the census checked. Perhaps the use of *tobacconist* furnishes a revealing aside on the Whig personality, for Democrats with large amounts of land and slaves contented themselves with the ordinary appellation *farmer*. Some Whigs did also, however.

11. *Green's St. Louis Directory for 1850*.

12. The reason there are fewer Democrats than Whigs in the St. Louis sample is that the latter party monopolized the city's representation to the General Assembly in both 1838 and 1850.

13. The sources used were W. V. N. Bay, *Reminiscenses of the Bench and Bar of Missouri; The United States Biographical Dictionary and Portrait Gallery of Eminent and Self-Made Men, Missouri Volume*; Henry Clay McDougal, *Recollections, 1844–1909*; Howard L. Conard, ed., *Encyclopedia of the History of Missouri, a Compendium of History and Biography for Ready Reference*; William Rufus Jackson, *Missouri Democracy, A History of the Party and Its Representative Members — Past and Present*, I; John F. Darby, *Personal Recollections*; Walter Bickford Davis and Daniel S. Durrie, *An Illustrated History of Missouri; Biographical Directory of the American Congress, 1774–1949*; Allen Johnson, ed., *Dictionary of American Biography*, 1–20. County histories in general proved disappointing for this purpose. Most were published between 1880 and 1900, and treatment of persons no longer living was exceptional. Those that did contribute were William F. Switzler, *History of Boone County, Missouri; History of Howard and Cooper Counties, Missouri*.

14. Besides two merchants, this category included a banker and one man who was described simply as "interested in business."

15. One banker, one who was frankly identified as a land speculator, one who dealt in "investments," one wholesaler, a manufacturer of shot, and four merchants. Two of these last were specifically lumber merchants.

16. Sixteen of the Democrats and 24 of the Whigs were born in Kentucky, a difference too small to explain the relative attractions of Transylvania.

17. For discussion of the aristocratic propensities of Transylvania, see Arthur K. Moore, *The Frontier Mind, A Cultural Analysis of the Kentucky Frontiersman*, 150–51, 224–26, 234–36. Moore feels it probable that the upper-class student body brought its political attitudes to the classroom instead of

acquiring them there. For evidence that prominent Whigs dominated the Transylvania trustees, see Robert and Johanna Peter, *Transylvania University, Its Origin, Rise, Decline, and Fall*, 125–26, 164–66. *Niles Weekly Register*, 37 (August 29, 1829), cited in Leonard D. White, *The Jacksonians, A Study in Administrative History, 1829–1861*, 99–100, is the source for the statistic.

18. Burnham, *Presidential Ballots*, 570–96. The vote was normally higher in the August state elections than in the November presidential balloting, but the results, including the proportion of the votes received by each party, were markedly similar. See tables in Leota M. Newhard, "The Beginnings of the Whig Party in Missouri, 1824–1840," 108–22; J. Claude Jones, "The Status of the Whig Party in Missouri, from 1848–1854," (unpublished Master's thesis, University of Missouri, 1930), 179–209; maps in Eula Blythe Baker, "The Distintegration of the Whig Party in Missouri, 1850–1856," (unpublished Master's thesis, University of Missouri, 1932), 63 ff.

19. Floyd Calvin Shoemaker, *Missouri and Missourians, Land of Contrasts and People of Achievements*, I, 225–27, provides a convenient table of county organization dates. See also Burnham, *Presidential Ballots*, 570–96.

20. Leota M. Newhard, "The Beginnings of the Whig Party in Missouri," *Missouri Historical Review*, 25 (January, 1931), 279–80.

21. For a convenient table of Missouri counties ranked according to population, see tables compiled by Samuel Asbury in Miscellaneous Manuscripts Collection (State Historical Society of Missouri, Columbia).

22. Viles, "Sections and Sectionalism in a Border State," 14–15; Newhard, "Beginnings of the Whig Party," 279–80; Cole, *Whig Party in the South*, 104. The assertion of a correlation between slavery and Whiggery is, of course, simply another aspect of the alleged rural, upper-class character of the Southern branch of the party.

23. Population tables compiled by Asbury. In actual numbers of slaves, these counties ranked 25th, 68th, 42nd, and 47th.

24. Cole, *Whig Party in the South*, 104; Paul Murray, *The Whig Party in Georgia, 1825–1853*, 175–80; Doherty, *Whigs of Florida*, 63–66.

25. Computations based on figures in J. D. B. DeBow, *Statistical View of the United States, . . . Being a Compendium of the Seventh United States: 1850*, 260–77; J. D. B. DeBow, *The Seventh Census of the United States: 1850*, 644–45, 676. In St. Louis County, which contained slightly less than one sixth of the total population of the state, the ratio was 1:34. If an individual "owned or managed" units that were not contiguous, the census enumerators were instructed to treat the entire holdings as one farm (xxiii). Figures for farm sizes are a result of "improved acres" divided by "number of farms."

26. One hundred counties were treated in the census. The discrepancy between this figure and the 108 which existed during the period under review stems from county mergers and the creation of some too late to be included in the census returns.

27. Reynolds, Ripley, Taney. In Shannon, Miller, Gasconade, DeKalb, Barry, and Atchison the Whig vote was regularly less than 20 per cent.

28. William M. Campbell to Abiel Leonard, May 1, 1838; Charles D. Drake to Abiel Leonard and others, January 30, 1844, in Leonard Collection; *Missouri Republican*, December 8, 1837, January 22, 1838; *Jeffersonian Republican*, February 10, 1838.

29. Switzler, *History of Boone County*, 763, 252–61; Frank F. Stephens, *A History of the University of Missouri*, 10–22.

30. Viles, "Sections and Sectionalism in a Border State," 15–19.

31. DeBow, *Statistical View of the Seventh Census*, 95; Bay, *Bench and Bar of Missouri*, 356–70.

32. "My Views on Religion," manuscript by James S. Rollins; James S. Rollins to James H. Rollins, May 11, 1858, in Rollins Papers; *Missouri Statesman*, April 10, 17, 1863; Switzler, *History of Boone County*, 934–38.

33. Switzler, *History of Boone County*, 746–47.

34. Samuel Bannister Harding, *Life of George R. Smith, Founder of Sedalia, Mo.*, 2–3, 40; George R. Smith to Friends of the Pacific Railroad in Cooper County, June 12, 1854, in George R. Smith Papers.

35. William B. Napton to C. F. Jackson, October 3, 1857, in Miscellaneous Manuscripts Collection (State Historical Society of Missouri, Columbia).

36. For examples of Missouri Democrats' characterizations of Whigs as aristocrats see *Missouri Argus*, April 24, May 6, 8, 1840; *Missouri Register* (Boonville), May 14, June 6, 1844; A. G. Harrison to Martin Van Buren, June 3, 1837, in Van Buren Papers. For a comprehensive survey of evidence that Democrats throughout the nation considered themselves at war with aristocracy, see Alfred Alexander Cave, "The Jacksonian Movement in American Historiography," (unpublished Ph. D. dissertation, University of Florida, Gainesville, 1951), 1–51.

37. *Missouri Argus*, September 23, November 18, December 16, 23, 1839; Chambers, *Old Bullion Benton*, 230–32. The leading student of American suffrage feels that although all politicians were resigned to universal white, male suffrage by the Whig period, more Whigs than Democrats earlier had reservations about full suffrage. Chilton Williamson, *American Suffrage from Property to Democracy, 1760–1860*, 260–61.

38. St. Louis *Mill Boy*, July 27, 1844.

39. Arthur M. Schlesinger, Jr., *The Age of Jackson*, 269–305; Robert Gray Gunderson, *The Log-Cabin Campaign*, 7–8.

40. Gunderson, *Log-Cabin*, 9.

41. *Missouri Whig and General Advertiser*, December 28, 1839; *Missouri Republican*, January 24, February 25, May 8, 1840; *Missouri Argus*, May 6, 7, 1840; Charles McCool Snyder, *The Jacksonian Heritage: Pennsylvania Politics 1833–1848*, 148–50; R. A. Ewing to Abiel Leonard, February 3, 1840, Leonard Collection.

CHAPTER 7

1. J. D. B. DeBow, *Statistical View of the United States, Being a Compendium of the Seventh Census*, 133, 266, 380.

2. Thomas S. Barclay, *The Movement for Municipal Home Rule in St. Louis*, University of Missouri Studies, XVIII, 14–16.

3. *Ibid.*, 23; L. V. Bogy to John F. Darby, January 2, 1841, Darby Papers; Clarence H. McClure, *Opposition in Missouri to Thomas Hart Benton*, George Peabody College for Teachers Contributions to Education, No. 37, 35–36.

4. *Missouri Republican*, April 1, 1839.

5. *Ibid.*, March 29, 1839, April 4, 1840; *St. Louis Daily Union*, March 27, 1848.

6. *Missouri Republican*, March 29, 1839; *St. Louis Daily Union*, March 27, 1848; Beriah Cleland, *An Historical Account of All the Mayors Since the Formation of the City Government of St. Louis to the Present — 1846* (Pamphlet [n.d.] at Missouri Historical Society, St. Louis).

7. Chilton Williamson, *American Suffrage from Property to Democracy, 1760–1860*, 269–72.

8. *Missouri Republican*, March 26, 1840.

9. *Ibid.*, April 8, 1840; *Missouri Argus* (St. Louis), March 14, April 4, 1840; J. Thomas Scharf, *History of St. Louis City and County, from the Earliest Periods to the Present Day: Including Biographical Sketches of Representative Men*, I, 672–73.

10. This was an unusual instance when St. Louis Whigs voted differently from other Whigs. So did Democrats, and the legislature defeated the measure by a large majority. *Journal of the House of Representatives of the State of Missouri at the Eleventh General Assembly*, 351–52; *Missouri Republican*, May 23, April 17, 1840; Walter R. Houf, "Organized Labor in Missouri Politics Before the Civil War," *Missouri Historical Review*, 56 (April, 1962), 244–54.

11. *Missouri Argus*, April 17, May 28, 1840.

12. In 1850 over half of the St. Louis population was foreign born. DeBow, *Compendium of the Seventh Census*, 399.

13. *Missouri Republican*, June 22, July 6, August 10, 1830. See note 2, Chapter 3.

14. Scharf, *History of St. Louis*, I, 653–76.

15. *Missouri Republican*, March 17, November 30, 1840.

16. *American Bulletin* (St. Louis), March 29, April 2, 4, 1842; *Missouri Republican*, April 1, 1842; Circular of the German Democratic Association, July 29, 1840, Political Papers (Missouri Historical Society, St. Louis).

17. George J. McHugh, "Political Nativism in St. Louis, 1840–1857," (unpublished Master's thesis, St. Louis University, 1939), 62–65; *Missouri Republican*, March 24, April 1, 1842; Beverly Allen to Abiel Leonard, April 10, 1842, Leonard Collection.

18. *American Bulletin*, April 2, 1842.

19. *Missouri Republican*, April 13, 15, 1842; *American Bulletin*, July 26 to August 14, 1842; McHugh, "Nativism in St. Louis," 66–67, 71.

20. *Missouri Republican*, April 1, 1843; McHugh, "Nativism in St. Louis," 67.

21. McHugh, "Nativism in St. Louis," 71–76; *Missouri Republican*, April 8, 1845. There was an "Independent" Democratic candidate for mayor who received a small vote.

22. McHugh, "Nativism in St. Louis," 88–90; Scharf, *History of St. Louis*, I, 675–77; John M. Krum to M. M. Marmaduke, March 22, 1848, Sappington Papers (Missouri Historical Society, St. Louis); *St. Louis Daily Union*, April 3, 1848.

23. *Missouri Statesman*, August 12, 1850.

24. Scharf, *History of St. Louis*, I, 683; *Missouri Republican*, August 3, 1854; for biographical sketch of Boernstein, see Walter B. Stevens, *St. Louis, The Fourth City, 1764–1909*, I, 217; McHugh, "Nativism in St. Louis," 104–5.

25. William Rufus Jackson, *Missouri Democracy, A History of the Party*

and Its Representative Members — Past and Present, with a Vast Amount of Informative Data, I, 141, 147.

26. McHugh, "Nativism in St. Louis," 42, 107; *Missouri Republican,* March 30, 1856.

27. Ironically, Henry Boernstein voted the Know-Nothing ticket in the presidential election of 1856. He preferred Fillmore to Buchanan; there were no Republican electors in Missouri. McHugh, "Nativism in St. Louis," 149.

28. *St. Louis Daily Union,* March 24, 27, 1848; *Missouri Republican,* March 27, April 3, 1848.

29. *St. Louis City Directory for 1848.* The directory did make it plain if the firm was a legal one.

30. Ray Allen Billington, *The Protestant Crusade, 1800–1860, A Study of the Origins of American Nativism,* 195, 323.

31. The occupations not accounted for in the text were miscellaneous listings. Each party had two physicians and one daguerreotypist; two watchmen and two sextons were Democrats. There was a Whig architect, two Whig measurers (of buildings), and a teacher at the Classical High School.

32. L. U. Reavis, *Saint Louis: The Future Great City of the World with Biographical Sketches of the Representative Men and Women of St. Louis and Missouri,* 483–88; Scharf, *History of St. Louis,* I, 180. Tax assessments over $20,000 appear in Scharf, 684–85. Scharf points out that the figures pertain only to real estate within the city limits and represent assessed rather than actual value.

33. Scharf, *History of St. Louis,* I, 674–75, 684–85; Reavis, *Saint Louis,* 477–81.

34. Scharf, *History of St. Louis,* I, 669–70. Bates and Gamble maintained residences outside of the city, which may account for their nonparticipation in city politics.

35. Stevens, *Fourth City,* I, 129, 137.

36. Scharf, *History of St. Louis,* I, 678; *Missouri Republican,* January 4, 1885; St. Louis (City) Tax List, Book I, A-L, 1847–1848, manuscript (Missouri Historical Society, St. Louis).

37. W. V. N. Bay, *Bench and Bar of Missouri,* 219.

38. Reavis, *St. Louis,* 419–24; 395–407; Scharf, *History of St. Louis,* I, 684–85.

39. Lee Benson, *The Concept of Jacksonian Democracy, New York as a Test Case,* 64.

40. Richard C. Wade, *The Urban Frontier,* 339–40.

CHAPTER 8

1. Richard P. McCormick, "New Perspectives on Jacksonian Politics," *American Historical Review,* 65 (January, 1960), 288–301.

2. *Ibid.,* 300; W. Dean Burnham, *Presidential Ballots, 1836–1892,* 570; *Jeffersonian Republican,* September 5, 1840; *Missouri Argus,* September 23, 1836; Duane Meyer, *The Heritage of Missouri — A History,* 236.

3. McCormick, "New Perspectives," 296–97, 300. McCormick employs a type of statistic which this writer feels misleadingly indicates a greater im-

provement in the Whig position in Missouri than actually occurred. He correctly notes that the difference between the percentage of votes received by the two parties was 21 in 1836 and 14 in 1840. It seems more meaningful to note instead that the Whigs advanced from slightly more than 39 per cent of the vote in 1836 to 43 per cent in 1840. The phrase "great commotion" is taken from the standard account of the campaign of 1840, Robert Gray Gunderson, *The Log-Cabin Campaign*. Gunderson cites only one piece of evidence from Missouri in support of the theme implied by this title of his first chapter, to wit, the caning of a Democratic editor by an overzealous Whig in St. Louis. See 1–12, 146.

4. *National Intelligencer* (Washington, D.C.), November 7, December 9, 1839; *Missouri Whig and General Advertiser*, December 28, 1839; *Missouri Republican*, January 9, 1840; R. A. Ewing to Abiel Leonard, February 3, 1840, Leonard Collection. See Charles Gibson Autobiography in Charles Gibson Papers (Missouri Historical Society, St. Louis), for a Whig's reminiscence which reflects distaste for his party's candidate and campaign of 1840.

5. *Boon's Lick Times*, August 1, 1839; Burnham, *Presidential Ballots*, 570–96.

6. Glyndon G. Van Deusen, *Thurlow Weed: Wizard of the Lobby*, 110–13; Gunderson, *Log-Cabin Campaign*, 108–13. Quotation is from Littleberry Hendricks to Abiel Leonard, July 22, 1840, Leonard Collection. See also Logan Hunton to James S. Rollins, March 4, 1840, Rollins Collection; *Missouri Whig and General Advertiser*, August 22, 1840; *Missouri Republican*, January 9, 1840.

7. Burnham, *Presidential Ballots*, 572, 592; Newhard, "The Beginnings of the Whig Party in Missouri," 109–22, provides tables for convenient comparison of state election returns of 1836 and 1840. A large Whig gathering took place in Hannibal (Marion County), but the newspaper account made no mention of log cabin or hard cider festivities. Instead, the Whig editor happily announced that "all was order and decorum." *Missouri Whig and General Advertiser*, August 8, 1840. The first political reference to log cabins in Missouri, to my knowledge, was in the *Missouri Republican*, April 14, 1840.

8. A. M. Davidson to Dr. William Bush, June 21, 1840, Political Papers (Missouri Historical Society, St. Louis). W. F. Switzler, *Illustrated History of Missouri from 1541 to 1877*, 255–57, and W. F. Switzler, *History of Boone County, Missouri*, 332–34, provide detailed accounts of the Rocheport meeting. Among the speakers were Chilton Allen of Kentucky and Fletcher Webster, a son of Daniel Webster. Although Switzler asserts that the state was "wild with excitement" during the 1840 canvass, he cites only the Rocheport meeting as an example of extraordinary campaign activity. Walter B. Davis and Daniel S. Durrie, *An Illustrated History of Missouri*, the only general history of the state published before Switzler's that is at all well known, does not single out the campaign of 1840 in any way. *Missouri Republican*, June 22, 23, 25, 1840, gives day-by-day accounts of the meeting. The *Republican* estimated the attendance between seven and ten thousand, which, even if exaggerated for partisan purposes, is not impressive when compared to the size of Whig rallies in other states. See Gunderson, *Log-Cabin Campaign*, 108–22.

9. James H. Birch to Joseph Bogy, March 12, 1840, appended to copy of *Address of the Central Committee to the People of the State of Missouri*

[n.d.] in library of Missouri Historical Society, St. Louis; James H. Birch to James S. Rollins, February 8, 1840, Rollins Collection; *Missouri Republican*, February 22, 1840; William Hyde and Howard L. Conard, eds., *Encyclopedia of the History of St. Louis, A Compendium of History and Biography for Ready Reference*, II, 948–49. By the spring of 1841 Moss was sufficiently recovered to seek federal patronage. Moss to Abiel Leonard, May 12, 1841, Leonard Collection. *Missouri Republican*, St. Louis, June 12, 1840.

10. James H. Birch to James S. Rollins, February 8, 1840; Logan Hunton to James S. Rollins, March 4, 1840, Rollins Collection; George C. Sibley to Abiel Leonard, June 6, 1840, Leonard Collection; E. M. Samuel to George C. Sibley, May 31, 1840, Sibley Papers; *Missouri Republican*, June 12, 1840; *History of Randolph and Macon Counties*, 508–9.

11. John Miller to M. M. Marmaduke, November 22, 1839, Sappington Papers.

12. Robert Gray Gunderson, *The Log-Cabin Campaign*, 65–66, 73–74, 169–70; *Boon's Lick Times*, June 6, 1840; printed circular of George C. Sibley to the Free and Independent Voters of Missouri, June, 1840, Sibley Papers.

13. *Address of the Central Tippecanoe Club of Callaway County to the Independent Voters of Callaway* (pamphlet [n.d.] at State Historical Society of Missouri, Columbia), 6–10.

14. James Harvey Birch, *Address to the People of the State of Missouri* (pamphlet [n.d.] at State Historical Society of Missouri, Columbia), 40–41, 15–22. For other examples of Whigs bluntly introducing the Independent Treasury issue into the campaign, see *Boon's Lick Times*, June 6, 1840, August 1, 1839; *Missouri Whig and General Advertiser*, June 6, 1840; *Missouri Republican*, January 11, May 13, 1840; George C. Sibley to the Free and Independent Voters of Missouri, June, 1840, Sibley Papers. Whigs in neighboring Illinois did reach a "high tide" of campaigning in 1840, according to the party's historian for that state. They did, however, openly embrace an economic program, similar to that advocated by the Missouri Whigs. Charles Manfred Thompson, *The Illinois Whigs before 1846*, IV (1915), 66–67, 87, 124–25.

15. In the state elections the Democratic candidates each received just under 29,000 votes. The Whigs received slightly over 20,000, except Clark who ran 1,000 votes ahead of the other state candidates of his party. Since he was the only Whig who conducted a full-scale canvass, perhaps this is evidence that political campaigns have some influence on election results. Van Buren electors carried the state 30,000 to 22,000. *Jeffersonian Republican*, September 5, 1840; Burnham, *Presidential Ballots*, 570. *Missouri Whig*, November 28, 1840.

16. John O'Fallon to Abiel Leonard, March 6, 1841, Leonard Collection; John O'Fallon to Charles W. Thruston, May 9, 1840; biographical sketch of John O'Fallon; John O'Fallon to William Henry Harrison, March 6, 1841, O'Fallon Papers (Filson Club, Louisville, Kentucky); George K. McGunnegle to John F. Darby, John F. Darby to Francis Granger, March 9, 1841, Darby Papers; T. J. Boggs to Abiel Leonard, February 10, 1841, Leonard Collection.

17. Samuel B. Churchill to Daniel Webster, January 11, 1841, Beverly Allen to Daniel Webster, December 31, 1840, Webster Papers (Library of

Congress). Both of these letters made suggestions for improving the Whig position in Missouri, now that the party controlled the national government. Churchill, a St. Louis editor and member of the legislature, urged that if the Administration would make Benton's pre-emption bill its own, the Whig cause in Missouri would be aided immeasurably. Allen dwelt on the benefits which would accrue to those who sponsored Missouri's cause in a dispute with Iowa over the boundary between the two states. The historians of patronage and government service are emphatic that the Whigs of 1840 utilized patronage on a grand scale. Thus, the Missouri situation was atypical and not merely a reflection of a national pattern. Leonard D. White, *The Jacksonians, A Study in Administrative History, 1829–1861,* 312–14; Carl R. Fish, *The Civil Service and the Patronage,* Harvard Historical Studies, XI, 151.

18. Unfortunately, there are no Birch papers. The following letters contain references either to requests made to Birch to use his influence or to the necessity of making such requests. John Dougherty to James H. Birch, March 15, 1841, Dougherty Papers (Missouri Historical Society, St. Louis); David Todd to Abiel Leonard, February 18, 1841, Woodson J. Moss to Abiel Leonard, May 12, 1841, Leonard Collection; George C. Bingham to James S. Rollins, August 3, 1841, Samuel B. Churchill to James S. Rollins, August 3, 1841, Rollins Collection; Archibald Gamble to George C. Sibley, July 13, 1841, Sibley Papers; James H. Birch to George R. Smith, February 15, 1841, George R. Smith Papers. For O'Fallon's estimate of Birch, see John O'Fallon to Abiel Leonard, March 6, 1841, Leonard Collection. *Missouri Republican,* August 26, 1841, gives the reaction of Missouri Whigs to Tyler's course. See also Oliver Perry Chitwood, *John Tyler, Champion of the Old South,* 217–34; Robert Seager, II, *And Tyler Too, A Biography of John and Julia Gardiner Tyler,* 151–63.

19. Archibald Gamble to George C. Sibley, July 13, 1841, Sibley Papers; Robert Wilson to John F. Darby, June 17, 1841, Darby Papers; *Missouri Republican,* August 26, 1841. It was not until after Tyler's veto of the second bank bill passed by the Whig majority in Congress that Whig members of his Cabinet resigned and a caucus of Whig congressmen officially repudiated him. Seager, *And Tyler, Too,* 159–63; Robert J. Morgan, *A Whig Embattled, The Presidency under John Tyler,* 23–57. Charles G. Sellers, Jr., feels that Southern Whigs most conclusively demonstrated their nationalistic character when all but three Virginians joined in denouncing the wayward President. Although Missouri Whigs, by virtue of their being unrepresented in Congress or Cabinet, did not participate in these events, they did persuasively demonstrate their nationalistic bent during the Tyler crisis. Sellers, "Who Were the Southern Whigs?" 339–40.

20. James H. Birch to George R. Smith, May 13, 1843; George R. Smith Papers; William Monroe to Meredith M. Marmaduke, January 24, 1845, Marmaduke Collection. White, *The Jacksonians,* 421, points out that land offices, with their opportunities for informed speculation, were much sought-after patronage appointments.

21. Manlius V. Thompson to George R. Smith, October 22, 1843, Thomas H. Blake to George R. Smith, April 17, 1843, Silas Reed to George R. Smith, May 20, 1843, January 12, 1844, V. Ellis to George R. Smith, June 3, July 5, 1843, George R. Smith Papers.

22. April 4, 1843, Leonard Collection; James H. Birch to George R. Smith, May 13, 1843, George R. Smith Papers [personal]. Massachusetts leader Daniel Webster remained in Tyler's Cabinet until a month after Birch's letter. Morgan, *Whig Embattled,* 74.

23. The George R. Smith Papers are the best source for information on the Tyler movement in Missouri. See letters from James H. Birch, Weston F. Birch, Vespasian Ellis, and Silas Reed to Smith, 1841–1844. Most of these are published in Samuel Bannister Harding, *Life of George R. Smith, Founder of Sedalia, Mo.* See also James F. Birch to James S. Rollins, May 26, 1843, Rollins Collection; James F. Birch to Abiel Leonard, April 4, 1843, Leonard Collection; Silas Reed to John Tyler, October 1, 1842, Tyler Papers (Library of Congress); Lyon G. Tyler, *The Letters and Times of the Tylers,* II, 471–75; McHugh, "Nativism in St. Louis," 66–67, 71; "Historical Notes and Comments," *Missouri Historical Review,* 20 (October, 1925), 128.

24. *Missouri Republican,* August 26, November 12, 1841; John Wilson to George R. Smith, August 4, 1842, George R. Smith Papers.

25. George C. Sibley, "Commonplace Book Number Three" (mss.), April-June, 1844, Sibley Papers; *Niles Weekly Register,* 66 (May 4, 1841), 145–48.

26. *Weekly Observer* (Boonville), September 18, October 10, 1844; William H. Russell to Henry Clay, May 7, 1844, Henry Clay Papers (Library of Congress); *Missouri Republican,* July 6, 1844; John Ruland to Meredith M. Marmaduke, May 15, 1844; Benjamin W. Sharp to Meredith M. Marmaduke, September 11, 1844, Sappington Papers; J. S. Smythe to John F. Darby, May 24, 1844, Darby Papers.

27. "Famous Personages of the Civil War in Missouri: Charles D. Drake," *Missouri Historical Review,* 56 (January, 1962), back cover; Charles D. Drake to Thomas Corwin, August 1, 1850, Thomas Corwin Papers (Library of Congress).

28. Drake to Fish, December 16, 1843; Fish to Drake, January 19, 1844 (Letterbook E), Hamilton Fish Papers (Library of Congress).

29. Charles Daniel Drake to Abiel Leonard and others, January 30, 1844, Leonard Collection; *Weekly Observer,* September 24, 28, October 10, 1844; *Missouri Whig,* September 23, 25, October 15, 20, 1844; *Mill Boy,* September 28, October 12, 1844. The *Mill Boy* was established especially for the Clay campaign. Howard's second rank is based on the Census of 1840; by 1850 Platte County had surpassed her.

30. John C. Richardson to Robert S. Rollins, December 6, 1844, Rollins Collection. Cass received 41,332 votes, Clay 31,206. Burnham, *Presidential Ballots,* 570. Richard P. McCormick indicates that Clay fared worse in Missouri than Harrison, but this is evidently based on miscalculation. The figures in Burnham, *Presidential Ballots,* which McCormick relies on, reveal that in both elections the Whigs received just over 43 per cent of the total votes. McCormick, "New Perspectives," 300.

31. Thomas H. Harvey to Meredith M. Marmaduke, July 9, 1844; John J. Lowry to Meredith M. Marmaduke, June 12, 1844, Sappington Papers; *Missouri Statesman,* November 8, 1844; Clarence Henry McClure, "Opposition to the Reelection of Thomas Hart Benton in 1844," (unpublished Master's thesis, University of Missouri, 1913), 118–20.

CHAPTER 9

1. Editorials reprinted in *Columbia Patriot*, November 6, 1841; W. V. N. Bay, *Bench and Bar of Missouri*, 331–34.

2. *Columbia Patriot*, November 6, 13, 20, 1841; *Boon's Lick Times*, November 9, 1841; William F. Switzler, *History of Boone County, Missouri*, 943–46.

3. William R. Ellett to Meredith M. Marmaduke, October 8, 1841, Sappington Papers; *Boon's Lick Times*, February 12, 1842; *Missouri Republican*, February 5, 1842.

4. George Penn to M. M. Marmaduke, October 8, 1841, Sappington Papers.

5. Clarence H. McClure, *Opposition in Missouri to Thomas Hart Benton*, 14–18; James Neal Primm, *Economic Policy in the Development of a Western State*, 41–43; Buel Leopard and Floyd C. Shoemaker, *The Messages and Proclamations of the Governors of the State of Missouri*, I, 454–57.

6. To John F. Darby, January 18, 1839, Darby Papers. A copy of the 1838 Currency Bill was printed in *Missouri Register*, April 9, 1844.

7. *Missouri Register*, April 9, 1844; McClure, *Opposition to Benton*, 18.

8. *Missouri Argus*, October 16, 20, December 29, 1840; *Jefferson Inquirer*, August 31, 1843; *Missouri Republican*, January 11, 1841; *Missouri Register*, February 25, 1841; McClure, *Opposition to Benton*, 33–35.

9. Articles quoted from *Ozark Eagle*, in *Jefferson Inquirer*, January 27, 1842; *Columbia Patriot*, June 2, 1842.

10. Thomas Reynolds to Meredith M. Marmaduke, March 29, 1842, James B. Marmaduke to Meredith M. Marmaduke, May 2, 1842, Marmaduke Collection.

11. "Missouriana," *Missouri Historical Review*, 35 (April, 1914), 259–60; *Boon's Lick Times*, June 18, 1842; *Jefferson Inquirer*, June 9, 1842.

12. *Boon's Lick Times*, June 18, 1842; Floyd C. Shoemaker, *Missouri and Missourians, Land of Contrasts and People of Achievements*, I, 412; "Missouriana," 259–60.

13. *Missouri Republican*, August 5, 12, 1842; *Columbia Patriot*, July 2, 29, 1842; *Boon's Lick Times*, July 9, 16, 1842; Shoemaker, *Missouri and Missourians*, I, 412.

14. George C. Sibley to D. D. Bernard, December 21, 1843; D. D. Bernard to George C. Sibley, January 4, 1844, Sibley Papers; *Mill Boy*, July 20, 1844.

CHAPTER 10

1. *Jefferson Inquirer*, July 28, 1842.

2. *Missouri Statesman*, February 24, September 1, 1843; *Jefferson Inquirer*, August 25, 1842, September 21, 1843; John Miller to Meredith M. Marmaduke, February 15, 1843, Sappington Papers; B. F. Stringfellow to Thomas Reynolds, September 20, 1842, Governor Thomas Reynolds Papers (Missouri Historical Society, St. Louis).

3. *Journal of the House of Representatives of the State of Missouri at the First Session of the Twelfth General Assembly*, 100–102; Richard Edwards and M. Hopewell, *Edward's Great West and Her Commercial Metropolis*,

Embracing a General View of the West, and A Complete History of St. Louis, from the Landing of Ligueste, in 1764, to the Present Time, 153–54; *Jefferson Inquirer,* December 15, 1842.

4. *Missouri Statesman,* April 21, 1843; *Missouri Republican,* June 20, 1843; *Jefferson Inquirer,* December 15, 29, 1842, January 5, 12, 17, 25, February 2, 1843.

5. Thomas Perkins Abernethy, *From Frontier to Plantation in Tennessee, A Study in Frontier Democracy,* 229–30; J. Thomas Scharf, *History of St. Louis City and County,* I, 686–87.

6. *Jefferson Inquirer,* January 5, 1843; *Missouri Register,* November 14, 1843. Clarence H. McClure, *Opposition in Missouri to Thomas Hart Benton,* 50–57, deals at length with Penn's letters.

7. William B. Napton to Governor Thomas Reynolds, October 11, 1843, Reynolds Papers; *Missouri Register,* November 14, 1843; William E. Parrish, *David Rice Atchison of Missouri: Border Politician,* 32–36.

8. John S. Phelps to Thomas Reynolds, January 11, 1844, Governors' Papers (Missouri Historical Society, St. Louis); J. Sanborn to [unknown], March 28, 1844, Miscellaneous Manuscripts Collection (State Historical Society of Missouri, Columbia).

9. *Missouri Register,* April 9, 16, 1844; *Jefferson Inquirer,* April 4, 1844.

10. *Missouri Register,* April 9, 30, 1844; *Jefferson Inquirer,* April 4, 1844.

11. *Missouri Republican,* December 23, 1843; *Missouri Register,* April 9, May 14, 1844; *Jefferson Inquirer,* April 18, May 23, 1844.

12. Thomas H. Harvey to Meredith M. Marmaduke, July 9, 1844; John J. Lowry to Meredith M. Marmaduke, June 12, 1844, Sappington Papers; *Jefferson Inquirer,* July 4, 1844; James C. N. Paul, *Rift in the Democracy,* 134–37; Thomas Hart Benton, *Thirty Years' View,* II, 581–85; Frederick Merk, *Manifest Destiny and Mission in American History, A Reinterpretation,* 42–44.

13. *Missouri Register,* June 11, 1844; *Missouri Republican,* November 21, 22, 1844; William H. Lyon, "Claiborne Fox Jackson and the Secession Crisis in Missouri," *Missouri Historical Review,* 58 (July, 1964), 422–25.

14. *Missouri Statesman,* September 1, 1843; *Missouri Republican,* October 5, 1844; *Missouri Register,* May 14, 21, June 4, August 27, 1844; William Nisbet Chambers, *Old Bullion Benton, Senator from the New West, 1782–1856,* 284–85; Alma West, "The Earlier Political Career of Claiborne Fox Jackson, 1836–1851," (unpublished Master's thesis, University of Missouri, 1941), 92–93.

15. William H. Russell to Henry Clay, May 7, 1844, Clay Papers.

16. *Mill Boy,* July 20, 27, 1844; *Missouri Statesman,* April 5, 1844.

17. The only exception to Hard victory was congressional candidate D. C. M. Parsons of Pike County, who died ten days before the election. Some voters either did not learn of his death or were fanatically loyal to the party, for he was the posthumous recipient of slightly over 18,000 votes. As a result, L. H. Sims of Greene County, who ran a few hundred votes ahead of the other Independents, was entitled to the fifth seat. According to a contemporary, Sims drew his mileage allowance and per diem, "and that was about the only thing he did during the two years he was in Congress." W. V. N. Bay, *Bench and Bar of Missouri,* 195–96.

18. Floyd Calvin Shoemaker, *Missouri and Missourians, Land of Contrasts and People of Achievements*, I, 410–13, 636–40, provides comprehensive election returns.

19. Chambers, *Old Bullion Benton*, 281–82. See Chapter 7, 88–91, for more detailed discussion of the presidential campaign of 1844 in Missouri.

20. George C. Sibley to the Voters of St. Charles and Warren (printed circular), July 4, 1844; Commonplace Book Number Three, Wednesday, July 31, 1844, Sibley Papers; McClure, *Opposition to Benton*, 75. The three occasions Whigs urged Sibley not to run were 1833, 1836 (for Congress), and 1844, for the office under discussion.

21. Commonplace Book Number Three, August 3, 1844, also June 24, July 15, July 31, 1844; John S. Waddell, John Bedford, D. D. Berry to George Sibley, July 17, 1844, Sibley Papers.

22. Commonplace Book Number Three, August 6, 1844, Sibley Papers.

23. *Ibid.*, August 12, 1844; W. Dean Burnham, *Presidential Ballots, 1836–1892*, 570–96.

24. *Mill Boy*, July 27, 1844; *Missouri Statesman*, September 1, 1843; *Jefferson Inquirer*, April 4, 11, 25, 1844; John S. Waddell and others to George C. Sibley, July 17, 1844, Sibley Papers.

25. *Missouri Register*, August 27, 1844; *Jefferson Inquirer*, August 16, 1844; *Missouri Statesman*, September 5, 1844.

26. *Missouri Republican*, November 21, 22, 1844.

27. William Monroe to Meredith M. Marmaduke, January 24, 1845, Marmaduke Collection; *Missouri Statesman*, January 2, 1845.

28. *Jefferson Inquirer*, December 7, 1844; *Revised Statutes of the State of Missouri, 1845* (St. Louis, 1845), 213–14.

29. *Journal of the House of Representatives of the State of Missouri at the Thirteenth General Assembly*, 39; McClure, *Opposition to Benton*, 94.

30. *Ibid.*, 40; *Missouri Republican*, November 25, 1844. It is an interesting aside that the most thorough study of the abortive effort to unseat Benton (McClure, *Opposition to Thomas Hart Benton*), mentions the Whigs only occasionally and incidentally. I feel that the perspective of McClure's careful study would have been enhanced by more attention to the Whigs, but certainly he is correct that the actuating spirit of the anti-Benton movement came from within the Senator's own party.

CHAPTER 11

1. *Missouri Statesman*, February 1, 1845; *Jefferson Inquirer*, November 21, 1844, January 24, 1845; Clarence H. McClure, *Opposition in Missouri to Thomas Hart Benton*, 96–98.

2. *Missouri Statesman*, July 3, 1846; William Nisbet Chambers, *Old Bullion Benton, Senator from the New West*, 308; McClure, *Opposition to Benton*, 103, 108–14; Frederick Merk, "Presidential Fevers," *Mississippi Valley Historical Review*, 47 (June, 1960), 17, 25, 32–33.

3. *Revised Statutes of the State of Missouri, 1845*, 213–14.

4. T. J. Boggs to Abiel Leonard, April 12, 1846, Leonard Collection; *Missouri Republican*, May 29, 1846.

5. Floyd Calvin Shoemaker, *Missouri and Missourians, Land of Contrasts and People of Achievements*, I, 637, 644, 651–52. John G. Miller should not

be confused with John Miller, a Democrat from Howard County, who served as Governor from 1825 to 1832 and as Congressman from 1832 to 1836, *ibid.*, 418–20.

6. Mary Phelps to George R. Smith, March 4, 1849, General George R. Smith Papers. Samuel Bannister Harding, *Life of George R. Smith, Founder of Sedalia, Mo.*, 68, 93–95. The work just cited reproduces verbatim virtually the entire George R. Smith Papers at the Missouri Historical Society. However, neither the collection nor the book contains correspondence between Richard M. Johnson and Smith. Harding refers to such letters, without mentioning dates, on p. 68.

7. *Missouri Republican*, May 29, July 20, 28, 30, August 6, 1846.

8. Shoemaker, *Missouri and Missourians*, I, 637; W. V. N. Bay, *Reminiscences of the Bench and Bar of Missouri*, 101–3, 185–88.

9. William Rufus Jackson, *Missouri Democracy, A History of the Party and Its Representative Members — Past and Present, With a Vast Amount of Informative Data*, II, 145; Shoemaker, *Missouri and Missourians*, I, 637.

10. *Missouri Statesman*, October 18, 25, 1848.

11. Charles M. Wiltse, *John C. Calhoun, Sectionalist, 1840–1850*, 173–81; McClure, *Opposition to Benton*, 60–63.

12. *Mill Boy*, July 27, 30, 1844; *Boon's Lick Times*, June 18, 1842.

13. Bay, *Bench and Bar in Missouri*, 101–3, 175–77, 191–98, 210–14, 499–509; Jackson, *Missouri Democracy*, II, 145.

14. *Ibid.*, 185–87, 271–76, 394–400, 462–66; Howard L. Conard, ed., *Encyclopedia of the History of Missouri, A Compendium of History and Biography for Ready Reference*, III, 397; Jackson, *Missouri Democracy*, II, 108–9, 145.

15. Microfilm copy of the original slave schedules of the Seventh Census of the United States (1850), State Historical Society of Missouri, Columbia; William B. Napton to Claiborne F. Jackson, October 3, 1857, Miscellaneous Manuscripts Collection (State Historical Society of Missouri, Columbia).

16. See McClure, *Opposition to Benton*, 65, for a summary of areas of Hard and Soft strength.

17. *Jefferson Inquirer*, April 4, 11, 25, June 6, 1844; *Missouri Register*, June 11, 1844; Thomas H. Harvey to Meredith M. Marmaduke, July 9, 1844, Sappington Papers.

18. *Missouri Republican*, June 12, 1838; John Wilson to George C. Sibley, August 24, 1832. Although fallacious if carried far, comparison of the Whig party in Missouri with the Republican party in the twentieth-century South is irresistible. One wonders what the effect on ante-bellum Missouri politics would have been if the direct primary system had been in use.

19. *Laws of the State of Missouri Passed at the Second Session of the Twelfth General Assembly*, 25.

20. *House Journal, Thirteenth General Assembly*, 158; McClure, *Opposition to Benton*, 24.

21. William M. Campbell to Abiel Leonard, December 20, 1840, Leonard Collection; Frederick Hyatt to John F. Darby, January 30, 1841, Darby Papers; *Missouri Republican*, January 15, 21, February 17, 1841, August 4, 1845, January 3, 1846.

22. *Missouri Republican*, August 1, 1846; C. F. Jackson to Meredith M. Marmaduke, January 24, 1845, Marmaduke Collection; J. P. Vaughan to

Abiel Leonard, July 24, 1845, Leonard Collection. McClure, *Opposition to Benton*, 22, and Shoemaker, *Missouri and Missourians*, I, 622–23, both link apportionment directly to the Hard-Soft controversy.

23. William Monroe to Meredith M. Marmaduke, January 24, 1834, Marmaduke Collection; J. P. Vaughan to Abiel Leonard, July 24, 1845, Leonard Collection.

24. *Constitution of the State of Missouri, 1845*, 17–18; James Neal Primm, *Economic Policy in the Development of a Western State, Missouri, 1820–1860*, 51–52.

25. Priscilla Bradford, "The Missouri Constitution Controversy of 1845," (unpublished Master's thesis, University of Missouri, 1936), 156–63.

26. James O. Broadhead to Garland C. Broadhead, December 22, 1846, James O. Broadhead Papers (Missouri Historical Society, St. Louis); L. U. Reavis, *Saint Louis: The Future Great City of the World with Biographical Sketches of the Representative Men and Women of St. Louis and Missouri*, 636–40.

CHAPTER 12

1. Hugh Bone, "Political Parties and Pressure Group Politics," *Annals of the American Academy of Political and Social Science*, 309 (September, 1958), 74; V. O. Key, Jr., *Politics, Parties, and Pressure Groups*, 221. See also William Nisbet Chambers, "Party Development and Party Action: The American Origins," *History and Theory: Studies in the Philosophy of History*, 3, No. 1 (1963), 92–93, 107–10.

2. Clarence Henry McClure, *Opposition in Missouri to Thomas Hart Benton*, 104–8; Gerald M. Capers, *John C. Calhoun — Opportunist: A Reappraisal*, 235–38; William Nisbet Chambers, *Old Bullion Benton, Senator from the New West, Thomas Hart Benton, 1782–1856*, 313–17.

3. James Neal Primm, *Economic Policy in the Development of a Western State, Missouri, 1820–1860*, 50–51.

4. Buel Leopard and Floyd C. Shoemaker, *The Messages and Proclamations of the Governors of the State of Missouri*, II, 103–11; *Jefferson Inquirer*, April 25, 1844; *Missouri Republican*, December 28, 1849.

5. Primm, *Economic Policy in Missouri*, 54, 58.

6. *Ibid.*, 45–50, 56–57.

7. *Missouri Republican*, January 27, 1849; J. Thomas Scharf, *History of St. Louis City and County from the Earliest Period to the Present Day; Including Biographical Sketches of Representative Men*, I, 924–25.

8. Arthur Charles Cole, *The Whig Party in the South*, 117–23; *Missouri Statesman*, January 2, 1845, January 7, 1848; *Missouri Republican*, July 11, 1846; Thomas Joyes to Abiel Leonard, May 30, 1846, Leonard Collection.

9. *Missouri Statesman*, November 19, June 25, December 24, 1847; *Missouri Republican*, July 11, 1846.

10. Walter B. Davis and Daniel S. Durrie, *An Illustrated History of Missouri Comprising Its Early Record and Civil, Political, and Military History*, 498–501; Floyd Calvin Shoemaker, *Missouri and Missourians, Land of Contrasts and People of Achievements*, I, 702–3.

11. Shoemaker, *Missouri and Missourians*, I, 703–14; Brainerd Dyer, *Zachary Taylor*, 268–83.

12. John Wilson to George R. Smith, April 23, 1847, General George R. Smith Papers; John Wilson to [James S. Rollins], July 14, 1847; Samuel B. Churchill to James S. Rollins, January 17, 1847, Rollins Collection.

13. T. M. Allen to James S. Rollins, December 16, 1847, Rollins Collection; *Missouri Republican*, April 7, 1848.

14. John Wilson to Abiel Leonard, October 12, 1847, Leonard Collection. Wilson offered also to support Leonard either for the governorship or for Congress. There is no evidence that the ever-reluctant Leonard even considered the proposition.

15. George C. Bingham to James S. Rollins, March 10, 184[8]; T. M. Allen to James S. Rollins, December 16, 1847, Rollins Collection. This is the only association of Democrats and donkeys I have encountered.

16. *Missouri Statesman*, April 7, 1848; *Missouri Republican*, April 7, 1848, November 7, 1849.

17. Howard Glyndon, *Notable Men in "The House,"* 30; Frank F. Stephens, *A History of the University of Missouri*, 12; Jonas Viles, *The University of Missouri, A Centennial History*, 14–19.

18. W. V. N. Bay, *Reminiscences of the Bench and Bar of Missouri*, 252–55; Luther T. Collier to Barton Bates, April 4, 1848, Bates Papers (Missouri Historical Society, St. Louis), Jesse H. McIlvain to John F. Darby, May 22, 1848, Darby Papers; *Missouri Statesman*, April 21, 1848; *Missouri Republican*, April 7, 1848. Littleberry Hendricks to Abiel Leonard, October 28, 1839, Leonard Collection.

19. *Missouri Statesman*, May 26, June 2, July 14, 28, 1848; J. Claude Jones, "The Status of the Whig Party in Missouri from 1848–1854," 36–39. In 1840 George C. Sibley and Edward M. Samuel energetically campaigned, but they entered the field as eleventh-hour replacements for the two convention nominees who withdrew.

20. Resolutions of the Whig Central Committee printed in *Boonville Observer*, September 2, 1847; *Missouri Statesman*, January 28, April 14, May 29, August 4, 1848; *Jefferson Inquirer*, May 13, July 22, 1848.

21. Quoted from *Missouri Whig and General Advertiser* in *Missouri Statesman*, November 16, 1849.

22. As noted in a previous chapter, Jackson's veto of the Maysville Road bill in 1830 was phrased in terms of the road's local character. Democratic politicians thenceforth preserved consistency by favoring federal aid for internal improvements only "of a truly national character." This category included river improvement and extension of the national road westward, the only improvements which Missourians really expected the federal government to aid them in anyway. On the justness of Whig claims that Democrats had usurped their issue, see Primm, *Economic Policy in Missouri*, 98–99.

23. July 16, 1847, General George R. Smith Papers. See also John Wilson to [James S. Rollins], July 14, 1847, Rollins Collection.

24. *Jefferson Inquirer*, June 17, 1848; *Missouri Statesman*, May 12, June 9, 1848.

25. September 5, 1848, Rollins Collection. Clay's use of the term *conservative* to describe his own party was unusual but not unheard of. However, when Whigs referred to the measures they advocated, they described them as *liberal*, that is, liberal banking policy, liberal incorporation, liberal system

of internal improvements. Once within the same letter John Wilson stressed the duty of the "conservative power [Whigs]" to exert itself so that it could control the government and create "private corporations — with liberal charters." To [James S. Rollins], July 14, 1847, Rollins Collection.

26. *Jefferson Inquirer*, October 7, 1848; *Metropolitan* (Jefferson City), August 15, 1849; *Missouri Statesman*, August 25, 1848; Shoemaker, *Missouri and Missourians*, I, 178–89.

27. Shoemaker, *Missouri and Missourians*, I, 637.

28. *Missouri Statesman*, September 22, August 25, 1848.

29. Rollins, 33,970; Hendricks, 32,976; Taylor, 32,303. Democratic totals were as follows: Austin A. King (Governor), 48,913; Thomas L. Price (Lieut. Governor), 48,170; Cass, 39,021. Shoemaker, *Missouri and Missourians*, I, 637. Norman A. Graebner, "1848: Southern Politics at the Crossroads," *Historian*, 25 (November, 1962), 14–16, makes the point that Taylor drew support from Southern Democrats.

30. C. F. Burnam to James S. Rollins, February 12, 1847, Rollins Collection; Albert D. Kirwan, *John J. Crittenden, The Struggle for the Union*, 202–7.

31. George Penn to Meredith M. Marmaduke, February 27, 1848, Sappington Papers; B. H. Reeves to Abiel Leonard, September 15, 1847, Leonard Collection; James S. Rollins to Logan Hunton, July 4, 1848, Rollins Collection. Holman Hamilton, *Zachary Taylor, Soldier in the White House*, 17, 20, 66–67; Glyndon G. Van Deusen, *The Life of Henry Clay*, 385; Norman A. Graebner, "Thomas Corwin and the Election of 1848; A Study in Conservative Attitudes," *Journal of Southern History*, 17 (May, 1951), 170–76; Malcolm C. McMillan, ed., "Joseph Glover Baldwin Reports the Whig National Convention of 1848," *Journal of Southern History*, 25 (August, 1959), 375.

32. James S. Rollins to Logan Hunton, July 4, 1848, Rollins Collection; *Jefferson Inquirer*, April 8, 1848.

33. William H. Russell to D. D. Mitchell, January 13, 1849, John J. Crittenden Papers; Bay, *Bench and Bar of Missouri*, 402–3; *Missouri Statesman*, June 23, 29, 1848.

34. Missouri delegates were "typical" Taylor delegates. Three-fourths of his support at the convention came from normally Democratic districts in slave states. Apparently in other states the stratagem worked and normally Democratic voters were lured to the support of Taylor. Kirwan, *John J. Crittenden*, 222.

35. *Missouri Statesman*, August 31, September 8, 29, October 27, 1848; Committee of Invitation for South Missouri Mass Meeting of Taylor Men to John F. Darby, August 10, 1848, Darby Papers; Whigs of Lafayette County to Abiel Leonard, November, 1848, Leonard Collection; Marvin R. Cain, *Lincoln's Attorney General; Edward Bates of Missouri*, 65–67.

CHAPTER 13

1. December 6, 9, 1848.

2. December 4, 1848, Leonard Collection; James Winston to John J. Crittenden, December 7, 1848, John J. Crittenden Papers.

3. December 11, 1848, Leonard Collection.

4. December 15, 1848, Leonard Collection.

5. John C. Richardson to Abiel Leonard, February 13, 1849; Abiel Leon-

ard to John C. Richardson, January 27, 1849, Leonard Collection; D. D. Mitchell to John J. Crittenden, February 5, 1849, Crittenden Papers. There is no direct evidence of any communication between Birch and Rollins before or after the appointment. The only letters in the Rollins Collection from Birch were written thirty years later and make no reference to the 1849 episode. Birch to Rollins, February 28, 1877, February 9, 1884, January 30, June 8, 1885, Rollins Collection.

6. John G. Miller to John J. Crittenden, January 12, 1849, Crittenden Papers. Crittenden's biographer points out that Crittenden's influence over appointments was not as great as expected. He also relates that Crittenden came to look with disfavor on office seekers. Albert D. Kirwan, *John J. Crittenden, the Struggle for the Union*, 248–49.

7. John Wilson to [James S. Rollins], July 14, 1847, Rollins Collection; Charles Daniel Drake to Abiel Leonard and others, January 30, 1844, Leonard Collection; Marvin R. Cain, *Lincoln's Attorney General*, 67–68.

8. John F. Darby, *Personal Recollections*, 371, 403; W. V. N. Bay, *Reminiscences of the Bench and Bar of Missouri*, 252–55. Bay was a Democratic congressman. Geyer served three terms in the Missouri House of Representatives during the 1820's (twice as Speaker) and one term in the early 1830's. After that he had no public offices until he became Senator in 1850. Allen Johnson, ed., *Dictionary of American Biography*, VII, 231–33.

9. Darby, *Personal Recollections*, 399; J. Thomas Scharf, *History of St. Louis City and County from the Earliest Period to the Present Day; Including Biographical Sketches of Representative Men*, II, 1466; *Niles Weekly Register*, 72 (August 7, 1845), 4–5. The Whigs of Missouri gave Bates another honorarium in 1848 when they endorsed him for the vice-presidency at their state convention in April. However, nothing developed from this favorite-son candidacy, and Missouri delegates voted for Millard Fillmore on both vice-presidential ballots at the national convention. Luther T. Collier to Barton Bates, April 4, 1848, Bates Papers; *Missouri Statesman*, June 23, 1848.

10. In 1859 Rollins informed his son that Bates was "a distant relative of your Ma," but the fact that he had so to inform his adult son indicates that the relationship was distant socially as well as genealogically. On the other hand, Rollins had read law in Leonard's office. The two occasionally collaborated on legal matters, and they exchanged advice about investments. See James S. Rollins to James Hickman Rollins, April 10, 1859, Rollins Collection.

11. John G. Miller to Abiel Leonard, February 5, 1849, Leonard Collection.

12. John C. Richardson to Abiel Leonard, February 13, 1849, Leonard Collection.

13. Ewing was, more accurately, Secretary of the Home Department. His department was created in 1849 and originally went by that name. Richard B. Morris, ed., *Encyclopedia of American History*, 210.

14. Copies of letters from Abiel Leonard to Thomas Ewing, May 22, June 1, 1849, to Jacob Collamer, June 1, 1849, to Zachary Taylor, February 7, 9, 1849, seven letters to Taylor, no date, Leonard Collection. See Leonard Collection December, 1848, to March, 1849, for numerous letters about patronage. See also Edward Bates Diary, February 5, 1849 (Missouri Historical Society, St. Louis).

15. John Wilson to George R. Smith, January, 1849, General George R. Smith Papers. Wilson names other Whigs he has written in this letter.

16. John Wilson to Abiel Leonard, March 7, 1849, Whig Members of Missouri Legislature to Zachary Taylor (copy), February, 1849, John C. Richardson to Abiel Leonard, May 25, 1849, Leonard Collection; John Wilson to John F. Darby, November 30, 1850, Darby Papers; Holman Hamilton, *Zachary Taylor, Soldier in the White House,* 207.

17. May 23, 1849, Leonard Collection; John G. Miller to Thomas Ewing, June 9, 1849, Thomas Ewing Papers (Library of Congress).

18. Besides those letters noted already in the Leonard Collection, see J. S. Martin to George M. Smith, January 28, 1849, General George R. Smith Papers; Greer M. Davis to James S. Rollins, January 23, 1849; John B. Clark to James S. Rollins, December 28, 1848, Rollins Collection; Edward Bates to Thomas Ewing, May 2, 1849, John O'Fallon to Thomas Ewing, June 16, 1849, Ewing Papers; C. F. M. Noland to John F. Darby, January 5, 1848, John Darby to John J. Crittenden, November, 1848, Crittenden Papers.

19. To George R. Smith, January, 1849, General George R. Smith Papers.

20. June 14, 1849, Leonard Collection.

21. A. B. Chambers to Thomas Ewing, June 9, 1849, Ewing Papers.

22. December 18, 1848, Darby Papers.

23. Scharf, *History of St. Louis,* II, 1438, 1467–69; Bay, *Bench and Bar of Missouri,* 288–97.

CHAPTER 14

1. *Missouri Intelligencer,* January 5, 1833; *Salt River Journal* (Boonville), July 18, 1840; *Missouri Republican,* September 13, 1836.

2. *Missouri Statesman,* April 4, 1848; *The Metropolitan,* July 4, 1848; Clarence Henry McClure, *Opposition in Missouri to Thomas Hart Benton,* 131–38; *Laws of the State of Missouri Passed at the Session of the Fifteenth General Assembly,* 667–68.

3. James B. Bowlin to Howell Cobb, June 6, 1849, quoted in U. B. Phillips, ed., *Correspondence of Robert Toombs, Alexander H. Stephens, and Howell Cobb,* American Historical Association Annual Report 1911, II, 159–60.

4. *Missouri Republican,* November 7, 1848.

5. George Penn to Meredith M. Marmaduke, March 27, July 25, 1849, Sappington Papers.

6. John J. Lowry to Meredith M. Marmaduke, May 13, 1849, Sappington Papers. See also G. W. Hough to Meredith M. Marmaduke, December 22, 1849, Marmaduke Collection; Lisbon Applegate to Meredith M. Marmaduke, May 30, 1849, John R. Pile to Meredith M. Marmaduke, May 30, 1849, Sappington Papers.

7. *Journal of the House of Representatives of the State of Missouri at the Fifteenth General Assembly,* 392–94, 479–82; *Jefferson Inquirer,* March 3, 1849; *Missouri Statesman,* May 18, 1849.

8. Charles Daniel Drake to James S. Rollins, February 19, 1849, Rollins Collection.

9. Edward Bates Diary, August 23, 1849, Bates Papers.

10. *Missouri Statesman,* July 5, 1850.

11. Samuel Ralston to Col. D. D. Jordan, September 15, 1849, quoted in

W. Darrell Overdyke, ed., "A Southern Family on the Missouri Frontier: Letters from Independence, 1843–1855," *Journal of Southern History*, 17 (May, 1951), 225.

12. Martha Leonard to Abiel Leonard, July 4, 1850, Thomas E. Birch to Abiel Leonard, July 24, 1850, Leonard Collection; *Jefferson Inquirer*, July 6, 1850.

13. E. Stanley to Abiel Leonard, July 17, July 26, 1850, Thomas E. Birch to Abiel Leonard, July 24, 1850, Leonard Collection; *Missouri Statesman*, July 5, 1850.

14. *Missouri Republican*, May 21, July 27, 1850; *Jefferson Inquirer*, March 16, June 3, 8, 1850. In Platte County the Democrats aroused the indignation of Whigs, who had come to take the majority party division for granted, by forming a joint Benton-anti-Benton ticket. Thomas E. Birch to Abiel Leonard, July 24, 1850, Leonard Collection.

15. *Missouri Statesman*, October 25, 1850; William McPherson to John F. Darby, January 23, 1851, Darby Papers; Floyd C. Shoemaker, *Missouri and Missourians, Land of Contrasts and People of Achievements*, I, 638.

16. *Jefferson Inquirer*, August 17, 1850; Baker, "The Disintegration of the Whig Party in Missouri, 1850–1856," 37. Miss Baker's conclusions are more correct than her mathematics. The Whig vote in each year was approximately 41 per cent, not 31 per cent, as she states. See *Missouri Statesman*, October 25, 1850.

17. *Jefferson Inquirer*, August 24, 1850; *Missouri Statesman*, August 30, 1850.

18. John C. Richardson to Abiel Leonard, August 3, 1850, Samuel T. Glover to Abiel Leonard, August 3, 1850, John G. Miller to Abiel Leonard, August 24, 1850, Leonard Collection; *Missouri Statesman*, September 13, 1850.

19. *Missouri Republican*, September 28, 1850; Samuel T. Glover to Abiel Leonard, September 27, 1850, Leonard Collection.

20. James S. Rollins to Thomas Hart Benton, August 31, 1850, Rollins Collection.

21. *Journal of the House of Representatives of the State of Missouri at the Sixteenth General Assembly*, 62, 86–88, 123–48; Samuel T. Glover to Abiel Leonard, September 27, 1850, Leonard Collection; Baker, "Disintegration of the Whig Party," 43–45.

22. *Ibid.*, 146–48. Abiel Leonard to his wife [Jeanette Leonard], January 18, 1851, Leonard Collection; *Missouri Republican*, January 6, 10, 1851.

23. James S. Rollins to Abiel Leonard, February 5, 1851, Samuel T. Glover to Abiel Leonard, January 24, 1851, Leonard Collection; Edward Bates Diary, February, 1851 (marginal note by entry for December 22, 1850), Bates Papers.

24. James S. Rollins to Abiel Leonard, February 5, 1851, James O. Broadhead to Abiel Leonard, February 7, 1851, Samuel T. Glover to Abiel Leonard, January 24, 1851, Leonard Collection.

25. *House Journal, Sixteenth General Assembly*, 17; Baker, "Disintegration of the Whig Party," 42; *Missouri Statesman*, January 10, 1851.

26. William McPherson to John F. Darby, January 23, 1851, Darby Papers. John B. Clark and Samuel Young, who had endorsed Clark's apostasy during the summer campaign, briefly voted with the Anti-Bentons. See also Wayman

Crow to John F. Darby, January 2, 1851; Joseph B. Crockett to John F. Darby, February 2, 1851, Darby Papers; Joseph B. Crockett to Abiel Leonard, February 6, 1851, Leonard Collection.

27. Joseph B. Crockett to John F. Darby, February 2, 1851, Darby Papers.

28. *House Journal, Sixteenth General Assembly,* 417; Frederic Arthur Culmer, *A New History of Missouri,* 300–301; Henry S. Geyer to James S. Rollins, February 28, 1851, Samuel T. Glover to James S. Rollins, February 14, 1851, Rollins Collection.

29. James S. Rollins to Abiel Leonard, May 30, 1852, Leonard Collection.

30. James O. Broadhead to Abiel Leonard, February 7, March 16, 1851, Leonard Collection.

CHAPTER 15

1. *Missouri Statesman,* April 9, 1852; George C. Bingham to James S. Rollins, November 24, March 30, 1851, Rollins Collection; A. S. Mitchell to Abiel Leonard, December 5, 1851, Leonard Collection; George Penn to Meredith M. Marmaduke, April 10, 1851, Austin A. King to Meredith M. Marmaduke, February 10, 1852, Sappington Papers.

2. Robert Prewitt to Abiel Leonard, April 12, 1852, Leonard Collection.

3. Benjamin Tompkins to Abiel Leonard, May 31, 1852; James S. Rollins to Abiel Leonard, June 4, 1852, Leonard Collection; W. V. N. Bay, *Reminiscences of the Bench and Bar of Missouri,* 379–81. *Missouri Statesman,* May 21, 28, 1852; James S. Rollins to Abiel Leonard, May 30, 1852, Leonard Collection.

4. James S. Rollins to Thomas Hart Benton, August 31, 1850; October 23, 1851 (copies), Rollins Collection. *Missouri Statesman,* November 7, 1851.

5. *Ibid.,* June 6, 1849, Rollins Collection.

6. Thomas Hart Benton to James S. Rollins, November 8, 1851; James S. Rollins to Thomas Hart Benton (copy), June 6, 1849, Rollins Collection.

7. *Missouri Statesman,* November 7, 14, 21, December 5, 12, 1851, April 12, 1852; George Caleb Bingham to James S. Rollins, November 24, December 12, 1851, James O. Broadhead to James S. Rollins, January 11, 1852, *The Metropolitan* (copy), no date, Rollins Collection; Frederic Arthur Culmer, *New History of Missouri,* 309.

8. James Winston to Abiel Leonard, May 18, 1852, Leonard Collection; *Missouri Statesman,* April 30, 1852.

9. James S. Rollins to Abiel Leonard, May 30, 1852, Leonard Collection.

10. *Missouri Statesman,* June 4, 18, July 2, 1852, January 14, 1853. Price 46,493; Winston 32,686.

11. James S. Rollins to Abiel Leonard, May 30, June 4, July 18, 1852, T. Shackleford to Abiel Leonard, July 20, 1852, John G. Miller to Abiel Leonard, July 2, 1852, Leonard Collection; *Missouri Statesman,* May 14, 1852; *Jefferson Inquirer,* July 31, October 2, 1852.

12. Austin A. King to Meredith M. Marmaduke, February 10, 1852, Sappington Papers; *Jefferson Inquirer,* October 2, 1852; Clarence Henry McClure, *Opposition in Missouri to Thomas Hart Benton,* 153–56.

13. B. Gratz Brown to Orlando Brown, May 9, 1847, Orlando Brown Papers (Filson Club, Louisville, Kentucky); *Missouri Statesman,* June 4, 1852; Norma Lois Peterson, *Freedom and Franchise, The Political Career of B. Gratz Brown,* 12–17.

14. *Missouri Republican,* August 5, 1852; James S. Rollins to Abiel Leonard, August 6, 1852, Leonard Collection.

15. Edward Bates to Millard Fillmore, August 1, 1850, Henry S. Geyer to Edward Bates, August 6, 1850, John F. Darby to Millard Fillmore, December 8, 1852, January 11, 1853, Millard Fillmore Collection (Buffalo and Erie County Historical Society, Buffalo, New York); Marvin R. Cain, *Lincoln's Attorney General: Edward Bates of Missouri,* 70–71.

16. Robert J. Rayback, *Millard Fillmore, Biography of a President,* 249–54, 356–57; *Missouri Statesman,* February 27, 1852; *Missouri Republican,* April 17, 23, 1852.

17. John G. Miller to Abiel Leonard, May 1, 1852, Leonard Collection; *Missouri Republican,* April 14, 17, 23, 1852; Charles Winslow Elliot, *Winfield Scott, the Soldier and the Man,* 609–13. Scott's only Missouri press support came from the *St. Louis Evening News,* whose editor, Abram S. Mitchell, confided to Abiel Leonard that the real motive for his unusual course was to "excite the public" and thereby increase circulation. Mitchell to Leonard, February 10, 1852, Leonard Collection.

18. Miller to James S. Rollins, October 15, 1851, Rollins Collection.

19. *New York Daily Times,* June 19, 21, 23, 1852; *Missouri Statesman,* July 2, 1852.

20. October 22, 1852; Baker, "Disintegration of the Whig Party," 69; Mount Vernon Scott Club to Abiel Leonard, August 12, 1852, Leonard Collection.

21. Pierce 38,353; Scott 29,962; Price 46,494; Winston 32,686. *Missouri Statesman,* February 4, 11, 1853. The Democratic vote customarily receded by about 25 per cent in the November election.

22. Charles G. Sellers, Jr., "Who Were the Southern Whigs?" *American Historical Review,* 59 (January, 1954), 335–46; Raynor G. Wellington, *The Political and Sectional Influence of the Public Lands, 1828–1842,* 6, 25, 86–88.

23. Henry R. Mueller, *The Whig Party in Pennsylvania,* 202; Arthur Charles Cole, *The Whig Party in the South,* 245–74.

24. Cole, *Whig Party in the South,* 274–82; E. Merton Coulter, "The Downfall of the Whig Party in Kentucky," *Kentucky Register,* 23 (May, 1925), 164–68; Herbert J. Doherty, *The Whigs of Florida, 1845–1854,* 57–58.

CHAPTER 16

1. James Neal Primm, *Economic Policy in the Development of a Western State, Missouri, 1820–1860,* 105.

2. Samuel T. Glover to James S. Rollins, no date, Rollins Collection. The letter has reference to an impending senatorial election, but from the context it is impossible to determine whether it was written in 1850 or 1854. Other letters in which Whigs lament that internal improvements are not the divisive issue in Missouri politics are: John G. Miller to Abiel Leonard, July 2, 1852, John J. Lindley to Abiel Leonard, April 4, 1854, Z. G. Draper to Abiel Leonard, November 26, 1850, Abiel Leonard to Z. G. Draper, December 14, 1850, Leonard Collection; Garland C. Broadhead to James O. Broadhead, January 23, 1853, James O. Broadhead Papers (Missouri Historical Society, St. Louis). See also *Missouri Republican,* August 13, 1852. The *Republican*

professed agreement with Benton on railroad matters, but resented his appropriation of "Whig doctrine."

3. *Journal of the House of Representatives of the State of Missouri at the Extra Session of the Seventeenth General Assembly*, 90–91; Primm, *Economic Policy in Missouri*, 66–68; 103–4.

4. Samuel Bannister Harding, *Life of George R. Smith, Founder of Sedalia, Mo.*, 153–75; Thomas T. January to James S. Rollins, December 13, 1853, January 10, 17, November 3, 18, December 3, 1854, James E. Tutt to James S. Rollins, June 28, September 3, 1853, January 21, November 28, December 23, 1855, Rollins Collection.

5. *St. Louis Intelligencer*, September 3, 1852; *Missouri Statesman*, September 3, 1852; J. Claude Jones, "The Status of the Whig Party in Missouri from 1848–1854," 141–42.

6. A. S. Mitchell to Abiel Leonard, September 3, 9, 1852, Leonard Collection; *House Journal, Seventeenth General Assembly, Extra Session*, 6–43; *Jefferson Inquirer*, February 2, 1853.

7. *Missouri Statesman*, September 2, 1852, March 4, 1853.

8. *Ibid.*, June 3, 1853.

9. J. P. Vaughan to James S. Rollins, March 24, 1853, Rollins Collection; John C. Richardson to Abiel Leonard, May 30, 1853, Leonard Collection.

10. John C. Richardson to Abiel Leonard, May 30, 1853, Leonard Collection; Frank P. Blair, Jr., to James S. Rollins, July 1, 1853, Rollins Collection; *Jefferson Inquirer*, June 25, 1853; *Missouri Statesman*, July 22, September 23, 1853.

11. *Missouri Statesman*, August 19, 22, 1853; *Jefferson Inquirer*, August 20, 1853.

12. *Jefferson Inquirer*, August 20, 1853.

13. A. S. Mitchell to Abiel Leonard, September 3, 1852, Leonard Collection; W. V. N. Bay, *Reminiscences of the Bench and Bar of Missouri*, 569–71.

14. Arthur Charles Cole, *The Whig Party in the South*, 305; *Missouri Statesman*, March 10, April 7, 1854; *The Congressional Globe, First Session, Thirty-Third Congress*, 27 (Washington, D. C., 1854), 874, 1209, 1222, 1254.

15. Cole, *Whig Party in the South*, 295–305; Joseph H. Parks, "The Tennessee Whigs and the Kansas-Nebraska Bill," *Journal of Southern History*, 10 (August, 1944), 308–30; Herbert J. Doherty, *The Whigs of Florida, 1845–1854*, 59.

16. Bingham to James S. Rollins, April 16, February 1, 1854, Rollins Collection; William Nisbet Chambers, *Old Bullion Benton, Senator from the New West, Thomas Hart Benton, 1782–1858*, 401–4.

17. James S. Rollins to Abiel Leonard, January 16, 1854, Notations by Leonard, January 7 and February 4, 1854, on letter from Whig Congressmen of Missouri to Abiel Leonard, January 7, 1854, Leonard Collection; John G. Miller to James S. Rollins, March 9, 1854, William T. Wood to James S. Rollins, March 18, 1854, Rollins Collection; *Missouri Statesman*, March 10, 1854; *Missouri Republican*, March 23, 1854.

18. James Lusk to Meredith M. Marmaduke, February 18, 1854, Sappington Papers.

19. William T. Wood to James S. Rollins, March 18, 1854, Rollins Collection; William T. Wood to Abiel Leonard, April 6, 1854, Leonard Collection.

CHAPTER 17

1. *Whig Messenger* (Hannibal), June 15, 1854; *Missouri Republican* (St. Louis), August 3, 1854.

2. Samuel T. Glover to James O. Broadhead, June 3, 1854, Broadhead Papers; James J. Lindley to Abiel Leonard, June 28, 1854, Frank P. Blair, Jr., to Abiel Leonard, July 18, 1854, Allen P. Richardson to Abiel Leonard, August 1, 1854, Abiel Leonard to Allen P. Richardson, July 20, 1854, Leonard Collection; *Jefferson Inquirer*, June 24, 1854; *Missouri Statesman*, October 13, 1854.

3. John G. Miller to James S. Rollins, March 9, 1854, Rollins Collection; *Missouri Statesman*, June 9, 23, 1854.

4. *Missouri Statesman*, February 10, 1854. For election returns, see *Missouri Statesman*, October 13, 1854. For information on Kennett, see J. Thomas Scharf, *History of St. Louis City and County from the Earliest Periods to the Present Day; Including Biographical Sketches of Representative Men*, I, 683.

5. *Missouri Statesman*, October 13, 1854; *Missouri Republican*, December 19, 1854.

6. Joe Davis to Abiel Leonard, December 27, 1854, Leonard Collection; R. S. Thomas to James S. Rollins, November 9, 1854, Rollins Collection; *A Statement of Facts and a Few Suggestions in Review of Political Action in Missouri* (pamphlet, 1856) at State Historical Society of Missouri, Columbia.

7. Joe Davis to Abiel Leonard, January 1, 1855, Leonard Collection; R. S. Thomas to James S. Rollins, November 9, 1854, Rollins Collection; letter from Edward Bates in *Whig Messenger*, February 8, 1855, cited in Frederic Arthur Culmer, *A New History of Missouri*, 322.

8. Abiel Leonard to W. V. N. Bay, November 11, 1854, Leonard Collection. Leonard's determination not to run for office unless he could be assured of both victory and the absence of opposition cannot be exaggerated. The following letters all contain assurances that Leonard would not be opposed for the judicial position. In most cases the context indicates that Leonard had requested such assurances. Letters to Leonard from Willard P. Hall, November 14, 1854; Samuel T. Glover, November 8, 1854; W. V. N. Bay, November 6, 1854; James O. Broadhead, November 3, 1854; Charles D. Drake, October 21, 1854; B. F. Stringfellow, December 6, 1854; J. J. Lindley, December 7, 1854, Leonard Collection. See Chapter 3, pp. 19–21, and Chapter 4, pp. 31–32, for discussion of the amendments struggle in the 1830's.

9. John C. Richardson to Abiel Leonard, October 30, 1854, Samuel T. Glover to Abiel Leonard, November 8, 1854, Leonard Collection.

10. Richardson's background was very similar to Rollins'. Both were from Kentucky; both had studied at Transylvania; Richardson was only three years younger than Rollins. As lawyers Richardson and Glover enjoyed far more recognition than Rollins did. W. V. N. Bay, *Reminiscences of the Bench and Bar of Missouri*, 513–15; Scharf, *History of St. Louis*, II, 1494–95.

11. James S. Rollins to John Dougherty, December 11, 1854, John Dougherty to James S. Rollins, Gilchrist Porter to James S. Rollins, September 7, 1854, Rollins Collection; James S. Rollins to Abiel Leonard, November 29, 1854, Leonard Collection.

12. Samuel T. Glover to Abiel Leonard, November 5, 1854, Joe Davis to Abiel Leonard, December 27, 1854, Leonard Collection.

13. *Journal of the House of Representatives of the State of Missouri at the First Session of the Eighteenth General Assembly*, 9.

14. A. S. Mitchell to James S. Rollins, November 25, 1851, Rollins Collection.

15. John C. McCoy to Pettis County Representatives, January 17, 1855, General George R. Smith Papers; *Missouri Statesman*, January 26, 1855; Edward Bates to James S. Rollins, February 2, 1855, Charles Daniel Drake to James S. Rollins, March 17, 1855, Thomas P. Rubey to James S. Rollins, January 25, 1855, Rollins Collection. Rubey was a Benton Democrat.

16. *Missouri Statesman*, February 9, 16, March 16, 1855.

17. *House Journal, Eighteenth General Assembly, First Session*, 112, 139–42; *A Statement of Facts and a Few Suggestions in Review of Political Action in Missouri*, 68–73; George Caleb Bingham to James S. Rollins, November 24, 1851, Rollins Collection.

18. *Missouri Statesman*, December 14, 1855.

19. *Journal of the House of Representatives of the State of Missouri at the Adjourned Session of the Eighteenth General Assembly*, 50–51.

20. Thomas B. Alexander, "Persistent Whiggery in the Confederate South, 1860–1877," *Journal of Southern History*, 27 (August, 1961), 305–30; Thomas B. Alexander, "Persistent Whiggery in Alabama and the Lower South, 1860–1867," *The Alabama Review*, 12 (January, 1959), 35–42; Thomas B. Alexander, "Whiggery and Reconstruction in Tennessee," *Journal of Southern History*, 16 (August, 1950), 291–305; David H. Donald, "The Scalawag in Mississippi Reconstruction," *Journal of Southern History*, 10 (November, 1944), 447–60; Daniel M. Robison, "The Whigs in the Politics of the Confederacy," *East Tennessee Historical Society Publications*, 11 (1939), 3–11. More general studies of American political parties also frequently take it for granted that the Whig party reincarnated in some form. See, for example, Wilfred E. Binkley, *American Political Parties, Their Natural History*, 195, 203; Seymour Martin Lipset, *Political Man, The Social Bases of Politics*, 380–84.

21. *Missouri Republican*, July 1, August 4, 1856; James O. Broadhead to James S. Rollins, March 16, 1856, George Caleb Bingham to James S. Rollins, June 2, 1856, Rollins Collection.

22. Gilchrist Porter to James S. Rollins, December 24, 1855, Rollins Collection. See also December 22, 1855.

23. *Letter of Hon. Mordecai Oliver, of Missouri, to Robert H. Miller, Esq., editor of the Liberty (Missouri) Tribune* (reprinted in pamphlet form, 1856 [available at Library of Congress]); *Letter of Samuel Caruthers to His Constituents Explaining His Past Action, Defining his Present Position, and the Position of Parties*; *Biographical Directory of the American Congress, 1774–1961*, 1220, 1859.

24. Howard K. Beale, ed., *The Diary of Edward Bates, 1859–1866*, Annual Report of the American Historical Association, 1930, IV, 136–38; William Ernest Smith, *The Francis Preston Blair Family in Politics*, I, 489–92; *Missouri Statesman*, June 8, 1860.

25. Thomas S. Barclay, *The Liberal Republican Movement in Missouri, 1865–1871*, passim.

BIBLIOGRAPHY

Manuscripts

Autobiography of Thomas L. Anderson. Western Historical Manuscripts Collection, University of Missouri, Columbia
Ashley Papers. Missouri Historical Society, St. Louis
David Rice Atchison Papers. Western Historical Manuscripts Collection, University of Missouri, Columbia
Bates Papers. Missouri Historical Society, St. Louis
Benton Papers. Missouri Historical Society, St. Louis
James H. Birch to Joseph Bogy, March 12, 1840, appended to copy of "Address of the Central Committee to the People of the State of Missouri" [n.p., n.d.]. Library of Missouri Historical Society, St. Louis
James O. Broadhead Papers. Missouri Historical Society, St. Louis
Orlando Brown Papers. Filson Club, Louisville, Kentucky
Henry Clay Papers. Library of Congress, Washington, D.C.
Thomas Corwin Papers. Library of Congress, Washington, D. C.
John J. Crittenden Papers. Library of Congress, Washington, D. C.
Darby Papers. Missouri Historical Society, St. Louis
Edward Dobyn Memoir. Missouri Historical Society, St. Louis
Dougherty Papers. Missouri Historical Society, St. Louis
Charles Daniel Drake Autobiography. State Historical Society of Missouri, Columbia
Daniel Dunklin Collection. Western Historical Manuscripts Collection, University of Missouri, Columbia
Rufus Easton Papers. Missouri Historical Society, Columbia
Millard Fillmore Collection. Buffalo and Erie County Historical Society, Buffalo, New York
Hamilton Fish Papers. Library of Congress, Washington, D. C.
Gamble Papers. Missouri Historical Society, St. Louis
Charles Gibson Papers. Missouri Historical Society, St. Louis.
Governors' Papers. Missouri Historical Society, St. Louis
Leonard Collection. State Historical Society of Missouri, Columbia. There are also Leonard Papers in the Western Historical Manuscripts Collection, University of Missouri, Columbia, and at the Missouri Historical Society, St. Louis. Only the collection at the State Historical Society is cited in this study.

Thomas Lenoir Letters. Western Historical Manuscripts Collection, University of Missouri, Columbia

Marmaduke Collection. State Historical Society of Missouri, Columbia

Miscellaneous Manuscripts Collection. State Historical Society of Missouri, Columbia

William B. Napton Diary. Missouri Historical Society, St. Louis

O'Fallon Papers. Filson Club, Louisville, Kentucky

Political Papers. Missouri Historical Society, St. Louis

Governor Thomas Reynolds Papers. Missouri Historical Society, St. Louis

Rollins Collection. State Historical Society of Missouri, Columbia

St. Louis (City) Tax List, Book I, A-L, 1847–1848. Missouri Historical Society, St. Louis

Sappington Papers. Missouri Historical Society, St. Louis. There are also Sappington Papers at the State Historical Socity of Missouri, but that collection is not cited in this study

Seventh Census of the United States, 1850. Microfilm copy in State Historical Society of Missouri, Columbia

Seventh Census of the United States, 1850, Slave Schedule. Microfilm copy in State Historical Society of Missouri, Columbia

George C. Sibley Papers. Missouri Historical Society, St. Louis

General George R. Smith Papers. Missouri Historical Society, St. Louis. There is a small George R. Smith collection at the State Historical Society of Missouri at Columbia that is not cited in this study.

Thomas A. Smith Collection. State Historical Society of Missouri, Columbia

Isaac Sturgeon Papers. Missouri Historical Society, St. Louis

Tate Family Papers. Western Historical Manuscripts Collection, University of Missouri, Columbia

Elmire P. Tesson Collection. Missouri Historical Society, St. Louis

Judge Samuel Treat Papers. Missouri Historical Society, St. Louis

John Tyler Papers. Library of Congress, Washington, D. C.

Martin Van Buren Papers. Library of Congress, Washington, D. C.

Daniel Webster Papers. Library of Congress, Washington, D. C.

Newspapers

Files of all Missouri newspapers listed below are in the State Historical Society of Missouri at Columbia, except where otherwise indicated.

American Bulletin, St. Louis

Boon's Lick Times, Fayette

Columbia Patriot

Farmers and Mechanics Advocate, St. Louis

Jefferson Inquirer, Jefferson City

Jeffersonian Republican, Jefferson City
Mill Boy, St. Louis
Missouri Argus, St. Louis
Missouri Intelligencer, Fayette and Columbia
Missouri Register, Boonville
Missouri Republican, St. Louis. Missouri Historical Society, St. Louis
Missouri Statesman, Columbia
Missouri Whig and General Advertiser, Palmyra
National Intelligencer, Washington, D. C.
New York Daily Times
Niles Weekly Register, Washington, D. C.
St. Louis Beacon
St. Louis Intelligencer
St. Louis Daily Union
Salt River Journal, Boonville
The Metropolitan, Jefferson City
Weekly Observer, Boonville
Western Emigrant, Boonville
Western Monitor, Fayette
Whig Messenger, Hannibal

Pamphlets

A Statement of Facts and a Few Suggestions in Review of Political Action in Missouri [n.p., 1856]. State Historical Society of Missouri, Columbia.

Address of the Central Tippecanoe Club of Callaway County to the Independent Voters of Callaway [n.p., n.d.]. State Historical Society of Missouri, Columbia.

Birch, James Harvey, *Address to the People of the State of Missouri* [n.p., n.d.]. State Historical Society of Missouri, Columbia.

Cleland, Beriah, *An Historical Account of All the Mayors Since the Formation of the City Government of St. Louis to the Present — 1846* [n.p., n.d.]. Missouri Historical Society, St. Louis.

Journal of the National Republican Convention which Assembled in The City of Baltimore, Dec. 12, 1831. Washington [n.p.], 1831. Library of Congress, Washington, D. C.

Letter of Samuel Caruthers to His Constituents Explaining his Past Action, Defending his Present Position, and the Position of Parties. Washington, Congressional Globe Office, 1856. Library of Congress, Washington, D. C.

Letter of Hon. Mordecai Oliver, of Missouri, to Robert H. Miller, Esq. of the Liberty (Missouri) Tribune [n.p., n.d.]. Library of Congress, Washington, D. C.

Government Publications

Biographical Directory of the American Congress, 1774–1961. Washington, D. C., Government Printing Office, 1961.

Congressional Globe, First Session, Thirty-Third Congress, Vol. 27. Washington, D. C., John C. Rives, 1854.

Constitution of the State of Missouri, 1845. Jefferson City, James Lusk, 1845.

DeBow, J. D. B., *Statistical View of the United States, Being a Compendium of the Seventh Census.* Washington, A. O. P. Nicholson, Public Printer, 1854.

————, *The Seventh Census of the United States: 1850.* Washington, R. Armstrong, Public Printer, 1853.

Journal of the House of Representatives of the State of Missouri at the Fifth General Assembly. Jefferson City, Calvin Gunn, 1829.

Journal of the House of Representatives of the State of Missouri at the Sixth General Assembly. Fayette, Western Monitor, 1831.

Journal of the House of Representatives of the State of Missouri at the Eighth General Assembly. Fayette, W. B. Napton, 1835.

Journal of the House of Representatives of the State of Missouri at the Tenth General Assembly. Jefferson City, Calvin Gunn, 1839.

Journal of the House of Representatives of the State of Missouri at the Eleventh General Assembly. Jefferson City, W. Lusk and Son, 1841.

Journal of the House of Representatives of the State of Missouri at the First Session of the Twelfth General Assembly. Jefferson City, W. Lusk and Son, 1843.

Journal of the House of Representatives of the State of Missouri at the Thirteenth General Assembly. Jefferson City, James Lusk, 1845.

Journal of the House of Representatives of the State of Missouri at the Fifteenth General Assembly. Jefferson City, James Lusk, 1849.

Journal of the House of Representatives of the State of Missouri at the Sixteenth General Assembly. Jefferson City, James Lusk, 1851.

Journal of the House of Representatives of the State of Missouri at the Extra Session of the Seventeenth General Assembly. Jefferson City, James Lusk, 1852.

Journal of the House of Representatives of the State of Missouri at the Adjourned Session of the Seventeenth General Assembly. Jefferson City, James Lusk, 1853.

Journal of the House of Representatives of the State of Missouri at the First Session of the Eighteenth General Assembly. Jefferson City, James Lusk, 1855.

Journal of the House of Representatives of the State of Missouri at the Adjourned Session of the Eighteenth General Assembly. Jefferson City, James Lusk, 1855.

Journal of the Senate of the State of Missouri at the Third General Assembly, St. Charles, Duff Green, 1825.

Journal of the Senate of the State of Missouri at the Fifth General Assembly. Jefferson City, Calvin Gunn, 1829.

Kennedy, J. C. G., *The Seventh Census, Report of the Superintendent of the Census for December 1, 1852 to which is Appended the Report for December 1, 1851*. Washington, Government Printing Office, 1853.

Laws of the State of Missouri Passed at the Fifth General Assembly. Jefferson City, Calvin Gunn, 1829.

Laws of the State of Missouri Passed at the First Session of the Ninth General Assembly. Jefferson City, Calvin Gunn, 1838.

Laws of the State of Missouri Passed at the Second Session of the Twelfth General Assembly. Jefferson City, James Lusk, 1844.

Leopard, Buel, and Floyd C. Shoemaker, eds. *The Messages and Proclamations of the Governors of the State of Missouri*, Vols. I and II. Columbia, The State Historical Society of Missouri, 1922.

Register of Debates in Congress. Twentieth Congress. Washington, D. C., Gales and Seaton, 1828.

Register of Debates in Congress. Twenty-First Congress, Vol. II. Washington, D. C., Gales and Seaton, 1828.

Revised Statutes of the State of Missouri. St. Louis, J. W. Dougherty, 1845.

Published Collections

Adams, Charles Francis, ed., *Memoirs of John Quincy Adams, Comprising Portions of His Diary from 1795–1848*. Philadelphia, J. B. Lippincott and Co., 1874–1877. 12 vols.

Bassett, John Spencer, ed., *The Correspondence of Andrew Jackson*. Washington, Carnegie Institution of Washington, 1926–1933. 6 vols.

Beale, Howard K., ed., *The Diary of Edward Bates, 1859–1866*. Annual Report of the American Historical Association, 1930, IV. Washington, United States Government Printing Office, 1933.

Fitzpatrick, John C., ed., *The Autobiography of Martin Van Buren*. Annual Report of the American Historical Association, 1918, I. Washington, United States Government Printing Office, 1920.

Lucas, John B. C., ed., *Letters of Honorable John B. C. Lucas from 1815 to 1836*. St. Louis, privately printed, 1905.

McGrane, Reginald, ed., *The Correspondence of Nicholas Biddle dealing with National Affairs — 1807–1844*. Boston, Houghton Mifflin and Company, 1919.

McMillan, Malcolm C., ed., "Joseph Glover Baldwin Reports the Whig National Convention of 1848," *Journal of Southern History*, 25 (August, 1959), 366–82.

Overdyke, W. Darrell, ed., "A Southern Family on the Missouri Frontier: Letters from Independence, 1843–1855," *Journal of Southern History*, 17 (May, 1951), 216–37.

Phillips, U. B., ed., *Correspondence of Robert Toombs, Alexander H. Stephens and Howell Cobb*. Annual Report of the American Historical Association, 1911, II. Washington, United States Government Printing Office, 1913.

Richardson, James D., ed., *A Compilation of the Messages and Papers of the Presidents, 1789–1902*. New York, Bureau of National Literature, 1897–1902. 10 vols.

Tyler, Lyon G., *The Letters and Times of the Tylers*. Richmond, Whittet and Shepperson, 1885. 2 vols.

Articles

Alexander, Thomas B., "Persistent Whiggery in Alabama and the Lower South, 1860–1867." *Alabama Review*, 12 (January, 1959), 35–52.

———, "Persistent Whiggery in the Confederate South, 1860–1877." *Journal of Southern History*, 27 (August, 1961), 305–29.

———, "Whiggery and Reconstruction in Tennessee." *Journal of Southern History*, 16 (August, 1950), 291–305.

Alexander, Thomas B., Kit C. Carter, and others, "Who Were the Alabama Whigs?" *The Alabama Review*, 16 (January, 1963), 5–19.

Anderson, Hattie M., "Frontier Economic Problems in Missouri, 1815–1828, Part II." *Missouri Historical Review*, 34 (January, 1940), 182–203.

Bone, Hugh A., "Political Parties and Pressure Group Politics." *Annals of the American Academy of Political and Social Science*, 309 (September, 1958), 73–83.

Chambers, William N., "Party Development and Party Action: The American Origins." *History and Theory: Studies in the Philosophy of History*, 3, No. 1 (1963), 92–114.

Cochran, Thomas C., "The 'Presidential Synthesis' in American History." *American Historical Review*, 53 (July, 1948), 748–59.

Collins, Arthur Loyd, "The Anti-Masonic Movement in Early Missouri." *Missouri Historical Review*, 39 (October, 1944), 45–52.

Coulter, E. Merton, "The Downfall of the Whig Party in Kentucky." *Kentucky Register*, 23 (May, 1925), 162–74.

Culmer, Frederic Arthur, "Abiel Leonard," *Missouri Historical Review*, 27 (January, 1933), 113–31.

Darling, Arthur B., "Jacksonian Democracy in Massachusetts, 1821–1848." *American Historical Review*, 29 (January, 1924), 271–87.

Donald, David H., "The Scalawag in Mississippi Reconstruction." *Journal of Southern History*, 10 (November, 1944), 447–60.

Dorsey, Dorothy B., "The Panic and Depression of 1837–1843 in Missouri." *Missouri Historical Review*, 30 (October, 1935), 132–61.

Eaton, Clement, "Southern Senators and the Right of Instruction, 1789–1860." *Journal of Southern History*, 18 (August, 1952), 303–19.

"Famous Personages of the Civil War in Missouri: Charles D. Drake." *Missouri Historical Review*, 56 (January, 1962), back cover.

Foley, William E., "The Political Philosophy of David Barton." *Missouri Historical Review*, 58 (April, 1964), 278–89.

Gates, Paul W., "The Railroads of Missouri, 1850–1870." *Missouri Historical Review*, 26 (January, 1932), 126–41.

Graebner, Norman A., "1848: Southern Politics at the Crossroads." *Historian*, 25 (November, 1962), 14–35.

———, "Thomas Corwin and the Election of 1848: A Study in Conservative Politics." *Journal of Southern History*, 17 (May, 1951), 162–79.

Haller, Mark H., "The Rise of the Jackson Party in Maryland, 1820–1829." *Journal of Southern History*, 27 (August, 1962), 307–26.

Higham, John, "Beyond Consensus: The Historian as Moral Critic." *American Historical Review*, 67 (April, 1962), 609–25.

Hoffman, William S., "Willie P. Magnum and the Whig Revival of the Doctrine of Instructions." *Journal of Southern History*, 22 (August, 1956), 338–54.

Houf, Walter R., "Organized Labor in Missouri Politics Before the Civil War." *Missouri Historical Review*, 56 (April, 1962), 244–54.

Krauthoff, L. C., "The Supreme Court of Missouri." *The Green Bag*, 3 (1891), 157–90.

Lyon, William H., "Claiborne Fox Jackson and the Secession Crisis in Missouri." *Missouri Historical Review*, 58 (July, 1964), 422–41.

McCormick, Richard P., "New Perspectives on Jacksonian Politics." *American Historical Review*, 65 (January, 1960), 288–301.

———, Review of Charles McCool Snyder, *The Jacksonian Heritage: Pennsylvania Politics, 1833–1848* (Harrisburg, 1958). *American Historical Review*, 64 (July, 1959), 967–68.

McWhiney, Grady, "Were the Whigs a Class Party in Alabama?" *Journal of Southern History*, 23 (November, 1957), 510–22.

Merk, Frederick, "Presidential Fevers." *Mississippi Valley Historical Review*, 48 (June, 1960), 3–33.

"Missouriana." *Missouri Historical Review*, 35 (April, 1941), 401–43.

Moore, Powell, "The Revolt Against Jackson in Tennessee, 1835–1836." *Journal of Southern History*, 2 (August, 1936), 335–59.

Newhard, Leota M., "The Beginnings of the Whig Party in Missouri." *Missouri Historical Review*, 25 (January, 1931), 254–80.

Nichols, Roy F., Review of Glyndon G. Van Deusen, *Thurlow Weed: Wizard of the Lobby* (Boston, 1947). *Mississippi Valley Historical Review*, 34 (September, 1947), 305–7.

Parks, Joseph H., "The Tennessee Whigs and the Kansas-Nebraska Bill." *Journal of Southern History*, 10 (August, 1944), 308–30.

Parrish, William E., "David Rice Atchison: 'Faithful Champion of the Old South.'" *Missouri Historical Review*, 51 (January, 1957), 113–25.

———, "David Rice Atchison, Frontier Politician." *Missouri Historical Review*, 50 (July, 1956), 339–54.

Phillips, Ulrich B., "The Southern Whigs, 1834–1854." In Guy Stanton Ford, ed., *Essays in American History Dedicated to Frederick Jackson Turner*. New York, Henry Holt, 1910, 211–35.

Pomeroy, Earl, "Toward a Reorientation of Western History: Continuity and Environment." *Mississippi Valley Historical Review*, 41 (March, 1955), 579–600.

Robison, Daniel M., "The Whigs in the Politics of the Confederacy." *East Tennessee Historical Society Publications*, 11 (1939), 3–11.

Sellers, Charles G., Jr., "Who Were the Southern Whigs?" *American Historical Review*, 59 (January, 1954), 335–46.

Sharp, James Roger, "Governor Daniel Dunklin's Jacksonian Democracy in Missouri, 1832–1836." *Missouri Historical Review*, 56 (April, 1962), 217–29.

Sydnor, Charles S., "The One-Party Period of American History." *American Historical Review*, 51 (April, 1946), 439–51.

Templin, Lucinda de Leftwich, "Two Illustrious Pioneers in the Education of Women in Missouri; Major George C. Sibley and Mary Easton Sibley." *Missouri Historical Review*, 21 (April, 1927), 420–37.

Van Deusen, Glyndon G., "Some Aspects of Whig Thought and Theory in the Jacksonian Period." *American Historical Review*, 63 (January, 1958), 305–22.

Viles, Jonas, "Sections and Sectionalism in a Border State." *Mississippi Valley Historical Review*, 21 (June, 1934), 3–22.

Wallace, Carolyn Andrews, "David Lowry Swain, The First Whig Governor of North Carolina." In J. Carlyle Sitterson, ed., *Studies in Southern History*, The James Sprunt Studies in History and Political Science, XLII. Chapel Hill, University of North Carolina Press, 1960, 62–84.

Winston, James E., "The Mississippi Whigs and the Tariff, 1834–1844." *Mississippi Valley Historical Review*, 22 (December, 1935), 505–24.

Theses and Dissertations

Unless otherwise indicated all theses and dissertations listed were completed at the University of Missouri, Columbia.

Anderson, Hattie M., "A Study in Frontier Democracy; the Social Bases of the Rise of the Jackson Group in Missouri." Doctoral dissertation, 1935.

Baker, Eula Blythe, "The Disintegration of the Whig Party in Missouri, 1850–1856." Master's thesis, 1932.

Bradford, Priscilla, "The Missouri Constitutional Controversy of 1845." Master's thesis, 1936.

Cave, Alfred Alexander, "The Jacksonian Movement in American Historiography." Doctoral dissertation, University of Florida, Gainesville, 1961.

Hall, Elizabeth Dorset, "William Franklin Switzler, Editor, Politician, and Humanitarian." Master's thesis, 1951.

Hartley, James Robert, "The Political Career of Lewis Fields Linn." Master's thesis, 1951.

Hensley, Orlana, "The Thomas Hart Benton Faction in Missouri Politics, 1850–1860." Master's thesis, 1931.

Herzer, Margaret B., "The Whig Party in Missouri, 1828–1831." Master's thesis, Washington University, St. Louis, Missouri, 1922.

Hines, A. Clarence, "The Beginnings of the Democratic Party in Missouri, 1824–1836." Master's thesis, 1930.

Houf, Walter R., "Fifty Years of Missouri Labor, 1820–1870." Master's thesis, 1958.

Hughes, Ora E., "The Attitudes of the Missouri Members of Congress toward the Oregon and Texas Questions, 1840–1846." Master's thesis, 1943.

Jones, J. Claude, "The Status of the Whig Party in Missouri from 1848–1854." Master's thesis, 1930.

McCandless, Perry M., "Thomas H. Benton, His Source of Political Strength in Missouri from 1815 to 1838." Doctoral dissertation, 1953.

McClure, Clarence Henry, "Opposition in Missouri to the Reelection of Thomas Hart Benton in 1844." Master's thesis, 1913.

McHugh, George J., "Political Nativism in St. Louis, 1840–1857." Master's thesis, St. Louis University, St. Louis, 1939.

March, David D., "The Life and Times of Charles Daniel Drake." Doctoral dissertation, 1949.

Newhard, Leota M., "The Beginnings of the Whig Party in Missouri, 1824–1840." Master's thesis, 1928.

Norton, Leslie M., "A History of the Whig Party in Louisiana." Doctoral dissertation, Louisiana State University, Baton Rouge, Louisiana, 1940.

Pegg, Herbert Dale, "The Whig Party in North Carolina, 1834–1861." Doctoral dissertation, University of North Carolina, Chapel Hill, North Carolina, 1932.

Ulbricht, John H., "Frank P. Blair, Jr., and Missouri Politics, 1856–1860." Master's thesis, 1936.

West, Alma, "The Earlier Political Career of Claiborne Fox Jackson, 1836–1851." Master's thesis, 1941.

Books

A *Memorial and Biographical Record of Jackson County, Missouri.* Chicago, National Historical Company, 1896.

Abernethy, Thomas Perkins, *From Frontier to Plantation in Tennessee, A Study in Frontier Democracy.* Chapel Hill, University of North Carolina Press, 1932.

Agar, Herbert, *The Price of Union.* Boston, Houghton Mifflin Company, 1950.

Atherton, Lewis E., *The Pioneer Merchant in Mid-America.* University of Missouri Studies, Vol. XIV. Columbia, University of Missouri, 1939.

Barclay, Thomas S., *The Liberal Republican Movement in Missouri 1865–1871.* Columbia, Missouri. State Historical Society of Missouri, 1926.

———, *The Movement for Municipal Home Rule in St. Louis.* University of Missouri Studies, Vol. XVIII. Columbia, University of Missouri, 1943.

Bay, W. V. N., *Reminiscences of the Bench and Bar of Missouri.* St. Louis, F. H. Thomas Company, 1878.

Beard, Charles A., *The American Party Battle.* New York, The Macmillan Company, 1928.

Benson, Lee, *The Concept of Jacksonian Democracy, New York as a Test Case.* Princeton, Princeton University Press, 1961.

Benton, Thomas Hart, *Thirty Years' View, or, A History of the Working of the American Government for Thirty Years, from 1820 to 1850.* New York, D. Appleton and Company, 1854. 2 vols.

Billington, Ray Allen, *The Protestant Crusade, 1800–1860, A Study of the Origins of American Nativism.* New York, The Macmillan Company, 1938.

Billon, Frederic L., *Annals of St. Louis in Its Territorial Days from 1804 to 1821.* St. Louis, privately printed, 1888.

Binkley, Wilfred E., *American Political Parties, Their Natural History.* New York, Alfred A. Knopf, 1943.

Brogan, D. W., *Politics in America.* New York, Doubleday & Company, Inc., 1954.

Burnham, W. Dean, *Presidential Ballots, 1836–1892.* Baltimore, Johns Hopkins University Press, 1955.

Cain, Marvin R., *Lincoln's Attorney General: Edward Bates of Missouri.* Columbia, University of Missouri Press, 1965.

Caldwell, Gaylon L., *American Government Today.* New York, W. W. Norton & Company, Inc., 1963.

Campbell, Angus, Gerald Gorin, and Warren E. Miller, *The Voter Decides*. Evanston, Illinois, Row, Peterson and Company, 1954.

Capers, Gerald M., *John C. Calhoun — Opportunist: A Reappraisal*. Gainesville, University of Florida Press, 1960.

Chambers, William Nisbet, *Old Bullion Benton, Senator from the New West, Thomas Hart Benton, 1782–1858*. Boston, Little, Brown & Company, 1956.

——, *Political Parties in a New Nation, The American Experience 1776–1809*. New York, Oxford University Press, 1963.

Chitwood, Oliver Perry, *John Tyler, Champion of the Old South*. New York, D. Appleton-Century Company, 1939.

Cole, Arthur Charles, *The Whig Party in the South*. Washington, American Historical Association, 1913.

Colton, Calvin, editor, *The Private Correspondence of Henry Clay*. New York, A. S. Barnes and Company, 1856.

Conard, Howard L., ed., *Encyclopedia of the History of Missouri, A Compendium of History and Biography for Ready Reference*. New York, Halderman, Conard and Company, 1901. 6 vols.

Connelly, William E., and E. Merton Coulter, *History of Kentucky*. Chicago, American Historical Society, 1922. 5 vols.

Culmer, Frederic Arthur, *A New History of Missouri*. Mexico, Missouri, McIntyre Publishing Company, 1938.

Current, Richard Nelson, *Daniel Webster and the Rise of National Conservatism*. Boston, Little, Brown & Company, 1955.

Darby, John F., *Personal Recollections*. St. Louis, G. I. Jones and Company, 1880.

Davis, Walter B., and Daniel S. Durrie, *An Illustrated History of Missouri, Comprising Its Early Record and Civil, Political, and Military History*. St. Louis, A. J. Hall and Company, 1876.

Doherty, Herbert J., Jr., *The Whigs of Florida, 1845–1854*. University of Florida Social Science Monographs, No. 1. Gainesville, Florida, University of Florida Press, 1959.

Dyer, Brainerd, *Zachary Taylor*. Baton Rouge, Louisiana State University Press, 1946.

Eaton, Clement, *Henry Clay and the Art of American Politics*. Boston, Little, Brown & Company, 1957.

Edwards, Richard, and M. Hopewell, *Edward's Great West and Her Commercial Metropolis, embracing a General View of the West, and a Complete History of St. Louis, from the Landing of Ligueste, in 1764, to the Present Time; with Portraits and Biographies of Some of the Old Settlers, and Many of the Most Prominent Business Men*. St. Louis, Office of "Edwards Monthly," 1860.

Elliot, Charles Winslow, *Winfield Scott, the Soldier and the Man*. New York, The Macmillan Company, 1937.

English, William Francis, *The Pioneer Lawyer and Jurist in Missouri.*

University of Missouri Studies, Vol. XXI. Columbia, University of Missouri, 1947.

Fish, Carl R., *The Civil Service and the Patronage*. Harvard Historical Studies, Vol. XI. Cambridge, Harvard University Press, 1905.

Fox, Dixon Ryan, *The Decline of Aristocracy in the Politics of New York*. New York, Columbia University Press, 1918.

Gammon, Samuel R., Jr., *The Presidential Campaign of 1832*. Johns Hopkins University Studies in Historical and Political Science, Vol. XL. Baltimore, Johns Hopkins University, 1932.

Glyndon, Howard, *Notable Men in "The House."* New York, Baker and Godwin, 1862.

Goebel, Dorothy B., *William Henry Harrison*. Indianapolis, The Bobbs-Merrill Company, 1926.

Greeley, Horace, ed., *Whig Almanac and Politicians Register for 1838*. New York, G. Dearborn and Company, 1838.

Green's St. Louis Directory for 1851 Containing the Names of the Inhabitants, Their Occupations, Places of Business, and Dwelling House. St. Louis, Charles & Hammond, Book and Job Printers, 1850.

Gunderson, Robert Gray, *The Log-Cabin Campaign*. Lexington, Kentucky, University of Kentucky Press, 1957.

Hamilton, Holman, *Zachary Taylor, Soldier in the White House*. Indianapolis, The Bobbs-Merrill Company, 1951.

Hammond, Bray, *Banks and Politics in America from the Revolution to the Civil War*. Princeton, Princeton University Press, 1957.

Harding, Samuel Bannister, *Life of George R. Smith, Founder of Sedalia, Mo.* Sedalia, privately printed, 1904.

Hartz, Louis, *Economic Policy and Democratic Thought: Pennsylvania, 1776–1860*. Cambridge, Harvard University Press, 1948.

History of Howard and Cooper Counties, Missouri. Chicago, National Historical Company, 1896.

History of Randolph and Macon Counties, Missouri. St. Louis, National Historical Company, 1884.

Hoffman, William S., *Andrew Jackson and North Carolina Politics*. The James Sprunt Studies in History and Political Science, Vol. XL. Chapel Hill, University of North Carolina Press, 1958.

Houck, Louis, *Memorial Sketches of Pioneers and Early Residents of Southeast Missouri*. Cape Girardeau, Naeter Brothers, 1915.

Hyde, William, and Howard L. Conard, eds., *Encyclopedia of the History of St. Louis, A Compendium of History and Biography for Ready Reference*, II. New York, The Southern History Company, 1899.

Jackson, William Rufus, *Missouri Democracy, A History of the Party and Its Representative Members — Past and Present, With a Vast Amount of Informative Data*. Chicago, S. J. Clarke, 1935. 3 vols.

Johnson, Allen, editor, *Dictionary of American Biography*. New York, Charles Scribner's Sons, 1928–36. 20 vols.

Key, V. O., Jr., *Politics, Parties, and Pressure Groups*. New York, Thomas Y. Crowell Company, 1956.

——, *Public Opinion and American Democracy*. New York, Alfred A. Knopf, Inc., 1961.

Kirwan, Albert D., *John J. Crittenden, The Struggle for the Union*. Lexington, Kentucky, University of Kentucky Press, 1962.

Lyon, William H., *The Pioneer Editor in Missouri, 1808–1860*. Columbia, University of Missouri Press, 1965.

McCarthy, Charles, *The Anti-Masonic Party*. Annual Report of the American Historical Association, 1902, I. Washington, United States Government Printing Office, 1903.

McClure, Clarence Henry, *Opposition in Missouri to Thomas Hart Benton*. George Peabody College for Teachers Contributions to Education, No. 37. Nashville, George Peabody College for Teachers, 1927.

McCormick, Richard P., *The Second American Party System: Party Formation in the Jacksonian Era*. Chapel Hill, University of North Carolina Press, 1966.

McDougal, Henry Clay, *Recollections, 1844–1909*. Kansas City, F. Hudson Publishing Company, 1910.

Merk, Frederick, *Manifest Destiny and Mission in American History, A Reinterpretation*. New York, Alfred A. Knopf, Inc., 1963.

Meyer, Duane, *The Heritage of Missouri — A History*. St. Louis, State Publishing Company, 1963.

Meyers, Marvin, *The Jacksonian Persuasion, Politics and Belief*. Stanford, Stanford University Press, 1957.

Miles, Edwin Arthur, *Jacksonian Democracy in Mississippi*. The James Sprunt Historical Studies in History and Political Science, Vol. XLII. Chapel Hill, University of North Carolina Press, 1960.

Million, John W., *State Aid to Railways in Missouri*. Chicago, University of Chicago Press, 1896.

Morgan, Robert J., *A Whig Embattled, The Presidency Under John Tyler*. Lincoln, University of Nebraska Press, 1954.

Moore, Arthur K., *The Frontier Mind, A Cultural Analysis of the Kentucky Frontiersman*. Lexington, University of Kentucky Press, 1957.

Morris, Richard B., ed., *Encyclopedia of American History*. New York, Harper and Brothers, 1953.

Mueller, Henry R., *The Whig Party in Pennsylvania*. Columbia University Studies in History, Economics, and Public Law, Vol. CI. New York, Columbia University Press, 1922.

Murray, Paul, *The Whig Party in Georgia, 1825–1853*. The James

Sprunt Studies in History and Political Science, Vol. XXIX. Chapel Hill, University of North Carolina Press, 1948.

Overdyke, William Darrell, *The Know-Nothing Party in the South.* Baton Rouge, Louisiana State University Press, 1950.

Parrish, William E., *David Rice Atchison, Border Politician.* University of Missouri Studies, XXXIV. Columbia, University of Missouri Press, 1961.

Paul, James C. N., *Rift in the Democracy.* Philadelphia, University of Pennsylvania Press, 1951.

Paullin, Charles O., *Atlas of the Historical Geography of the United States.* New York, Carnegie Institution of Washington and American Geographic Society of New York, 1932.

Pease, Theodore Calvin, *Illinois Election Returns, 1818–1848.* Collections of the Illinois State Historical Library, Vol. XVIII. Springfield, Illinois State Historical Library, 1923.

Peter, Robert, and Johanna Peter, *Transylvania University, Its Origin, Rise, Decline, and Fall.* Louisville, Filson Club, 1896.

Peterson, Norma L., *Freedom and Franchise: The Political Career of B. Gratz Brown.* Columbia, University of Missouri Press, 1965.

Poage, George R., *Henry Clay and the Whig Party.* Chapel Hill, University of North Carolina Press, 1936.

Primm, James Neal, *Economic Policy in the Development of a Western State, Missouri, 1820–1860.* Cambridge, Harvard University Press, 1954.

Rayback, Robert J., *Millard Fillmore, Biography of a President.* Buffalo, Buffalo Historical Society, 1959.

Reavis, L. U., *Saint Louis: The Future Great City of the World with Biographical Sketches of the Representative Men and Women of St. Louis and Missouri.* St. Louis, C. R. Barnes, 1876.

Remini, Robert V., *The Election of Andrew Jackson.* Philadelphia, J. B. Lippincott Company, 1963.

Rossiter, Clinton, *Parties and Politics in America.* Ithaca, Cornell University Press, 1960.

St. Louis Directory for the Year 1848. St. Louis, Chambers & Knapp, 1848.

Savage, John S., *Our Living Representative Men.* Philadelphia, Childs and Peterson, 1860.

Scharf, J. Thomas, *History of St. Louis City and County from the Earliest Periods to the Present Day, including Biographical Sketches of Representative Men.* Philadelphia, Louis H. Evarts and Company, 1883. 2 vols.

Schlesinger, Arthur M., Jr., *The Age of Jackson.* Boston, Little, Brown & Company, 1945.

Schurz, Carl, *Life of Henry Clay.* Vol. I. New York, Houghton Mifflin Company, 1891.

Seager, Robert, II, *And Tyler Too, A Biography of John and Julia Gardiner Tyler.* New York, McGraw-Hill Book Company, Inc., 1963.

Sellers, Charles G., Jr., *James K. Polk, Jacksonian, 1795–1843.* Princeton, Princeton University Press, 1957.

Shoemaker, Floyd Calvin, *Missouri and Missourians, Land of Contrasts and People of Achievements.* Vol. I. Chicago, The Lewis Publishing Company, 1943.

Simms, Henry Harrison, *The Rise of the Whigs in Virginia, 1824–1840.* Richmond, The William Byrd Press, 1929.

Smiley, David L., *The Lion of White Hall, The Life of Cassius M. Clay.* Madison, University of Wisconsin Press, 1962.

Smith, Elbert R., *Magnificent Missourian, The Life of Thomas Hart Benton.* Philadelphia, J. B. Lippincott Company, 1958.

Smith, William Benjamin, *James Sidney Rollins, Memoir.* New York, De Vinne Press, 1891.

Smith, William Ernest, *The Francis Preston Blair Family in Politics.* New York, The Macmillan Company, 1933. 2 vols.

Snyder, Charles McCool, *The Jacksonian Heritage: Pennsylvania Politics, 1833–1848.* Harrisburg, Pennsylvania Historical and Museum Commission, 1958.

Stephens, Frank F., *A History of the University of Missouri.* Columbia, University of Missouri Press, 1962.

Stevens, Walter B., *Missouri, The Center State, 1821–1915.* Chicago, S. J. Clarke, 1915. 2 vols.

———, *St. Louis, The Fourth City, 1764–1909.* St. Louis, S. J. Clarke, 1911. 2 vols.

Stewart, A. J. D., ed., *The History of the Bench and Bar of Missouri.* St. Louis, The Legal Publishing Company, 1898.

Streeter, Floyd Benjamin, *Political Parties in Michigan, 1837–1860.* Lansing, University of Michigan Press, 1918.

Switzler, William F., *History of Boone County, Missouri, Written and Compiled from the Most Authentic Official and Private Sources including a History of Its Townships, Towns, and Villages.* St. Louis, Western Historical Company, 1882.

———, *Illustrated History of Missouri from 1541 to 1877.* St. Louis, C. H. Barnes, 1879.

Thompson, Charles Manfred, *The Illinois Whigs before 1846.* University of Illinois Studies in the Social Sciences, Vol. IV. Urbana, University of Illinois Press, 1915.

The United States Biographical Dictionary and Portrait Gallery of Eminent and Self-Made Men, Missouri Volume. New York, The United States Biographical Publishing Company, 1878.

Van Deusen, Glyndon G., *The Jacksonian Era, 1828–1848.* New York, Harper and Brothers, 1959.

————, *The Life of Henry Clay*. Boston, Little, Brown & Company, 1937.

————, *Thurlow Weed: Wizard of the Lobby*. Boston, Little, Brown & Company, 1947.

Viles, Jonas, *The University of Missouri, A Centennial History*. Columbia, University of Missouri, 1939.

Violette, Eugene M., *A History of Missouri*. New York, D. C. Heath & Company, 1918.

Wade, Richard C., *The Urban Frontier*. Cambridge, Harvard University Press, 1959.

Weed, Thurlow, *Autobiography of Thurlow Weed*, Harriet A. Weed, ed. Vol. I. Boston, Houghton Mifflin Company, 1884.

Weisenburger, Francis P., *The Passing of the Frontier, 1825–1850*. Columbus, Ohio State Archaeological and Historical Society, 1941.

Wellington, Raynor G., *The Politics and Sectional Influence of the Public Lands, 1828–1842*. New York, Riverside Press, 1914.

Weston, Florence, *The Presidential Election of 1828*. Washington, The Ruddick Press, 1938.

White, Leonard D., *The Jacksonians, A Study in Administrative History, 1829–1861*. New York, The Macmillan Company, 1954.

Williams, Walter, ed., *A History of Northwest Missouri*. Chicago, National Historical Company, 1915. 3 vols.

————, and Floyd C. Shoemaker, *Missouri, Mother of the West*. New York, The American Historical Society, 1930. 5 vols.

Williamson, Chilton, *American Suffrage from Property to Democracy, 1760–1860*. Princeton, Princeton University Press, 1960.

Wiltse, Charles M., *John C. Calhoun, Sectionalist, 1840–1850*. Indianapolis, The Bobbs-Merrill Company, 1951.

Wise, Henry A., *Seven Decades of the Union*. Philadelphia, J. B. Lippincott Company, 1881.

County Organization of Whig Party

The Whig Party in Missouri

County Organization of Whig Party*

COUNTY	DATE OF COUNTY ORGANIZATION	PRESIDENTIAL ELECTIONS IN WHICH COUNTY YIELDED WHIG MAJORITIES
Audrain	1836	1844–1852
Bates	1841	1848
Boone	1820	1836–1852
Callaway	1820	1840–1852
Cape Girardeau	1812	
Chariton	1820	
Clark	1836	1840–1852
Clay	1822	1844–1852
Clinton	1833	1848
Cole	1820	
Crawford	1829	

*Shaded areas are predominantly Whig counties.

COUNTY	DATE OF COUNTY ORGANIZATION	PRESIDENTIAL ELECTIONS IN WHICH COUNTY YIELDED WHIG MAJORITIES
Franklin	1818	
Gasconade	1820	
Grundy	1841	1848–1852
Henry	1834	1848–1852
Howard	1816	1844
Jackson	1826	
Jasper	1841	1852
Jefferson	1818	
Lafayette	1820	1840–1852
Lincoln	1818	
Marion	1826	1836–1852
Monroe	1831	1840–1852
Montgomery	1818	1836–1852
New Madrid	1812	1840–1852
Pemiscot	1851	1852
Perry	1820	
Pike	1818	1844–1852
Ralls	1820	1840–1852
Randolph	1829	1840–1848
Ray	1820	
Saint Charles	1812	1836–1840
Sainte Genevieve	1812	
Saint Francois	1821	1844–1848
Saint Louis	1812	1836–1848
Saline	1820	1840–1852
Schuyler	1845	1848
Scott	1821	
Shelby	1835	1844
Warren	1833	1844–1852
Washington	1813	1844–1852
Wayne	1818	

INDEX

ABOUT THE AUTHOR

JOHN VOLLMER MERING was born in Kansas City, Missouri, and attended the Pembroke-Country Day School there. After taking his Bachelor's degree (1953) at the University of Missouri at Columbia, he served in the United States Army for two years. He then returned to the University of Missouri for graduate study in History (M.A., 1957; Ph.D., 1960).

Currently, Dr. Mering is Visiting Associate Professor of History at the University of Rhode Island (1966–1967), on leave from the University of Florida, where he teaches Social Science and History.